KING OF SPIES

Blaine Harden is a reporter for PBS Frontline and a contributor to *The Economist*, based in Seattle, having completed a tour as the *Washington Post*'s bureau chief in Tokyo. He is the prize-winning, acclaimed author of *Escape from Camp 14*; *Africa: Dispatches from a Fragile Continent*; *A River Lost: The Life and Death of the Columbia* and *The Great Leader and the Fighter Pilot*.

KING OF SPIES

THE DARK REIGN OF AMERICA'S SPYMASTER IN KOREA

BLAINE HARDEN

PAN BOOKS

First published 2017 by Viking, an imprint of Penguin Random House LLC

First published in the UK 2018 by Mantle

First published in the UK in paperback 2019 by Pan Books
an imprint of Pan Macmillan
20 New Wharf Road, London N1 9RR
Associated companies throughout the world
www.panmacmillan.com

ISBN 978-1-5098-1579-1

Visit **www.panmacmillan.com** to read more about all our books
and to buy them. You will also find features, author interviews and
news of any author events, and you can sign up for e-newsletters
so that you're always first to hear about our new releases.

Ask yourself: Is there a man capable of never misusing his legal license to murder?

—Major Donald Nichols

How long can we defend ourselves—you and we, by methods of this kind, and still remain the kind of society that is worth defending?

—John le Carré

CONTENTS

PART III
RUINED SPY

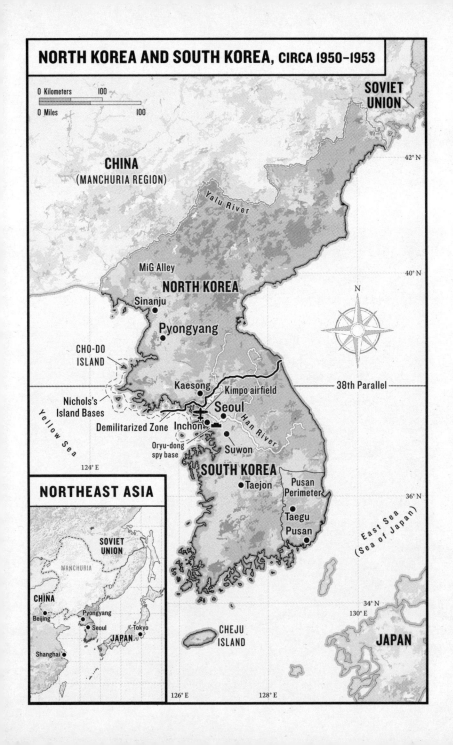

INTRODUCTION

The Spy Who Came in from the Motor Pool

During World War II, Donald Nichols worked in a U.S. Army motor pool and a makeshift morgue. He repaired trucks bound for Burma and embalmed GIs bound for home. The soldiers died of malaria, dengue fever, or amoebic dysentery—diseases that hospitalized but could not kill Nichols. For his grit and his gumption, he was promoted in India to master sergeant at the age of nineteen, making him one of the youngest men of that rank in the army. By the spring of 1946, the war was over and Nichols was no longer pumping embalming fluid into his dead comrades. But he was still stuck in the motor pool, this time on Guam, a sleepy speck of American-owned sand in the western Pacific. In Washington, President Harry S. Truman was gutting the defense budget and the army was imploding. So were the chances that Nichols could make a career in the military—until he caught the eye of recruiters from the Counter Intelligence Corps, an army unit that hunted saboteurs near military bases. The army flew him to Tokyo, gave him three months' training, and sent him to Korea.

There, at the dawn of the cold war, the motor pool mechanic metamorphosed into a black-ops phenomenon. He became a spymaster with his own base, his own secret army, and his own rules. His target: North

Korea, the Soviet puppet regime that would become the world's longest-lasting totalitarian state. Nichols was wildly ambitious, virtually unsupervised, and just twenty-three years old. He would build an eponymous intelligence outfit, known as NICK, that outhustled and outspied the Central Intelligence Agency and the massive military intelligence apparatus under General Douglas MacArthur. He warned months in advance—with precise details on troops, tanks, and aircraft—about the Soviet-supported North Korean invasion that would catch the United States flatfooted in June 1950. In the early, desperate days of the Korean War, when GIs were panicking, retreating, and dying, his team of Korean cryptographers broke North Korean army codes, which helped American forces hold the line, saving them from being pushed off the southern tip of the Korean Peninsula. Nichols also saved countless lives by penetrating enemy lines to discover vulnerabilities in Soviet tanks and MiG fighter jets. He and his operatives found most of the targets for the bombing of North Korea. He swiped photographs of Stalin and Mao from the office of North Korean leader Kim Il Sung in Pyongyang. He also took the Great Leader's swivel chair. His commanding general called him "magnificent," "wonderful," and a "one man war" who "didn't know what it was to be scared of anything."

More than any American, Nichols was ready for war in Korea. Years before it started, when the Korean Peninsula was a backwater and he was a nobody, he insinuated himself into the affections of an extreme right-wing politician who would become South Korea's founding leader. President Syngman Rhee had a PhD from Princeton and a penchant for exterminating Koreans he believed to be Communists. He led South Korea for a dozen years and Nichols became his "son." As such, Nichols entered a demimonde of torture, mass killings, and chopped-off heads as Rhee and his security forces prosecuted a savage civil war against South Koreans suspected of loyalty to the Communist North. Rhee's anti-Communist crusade—tacitly supported and covered up by the United States—would kill tens of thousands of South Korean civilians, many of them women and children.

For an American spy immersed in war, torture, and extrajudicial killings, Nichols had an astonishingly long tenure—eleven years. His officer efficiency reports described him as "highly aggressive" and "audacious." His superiors had never seen an agent work so hard for so long. Spying was all he knew, they said in their evaluations of Nichols, and all he was suited for. Year after year, he rarely took a day off. "He is the only one of his kind I have ever known," his commanding colonel wrote.

Nichols did not look, dress, or behave like the spies we know from books and movies. Quick tempered and pushy, fast talking and fleshy, he drank Coca-Cola by the case and ate candy bars by the box. Butterfingers, when he could find them; Hershey's, when he could not. He did not smoke and rarely touched alcohol. He had zero interest in women, often telling his men that he "hated" them. Among Koreans, he was an American colossus: six feet two inches tall, weighing up to 260 pounds. "No Korean could match his height or fatness," said Chung Bong-sun, who worked for Nichols for eight years as an intelligence officer in the South Korean air force. "But he was very agile and could run fast."

By breeding and background, Nichols had nothing in common with the upper-crust spies who ran covert operations for the CIA. Unlike the agency's very best men, he had not attended an East Coast boarding school or gone to Yale or worked on Wall Street or summered in the Hamptons. Even compared with other American military intelligence agents, he was astoundingly unschooled, with no college and no high school. Twelve weeks of spy class in Tokyo were as close as he ever came to higher education. A child of America's Great Depression, he grew up poor, ill clothed, unwashed, and hungry. When he was seven, his mother abandoned him and his three older brothers. His father took the four boys from Hackensack, New Jersey, to South Florida, where they stumbled miserably through the 1930s. Donald dropped out of school in seventh grade and became a scavenger, stealing everything from tomatoes to tractor parts. He enlisted in the army at seventeen for the "big pay day" of twenty-one dollars a month. He sent sixteen dollars to his brothers to help them buy false teeth for their father.

Nichols grew into adulthood with a distinctly sophomoric sense of humor. In Korea, he told his interpreter to put a can of shaving cream up to his ear, squeeze the spray button, and "hear the music." In his midthirties, when he was back in Florida, his behavior veered from quirky to criminal. He stashed hundreds of thousands of dollars—loot he brought back from Korea—in his brother Judson's freezer. He kept big wads of it in his pocket and flashed it in front of strangers, stuffing it in his knee socks when crossing national borders. He became a fugitive from justice in the 1960s and was wanted by the Federal Bureau of Investigation. At forty-three, bound for Mexico while fleeing a felony morals charge, he left a paper sack containing twenty-five thousand dollars in cash on a coffee shop counter.

For all his failure to conduct himself with the panache of James Bond, the prudence of George Smiley, or even the common sense that God gave a goose, Nichols had an exquisite gift for clandestine operations. He wowed generals in the Far East Air Forces by conceiving, organizing, and leading covert missions inside North Korea. They described him as "an invaluable man" and "the best intelligence operator in the theater." General George E. Stratemeyer, commander of Far East Air Forces, wrote in his diary during the first year of the Korean War that Nichols had "performed the impossible."

Nichols, who moved from the army to the air force in 1947, when the latter became a separate service, was promoted faster than regulations normally allowed, moving from master sergeant to chief warrant officer to lieutenant to captain to major. The speed of his rise raised eyebrows in Washington. In a cable from Tokyo, General Stratemeyer had to explain that because Nichols was clearly the best intelligence agent in the Far East, his promotions were "a completely justifiable exception" to military policy. As his power and political connections grew, Nichols ascended to a unique perch, operating above and beyond conventional calibrations of military rank. He wore civilian clothes or plain military fatigues that bore no insignia of military branch, unit, or rank. American airmen assigned to his unit were told that his rank was a secret. They knew only that he was "a big shot" and they called him "Mr. Nichols."

To keep Mr. Nichols happy and to ward off attempts by army intelligence or the CIA to poach his services, air force generals gave him his own intelligence base, funded it generously, and allowed him to run it largely as he pleased. There was no base like it in Korea or anywhere else in the American military. From "Nick's place," as his commanding general called it, he supervised up to fifty-eight American intelligence officers and airmen, two hundred South Korean intelligence officers, and more than seven hundred agents, most of them defectors and refugees from North Korea. The agents were his eyes and ears—and they were disposable. When he sent them inside North Korea, Nichols expected most would be captured, tortured, or killed. On his watch, as many as eight out of ten of the agents who parachuted over North Korea never came back. Nichols said his bosses "wanted the answers. And in some cases didn't want to be told how I got them. They knew it meant lives, sometimes many."

In constant need of new agents, Nichols frequented refugee camps and prisons, where he recruited gangsters, murderers, and thieves. If they survived a mission, he offered pardons and commissions in the South Korean air force, which Nichols helped create and which was run by a general he helped select. While his agents were in the North, Nichols gave rice to their families. At other times, to control their behavior, he threatened those families. For the few who made it back, he provided "a clean bed, a hot meal, a pretty body. . . ." During the first year of the war a group of his agents, furious over the death of so many of their comrades and afraid they might be next, attacked Nichols at night in his quarters. He shot several of them.

The CIA and army intelligence grumbled about Nichols, tried to rein him in, tried to fire him, and tried to hire him. But air force generals stood jealous guard, keeping him happy with promotions, a big budget, and medals—at least twenty-one of them. One of those was the Distinguished Service Cross, America's second-highest military honor, which he received for salvaging key parts from a crashed Russian-made fighter jet inside North Korea. A South Korean intelligence officer who was on that mission and later became director of his country's central intelligence agency said Nichols fabricated a self-serving story about what happened on the ground during that mission in order to win the medal. This was not a one-off lie. Nichols was smart and bold, but he embellished his achievements to make himself look even more so.

Inside North Korea, Nichols was sometimes called "the King of U.S. spies." His espionage efforts were recounted at the end of the war with considerable accuracy in a Pyongyang courtroom during a sensational, Stalinist-style show trial. North Korea also put a bounty on his head. When one would-be assassin was arrested near Seoul and confessed to having come from the North to kill him, the suspect was summarily shot and buried on a hill above the office where Nichols worked.

Nichols claimed the air force gave him a "license to murder," which he used to dispose of "double agents," pushing them out of boats and dropping them from airplanes. Worried about assassination, he lived with a large pack of snarling dogs. His dogs joined him for meals in the officers' mess, where they occasionally bit other officers.

Before and during the Korean War, Nichols attended mass executions of suspected Communists, including one of the most notorious atrocities of the Rhee era, when South Korean police and army forces shot thousands of civilians in early July 1950 and buried their bodies in ditches near the town of Taejon. For decades, the official U.S. military history of the Korean War wrongly blamed this massacre on North Korean soldiers. Nichols never disputed this false claim and never publicly acknowledged his presence at the Taejon killings.

For nearly fifty years the government of South Korea refused to investigate what happened at places like Taejon. When a truth commission was created by reform governments in Seoul at the beginning of the twenty-first century, South Korean intelligence and defense ministries refused to open their files. But investigators found forensic and eyewitness evidence of the killings of at least a hundred thousand civilians. After less than a decade of semiopenness, Korea's elected leaders reversed course in 2010, shutting down the inquiries and ignoring their findings. The massacres have again become a taboo subject, obscured by denial and stonewalling. The nation's War Memorial museum in Seoul bears no mention of them.

The friendship between Nichols and South Korea's founding leader was deep and durable. Nichols would always praise Syngman Rhee as "one of history's great men." Few share this view. In the judgment of history, Rhee was a prickly ideologue who mismanaged the economy, murdered his rivals, and stayed in power far too long. Street protests in South Korea forced him out in 1960, when the United States put him on a military plane and flew him into exile in Hawaii.

———

Nichols, too, was forced out of Korea. In the autumn of 1957, the air force flew him to Eglin Air Force Base Hospital in Florida, checked him into a psychiatric ward, and sedated him with extralarge doses of Thorazine. When he would not calm down, he was forced to submit to electroshock treatment. "He demonstrated considerable organic confusion" after his eighth consecutive daily treatment, his clinical record says. Psychiatrists then gave him six more rounds of electroshock on six consecutive days. "They are trying to destroy my memory," he told his family.

Within a few months, he agreed to retire from the air force on a medical disability. Had he not done so, air force investigators said, he would have been thrown out.

Family members did not know then—and would not know for six decades—the scope and significance of what Nichols had done in Korea. Nor did they know why he had left the air force so abruptly. They found his war stories fantastical. They found him spooky, selfish, and strange. "With Uncle Don, you never knew what to believe," said a niece who lived with him for several years. Nichols himself began to wonder how he had managed to become what he had been. In an autobiography he paid to have published in a small-town Florida print shop, he asked: "How did I, an uneducated, non-trained, non-experienced individual possess the knowledge that I did/do about ways and means to conduct sabotage/espionage????"

He acknowledged that his years as a spy ended in disgrace, but he did not explain why. He concealed his electroshock treatment. What he did not hide was the numbness and confusion he felt as an ex-spy adrift in the United States. "I was a fifth wheel . . . a misfit wherever I went." He joined what he called the ranks of the "living dead." Jobless and unemployable, he wandered zombielike among countrymen who ignored him and his war.

World War II had affirmed American values by crushing Nazi Germany and imperial Japan. It set the table for decades of prosperity and global dominance. The Korean War affirmed nothing and ended in a way that was impossible to celebrate: in a tie that cost more than 33,000 American combatants their lives. And it was soon eclipsed by slow-motion defeat in Vietnam, where failure featured drugged-out GIs, covered-up civilian massacres, secret bombings, napalmed children, and a decade of presidential lies. That war, the first to be televised, spilled combat into living rooms and seared itself into popular culture in a way that Korea never did. The Vietnam War's hallucinogenic mix of technology, pointlessness, and death forced Americans to reconsider what their country stood for. As historian Ronald Steel explained, Vietnam was "the graveyard of an image we held of ourselves."

Yet civilian killings and napalmed villages, high-level lies and long-running cover-ups, were hardly new in Vietnam. A decade earlier—when Americans were paying less attention, when the press asked fewer questions—Korea had them all. Those black threads are woven into the reign and ruin of Donald Nichols. He cozied up to a fanatical foreign leader, sat in on torture sessions, attended mass killings (without reporting them), sent hundreds of Koreans to near-certain death, and targeted civilians for incendiary bombs. Like Kurtz in Conrad's *Heart of Darkness* and Colonel Kurtz in *Apocalypse Now*, Nichols was an uncontrolled commander in a faraway shadowland. But he was no fictional archetype. He was a highly decorated U.S. Air Force intelligence officer who ran his own secret war for more than a decade, while losing touch with propriety, with morality, with legality—even with sanity, if military psychiatrists are to be believed.

The air force credited Nichols, more than anyone else, with finding bomb targets in North Korea. That U.S. bombing campaign, which continued for three years, destroyed nearly all of the country's cities and towns. Napalm and conventional explosives razed 85 percent of its buildings. The North Korean government never released numbers on civilian deaths, but the population of the country officially declined during the war by 1,311,000, or 14 percent. General Curtis E. LeMay, head of the Strategic Air Command during the war, guessed that American bombs killed even more: about 20 percent of the North Korean population, roughly 1,900,000 people. Americans would never pay much attention to these deaths, but outside of the United States the bombing was widely regarded as a war crime. It still resonates as Yankee genocide inside North Korea, where the Kim family dictatorship endlessly warns that the Americans will come again with bombs and fire and death.

While Korea would become "the forgotten war," Americans would not forget Donald Nichols. They never heard of him. Not from their government, not from the press, not in the 1950s, not for nearly half a century.

With the help of his autobiography and some archival records, military historians pieced together scattered fragments of his career in the 1990s, usually in book chapters and articles written for intelligence specialists and published by the Naval Institute Press or the Air University Press. In some of those partial portraits, he was presented as a working-class war hero, an alcoholic pirate, or a two-dimensional rib tickler. An otherwise excellent book on the air war in Korea calls him "one of those colorful, larger-than-life, bold, and outlandish characters that occasionally appear and add sparkle to tedious histories." None of these historians learned how the U.S. military ended his career. And only one Korean War–era journalist, John Dille, a writer for *Life* magazine, seems to have understood his significance as an intelligence operative. Dille, though, disguised Nichols's identity, calling him "Bill." After interviewing Nichols in Seoul, he praised him without qualification, writing that "Bill" was "responsible, more than anything else" for America's success in Korea.

Nichols was more candid. He acknowledged that his years in Korea were steeped in civilian blood. In his autobiography he described himself as a "thief, assassin, judge, jury and executioner." He said he wrote the book as "an expiation, an apology to a multitude of unnamed men, women, and children whose sufferings and deaths related to events in my life." But it spells out little of what he apologized for. His exploits, he wrote, were "better left un-detailed for reasons of sensitivity, as well as for security." The air force, in some ways, has followed suit. In an unusual and obdurate insistence on secrecy, it continues to classify and withhold documents related to spy operations that Nichols led more than sixty years ago. In the National Archives in College Park, Maryland, hundreds of intelligence reports written by Nichols have been pulled off shelves since 2011 at the request of the air force and replaced with blue sheets of paper stamped "access restricted."

An internal air force publication described Nichols as one of the "founding fathers" of its covert operations. Yet the air force has given no awards in his name. No buildings, streets, or schools are named after him. His photograph is not displayed at the Air Force Special Operations Command headquarters at Hurlburt Field in Florida. Instructors there do not tell their students about him. Herb Mason, the command historian at air force special-ops headquarters, used to mention Nichols in intelligence lectures. But several years ago he stopped, deciding it was best to say nothing about the spy who came in from the motor pool.

"We couldn't tell his whole story, so I chose not to bring him up anymore," said Mason. "As far as I know, the air force has never even considered an honor for Nichols. He had a dark side. In wartime, he was the guy you want on your team. In peacetime, you lock him up."

In *King of Spies*, I have tried to unlock Donald Nichols and, for the first time, tell the story of his life and legacy. Drawing upon his previously unreleased military service record, his psychiatric treatment notes, newly declassified air force documents, Syngman Rhee's presidential papers, unsealed civilian court records, private letters, and interviews with family members and his former intelligence colleagues in the United States and South Korea, the book reveals an American intelligence commander who was a fearless war hero and a postwar outlaw, a special-ops innovator and a shameless liar, a self-invented spymaster and a sexual predator who succeeded for years in covering his tracks. Nichols was the best and the worst kind of American warrior: ferocious, creative, and unbreakable. Yet he was oblivious to the rules of war and wasteful of human life. The air force gave him an astonishingly long leash and allowed him to play whatever role he chose—until it suddenly and secretly jerked him out of Korea, incorrectly diagnosed him as severely schizophrenic, and pushed him out into civilian life. Nichols never detailed the full scope of his wartime triumphs; neither has the U.S. military. His achievements were too closely linked to atrocities, too twisted up in allegiance to a foreign autocrat, too tainted by what happened after he was sent home. As such, his extraordinary and tragic story was allowed to sink into the murk of America's forgotten war—until now.

PART I

MOST VALUABLE SPY

CHAPTER 1
Nichols of Korea

To understand the improbable rise of Donald Nichols, it is useful—up to a point—to think of him as a supersized American version of T. E. Lawrence, the diminutive British military officer who became known as Lawrence of Arabia. Thomas Edward Lawrence was a lowly second lieutenant assigned to intelligence in Cairo in 1914 when he united fractious desert tribes, led an Arab revolt that defeated the Turks, and helped Great Britain win World War I. Lawrence and Nichols were both in their twenties when they performed their respective miracles. Both were cheeky, creative, and skilled at wringing personal power out of chaos. They were also natural leaders, brave, and wonderfully lucky under fire. Their adversaries—the Turks and the North Koreans—repeatedly failed to kill them. Though Lawrence was an Oxford-trained scholar, an archaeologist, and a translator of the classics, his ascendancy in Arabia, much like Nichols's in Korea, was largely rooted in good timing.

Lawrence arrived in the Middle East in 1910, four years before World War I, when the Great Powers were not yet paying attention to the region. It was, as Lawrence said, "a sideshow of a sideshow." His early arrival gave him time to master Arabic, understand fundamentalist Islam, learn how to survive in the desert, acquire a nuanced firsthand understanding of the region's geography and trade routes, and make personal contacts with key tribal and political leaders. When war came, Lawrence was better prepared than any other Englishman.

Nichols's sideshow was the Korean Peninsula in the mid-1940s. Except for a few hundred Protestant missionaries, who had been proselytizing and teaching there since the late nineteenth century, few Americans traveled to or knew anything about the place. There were no important American commercial interests in Korea. After Nichols was sent there in 1946, the Joint Chiefs of Staff declared it to be of "little strategic value." The focus of postwar American interest in the Far East was Japan, where General Douglas MacArthur, the supreme commander of American forces in the Pacific, had become shogun. In the late 1940s he was using his nearly unlimited authority to reinvent the country as a peaceful, productive, and democratic ally of the United States. MacArthur succeeded in this mission beyond all expectations. Korea is less than forty miles from the westernmost islands of Japan, but it existed on the dim edge of MacArthur's lordly attention span.

Everything changed in late June 1950 when North Korea, backed by the Soviet Union, launched a massive armored invasion of its U.S.-supported neighbor to the south. The exceptionally bloody three-year war that followed drew combatants from twenty nations on six continents. About 1.2 million soldiers were killed. The number of civilian dead has been estimated at 2.7 million. For the first and only time in history, American fighter pilots faced off in jets against Russian fighter pilots. The Korean War, as historian William Stueck wrote, "served in many ways as a substitute for World War III." Yet the states that were fighting and financing it chose to corral the chaos, keeping nearly all the death and destruction inside the borders of the Korean Peninsula, a geographic space about the size of Minnesota.

Like Lawrence, Nichols arrived early for his war—four years early. He had no way of knowing what lay ahead. Nonetheless, he worked relentlessly to get ready. He traveled widely, sometimes in disguise. He made powerful friends. He taught himself the local language.

But similarities between Lawrence and Nichols go only so far. Lawrence was angered and embarrassed by Britain's colonial ambitions in the Middle East. More scholar than spy, more diplomat than soldier, he was a paradoxical man, painfully shy but also a brilliant self-promoter. In Arab garb and riding a camel, he posed for photographs that made him an international celebrity.

Nichols was no scholar, no diplomat, no seeker of fame. In South Korea, he was invisible outside the world of military intelligence. Even in that world he avoided cocktail parties and crowded receptions. An evaluation of his performance as an officer said "he has a pronounced lack of interest in social activities and this might tend to limit his growth potential to [spying]." He often ate dinner alone in his compound and dressed in a way that attracted little attention. "One who has been engaged in intelligence work for years subconsciously strives to stay in the background," Nichols later wrote in a letter to his commanding general, saying it is a "natural tendency that is difficult to overcome."

Nichols rarely read a book and did not acquire a nuanced historical understanding of Korea. He paid little attention to the news. A streetwise hustler, he had a good ear for language, although he was not nearly as proficient in Korean as Lawrence was in Arabic. Instead, Nichols excelled in bare-knuckle bullying. "I soon learned one of the most effective ways to control high level politicians is through a state of fear," he wrote. "Everyone has a skeleton to hide. Find out what, where or who it is, and you have your man more or less under control."

Unlike Lawrence, Nichols did not aspire to shape the fate of nations or challenge the policies of his government. He played the anti-Communist cards his government and Syngman Rhee dealt him. He made his generals look good. In return, they gave him the keys to his own spy kingdom.

After World War II, most American servicemen were desperate to go home. From Austria to the Philippines, tens of thousands of them marched and protested, sometimes violently, to speed up the pace of demobilization.

Within two years, nine out of ten had returned to the States, where they stashed their uniforms in the attic and rejoined civilian life. Between 1945 and 1947, the number of U.S. military personnel plummeted from more than 12 million to fewer than 1.6 million.

For American officers and enlisted men who remained overseas as postwar occupiers, the place to be in the Far East was Japan. Even a private could feel rich and eat well there. It was safe. Soldierly responsibilities were few. "Shack girls" were abundant and affordable; easy money could be made on the black market. Back in the States, "Have Fun in Japan" was an army recruitment pitch.

Korea was seen as a hellhole. Soldiers and airmen stationed there complained about the stink of human excrement, which was used to fertilize rice paddies. Housing was limited, food bad, roads poor, and weather extreme, with harsh winter winds that blew in from Siberia and sweltering summers punctuated by long bouts of rain. Mud brown was the color of a GI's life in Korea. For American troops lucky enough to be stationed in Japan, an American general said there were only three things to fear: "gonorrhea, diarrhea, and Korea."

Losers, it was said, were posted there. "It was an article of faith in the U.S. Army officer's corps that assignment to Korea was one short step away from being cashiered out of the service," wrote Ed Evanhoe, a combat infantryman and later an army intelligence officer in Korea. "Few of the better army officers volunteered. . . ."

Nichols saw it differently.

For him, anywhere the army sent him was an improvement on the life he had known growing up. His family was operatically dysfunctional. Back in Hackensack, before his mother left the family, she bathed naked in the kitchen sink and had sex with male suitors in the living room while his father, Walter, a postman, was out delivering the mail. His mother's behavior haunted him all his life. During the Korean War, Nichols often spoke disparagingly of women, explaining to his men that it was because his mother had abandoned him.

Walter Nichols left New Jersey in 1933 and took his four boys, including ten-year-old Donald, to South Florida, but he could not find work and would not get over the collapse of his marriage. He brooded for years over his gallivanting wife and periodically beat his sons. Once, while sharpening knives in the kitchen, he threatened to kill himself, but only after he had slit his boys' throats.

When Miami proved too expensive, Walter took his sons to the low-rent outskirts of Hollywood, Florida, a resort town that had been carved out of mangrove swamps and salt marshes during a real-estate boom in the early 1920s. Its developers had tried to give the place more swank than other upstart coastal resorts by bringing in titled Europeans, hiring tennis champions, and building a "tailor-made" city of shops, hotels, and apartments in white and pink stucco. The Nichols family lived on the bleak, sun-blasted fringes of all this in a shack with a tar-paper roof, no running water, and walls black from kerosene smoke. The boys rarely had money for soap. Most of their food and clothing throughout the 1930s came from the Salvation Army and from government assistance. To help his father put food on the table, Donald, starting as a preteen, shoveled chicken manure, picked fruit, pumped gas, and burglarized neighbors. Still, there was rarely enough food and he often went to bed hungry. Chronic childhood hunger, he would later say, was the cause of his life-long struggle with obesity and his "psychopathic" bingeing on Coke and chocolate.

Donald attended elementary school in the nearby town of Dania, usually without bathing and sometimes without shoes. As the youngest boy in his family, he wore hand-me-down pants that often had holes in the rear end. He had no underwear. He believed his classmates saw him as white trash and was quick to take offense. When a sympathetic classmate, Nora Mae Swengel, who thought Donald had nice green eyes, gave him four pencils, he broke them in half and threw them on the floor. Often, though, he had to swallow his pride; he begged a dentist to fix a toothache. Nichols dropped out of school when he was fourteen and found full-time work as a dishwasher in the Hollywood Beach Hotel, an expensive resort that served roast beef, tenderloin, and other delicacies that he had heard about but rarely eaten. The best part of his $2.50-a-day job was returning home with the half-eaten scraps of rich tourists. Nichols joined Franklin Roosevelt's Civilian Conservation Corps, a jobs program during the Depression, and helped build federal parks in the Florida Keys. At seventeen, after three years of mixing low-wage work with petty crime, he concluded that he could "only find hope in the big pay offered by the United States Army."

After he enlisted in the spring of 1940, his father lived alone and struggled to pay his boardinghouse rent. Walter wrote mournful, self-pitying letters to his youngest son, an army private at MacDill Field near Tampa. The letters, which arrived once or twice a week, begged for money and complained about a life that was "nothing but trouble." After Donald sent money, his father wrote back with passive-aggressive pleas for more: "I am sorry I had to write you for that $5.00. I had to have it for my room rent. . . . Even now I have to get a day's work so that I can eat."

Besides money problems, the letters wallowed in uxorious torment. Walter was unable to forget and unwilling to forgive his flamboyantly unfaithful wife, whom he called "Peanut." His letters surely must have tormented Donald, who was reading them in an army barracks in his first months away from home. In one letter, Walter asked Donald, who rarely saw or communicated with his mother, to somehow bring Peanut back to him. "I need her now," he wrote. "I want her and you can help me by writing her a nice letter. Call her and she will be tickled to death."

In another letter, Walter mentioned that his sons Judson and Bill had seen Peanut in bed with another man. "I wanted her but have changed my mind," he wrote. "I am going to divorce her as soon as I get the money. To hell with her now."

Walter did not divorce his Peanut. In the late autumn of 1940, at age fifty-three, he died pining for her. Doctors blamed a bad heart. The three eldest boys blamed their mother. Army private Donald Nichols, still seventeen and still based in Tampa, blamed himself. "My biggest regret in life is, has always been, and will always be, that of leaving my Dad when he needed me," he wrote. "I should have remained with my Dad. He died of loneliness, nothing else."

Nichols shipped out to the Pacific war zone in January 1942, a month after Japan attacked Pearl Harbor. Trained as a carburetor repairman, he was assigned to a sprawling army motor pool in the South Asian port city of Karachi, where he helped keep thousands of trucks on the road to Burma. The trucks carried men and supplies to war zones in China and Southeast Asia. While there were no battle casualties in Karachi, large numbers of army mechanics succumbed to malaria and intestinal disease. The army could not keep up with the corpses that needed to be prepared for a long voyage home. "Our higher brass evidently forgot that people were going to die," Nichols wrote in his autobiography. So he volunteered to become an embalmer. Working in the motor pool during the day and in a morgue at night, he was soon exhausted, became deathly ill, and was hospitalized for several weeks.

After his recovery, Nichols got his first taste of undercover work. He was assigned to police the docks in Karachi, where he quickly learned how to fiddle with the paperwork on newly arrived supply crates, redirecting them from other army units to his own. Soon, mechanics in his automotive shop had all the tools and truck parts they needed, as well as "crates of other items of necessity to our unit and to ourselves." His commanding officers were pleased and promoted Nichols to master sergeant. The lesson he learned on Karachi's docks would serve him well in Korea: if you make the bosses happy, they won't question your methods.

He returned to the United States in the spring of 1945, as World War II was drawing to an end, but for only a few months, much of it spent in military hospitals. When he landed in New York in a C-54 army transport plane, he weighed eighty-seven pounds and needed weeks of treatment for dysentery and other lingering infections of the gut. Doctors also performed an appendectomy. Nichols did not consider leaving the army and going home to Florida. With his father dead, there was no family home to go home to. He learned from his brothers that his mother was still sleeping around in Hackensack—and sometimes South Florida—with a changing cast of no-account men. As a teen, Donald had never shown any romantic interest in girls; he certainly did not have one waiting for him. His brothers were scattered geographically, and when they got together, they did not get along. Judson, the second born and most congenial of the brothers, dropped out of high school to pick tomatoes up and down the East Coast. William, the third son, went to war and came home an alcoholic. He quarreled with his oldest brother, Walter Jr., a policeman in Hollywood, Florida, who suspected that William was sleeping with Walter's wife, Fern. Walter Jr. and William would spend much of their lives not speaking to each other. "The Nichols brothers were an explosion waiting to happen," said Donald H. Nichols, Judson's eldest son.

Nichols's first enlistment tour in the army ended in October 1945, when he was living in an army air base near Salt Lake City. But he gave no thought to leaving the military, reenlisting immediately and, in early 1946, shipping out to a B-29 bomber base on Guam, which put eight thousand miles between him and the wreckage of his family. He traveled to the Far East with heavy baggage: guilt about his father, loathing of his mother, and repressed confusion about his sexuality.

The police work Nichols had done on the docks in Karachi had piqued his interest in intelligence operations. He saw it as his best way out of the motor pool. When he learned that representatives of the army Counter Intelligence Corps were coming to Guam to interview potential agents, he applied and won a spot at a CIC training school in Tokyo. He graduated with a score of 98, the highest in his class, according to his autobiography, although there is no confirmation of this in his military record. In any case, as soon as he finished the three-month course, the army flew him to South Korea.

Chaos awaited him there. Rioters and police began killing each other in appalling ways in the autumn of 1946—disemboweling, beheading, burying alive. The American public took no notice of the fratricidal civil war that was taking hold. The political culture of Korea had been crushed by more than three decades of colonial servitude. From 1910 to 1945, imperial Japan dominated the Korean Peninsula and humiliated the Koreans. The mistreatment only worsened during World War II, when

Koreans were forced to abandon their names, language, and religious shrines. Korean men had to fight for Emperor Hirohito; about two hundred thousand Korean women were forced to become sex slaves for his troops.

As a colonizer, Japan subjugated and industrialized Korea at the same time. It built state-of-the-art chemical factories, erected hydroelectric dams, and delivered electricity to major cities. It also increased food production and assembled the developing world's best network of railroads, ports, and highways. But most of the food grown in Korea was exported and eaten in Japanese cities, while Koreans endured chronic hunger. Similarly, Japanese companies kept the profits from manufacturing. Four out of five Koreans had menial jobs, usually as tenant farmers. Most of the peninsula's thirty million people were uneducated and landless.

The defeat of Japan in 1945 released decades of pent-up hatred—for the Japanese and for the well-heeled Koreans who had collaborated with them. The Korean people wanted a strong, independent government that would redistribute wealth and redress colonial injustices. The landless majority was attracted to the policies of the Left, which demanded comprehensive land reform and punishment of collaborators. The Korean Right was controlled and financed by a small number of wealthy collaborators seeking to preserve vested property rights. They championed an American-style, free-market economy that they intended to dominate.

When Nichols arrived in Korea, the Right had far fewer supporters than the Left. But the Right cloaked itself in anti-Communist rhetoric and paid young men to beat up leftists in the streets. Neither the Right nor the Left was open to compromise; both sides were eager to kill and willing to die. Disagreements were sorted out by mobs, arson, and assassinations.

Nasty as all this was, the Korean Peninsula had an infinitely more explosive and globally significant problem. In early maneuvers of the cold war, the world's two most powerful nations had sliced Korea in half and were picking sides in the emerging civil war.

The Soviet Union occupied the North, the part with heavy industry and hydroelectric dams. The Russians rolled in on trucks in August 1945

and soon deployed about 100,000 troops in what would become the Soviet zone, later North Korea. The United States occupied the South, home
to two thirds of the Korean population, most of the fertile land, and the
capital, Seoul. Soon after the U.S. Army's XXIV Corps arrived in September, there were 45,000 soldiers in the American zone, which would
become South Korea.

Between them lay the thirty-eighth parallel, an entirely arbitrary border drawn after midnight on August 11, 1945, by two American colonels
using a small *National Geographic* map. The Americans had divided Korea
in the waning days of World War II because they feared, with good reason, that the Soviets would otherwise take the entire peninsula. To Washington's surprise, Soviet leader Joseph Stalin honored the border and kept
his army north of it. The U.S. government hoped division could be a temporary tool, one that would contain the Soviet Union above the thirty-
eighth parallel and limit postcolonial chaos below it, as the Japanese were
gradually rounded up and sent home. American officials promised Koreans a democratic government, but only in "due course," after they showed
enough political maturity.

In addition to being high-handed and insulting, American plans for
the peninsula's future were delusional. Division proved to be an irrevers-
ible blunder. The nonsensical new border squeezed the life out of Korea's
already anemic economy. Electricity stopped flowing south. Food stopped
moving north. Store shelves emptied. Much more dangerously, division
transformed a relatively insignificant postcolonial struggle between landed
and landless Koreans into a proxy fight between superpowers.

From Tokyo, MacArthur sensed trouble. Days after American soldiers arrived in Seoul, he sent a top-secret cable to Secretary of State
George Marshall: "The splitting of Korea into two parts for occupation
by force of nations operating under widely divergent policies and with no
common command is an impossible situation."

No fool, MacArthur assigned day-to-day management of this emerging
mess to a subordinate commander, Lieutenant General John R. Hodge, telling him to "use your best judgment as to which action is to be taken."

Hodge was a much-decorated hero of the war in the Pacific and an accomplished leader of men on the battlefield. He learned quickly and had good advisers. But he had no experience as an occupation administrator. Like nearly all Americans, he was ignorant of Korea's colonial history and did not understand the reasons behind the civil war he was presiding over. During his first week in Seoul, this inexperience and naïveté showed. He was quoted by the press—inaccurately and out of context, American officials would later claim—as saying that Koreans were "the same breed of cats" as the Japanese. He also said that, for the sake of efficiency, Japanese officials would be temporarily retained at their posts.

The general could not have struck a more discordant note. Koreans in the American zone howled that he was a racist and a dictator. Press coverage was scathing in Korea and the United States. The State Department and the Truman White House overruled Hodge and apologized. "The Japanese warlords are being removed. . . . The American people rejoice in the liberation of Korea," Truman said in a damage-control statement hurriedly written by the State Department.

Hodge hustled the Japanese out of Korea. Within four months, nearly four hundred thousand of them were gone. But the damage had been done. Americans were perceived to have taken sides in favor of the landowners while turning their back on the landless poor.

This perception was largely correct, as the United States viewed political struggle in Korea through filters of paternalism and anti-Communist paranoia. MacArthur spelled out the father-knows-best role the Americans would try to play. "The Koreans themselves have for so long a time been down-trodden that they cannot now or in the immediate future have a rational acceptance of this situation and its responsibilities." He argued that Left-leaning political groups in Korea "are being born in emotion." The wise course, MacArthur wrote, was to embrace and empower the Right: "Some older and more educated Koreans despite being now suspected of collaboration are conservatives and may develop into quite useful groups." MacArthur mentioned the "desirability" of importing Syngman Rhee, a U.S.-based Korean politician of the extreme Right.

The United States chose sides in Korea's civil war while paying little attention to questions of social justice, economic equity, or majority will.

It was a blinkered decision similar to those Washington would later make in Iran, Southeast Asia, Africa, and Latin America. Hodge was an inflexible anti-Communist who could not stomach the sweeping land reforms most Koreans wanted. In a cable to MacArthur, he said that events on the ground in Korea were forcing him into a "declaration of war" on "communistic elements."

Still, Americans did not come to Korea to crush human rights. Hodge's orders were to make Korea "a free and independent nation." To that end, he pushed hard to create a governing coalition with participation from the Left and the Right. When they refused to find common ground, he came to hate extremists on both sides. In late 1945, the general, who was a self-lacerating writer, acknowledged his failures in a glum cable to MacArthur.

"The U.S. occupation of Korea under present conditions and policies is surely drifting to the edge of a political-economic abyss from which it can never be retrieved with any credit to United States prestige in the Far East.... Under present conditions with no corrective action forthcoming I would go so far as to recommend we give serious consideration to an agreement with Russia that both the U.S. and Russia withdraw forces from Korea simultaneously and leave Korea to its own devices and an inevitable internal upheaval for its self purification."

North of the thirty-eighth parallel, there was no such hand-wringing among Soviet generals, no talk of giving up and going home. Much more quickly than in the South, hated pillars of Japanese colonial rule crumbled in North Korea. The generals did what Stalin told them to do. They gave power to compliant Koreans of the Left, while exiling, locking up, or executing everyone else. In the first weeks of occupation, Soviet soldiers ran wild, looting, raping, and terrifying Koreans. But after Stalin personally ordered the troops to "not offend the population," the Soviet zone became much quieter and more manageable than the American-occupied South. Soon, Soviet-style reforms redistributed farmland, nationalized factories, and began teaching millions of poor Koreans to read. Many peasant farmers supported the reforms and grew more food. As the CIA and the State Department would soon secretly acknowledge, the Soviets got off to a much smoother start in Korea than the Americans did.

The Soviets chose Kim Il Sung, who had impeccable Communist credentials and genuine local support, to lead their puppet state. He was also handsome, charismatic, and young, just thirty-four when the Soviets first occupied northern Korea. He had been a captain in the Soviet army, although the Soviets kept that a secret. Instead, the generals celebrated and publicized his record as a Korean nationalist hero. Many Koreans already knew of Kim Il Sung. As a guerrilla leader based in northeast China in the 1930s, he had bedeviled the Japanese police, who put him on their list of most-wanted Communist bandits. By the end of World War II, he had become a legend. Some Koreans believed he could walk on water and make himself invisible.

Kim, of course, would prove to be much more than a Soviet puppet. For nearly half a century, he dominated North Korea as a self-proclaimed god. The publicists who wrote his autobiography called him "the sun of mankind and the greatest man who has ever appeared in the world." He became the Great Leader, crushing dissent and sorting his people geographically based on his perception of their loyalty. Those he trusted were allowed to live in Pyongyang. Those he had doubts about were dispatched to the boondocks. Those he did not trust at all were taken away at night by his secret police to a gulag of concentration camps, which exists to this day. There, hundreds of thousands of North Koreans have been starved, raped, murdered, and worked to death. Kim Il Sung created the only totalitarian state to be ruled by a family dynasty. Upon his death in 1994, his son Kim Jong Il seized power; his grandson Kim Jong Un took over in 2011.

In the 1940s, Kim Il Sung played the toady with calculated patience. He flattered and groveled before Stalin while scheming to seize control of the entire Korean Peninsula. During several secret trips to Moscow, Kim begged Stalin to provide him with enough arms, aircraft, and money to invade and defeat South Korea. At the same time, he found ways to relieve political discord in the North: Koreans who found themselves north of the thirty-eighth parallel did not have to put up with the Great

Leader if they did not want to. For a couple of years after he took power, those who owned property or had a college degree or had collaborated with the Japanese were allowed to give up everything they owned and flee south. About two million of them did, bringing more confusion and dislocation into the already roiling politics of South Korea. Some who claimed to be refugees were in fact spies for Kim Il Sung, sent to support the leftists, discredit the Americans, and raise hell. Thanks to a bumbling and sometimes brutal U.S. occupation, they found fertile ground. They also gave the South Korean government the excuse it needed to jail, torture, and kill anyone suspected of being a Communist sympathizer.

When Nichols showed up in Seoul on June 29, 1946, grassroots disgust with the Americans was beginning to boil over.

A cholera epidemic had spread across the American zone, killing nine thousand Koreans. Inflation was rampant and unemployment soared as consumer goods disappeared from stores. The supply of electricity coming in from the Soviet zone declined with each passing month. As crimes against Koreans and their property rose, General Hodge warned his officers to crack down on the boorish and sometimes violent behavior of occupying American soldiers. Land reform had stalled. A shortage of fertilizer and floods had damaged crops, creating rice shortages. In one of his most ill-advised moves, Hodge ordered the Korean National Police to collect rice from farms and distribute it in cities. The police made a bloody hash of it, stealing rice, beating up farmers, and giving a propaganda gift to the Left.

Nichols reported to Sub-Detachment K of the 607th Counter Intelligence Corps, a three-man unit based at Kimpo airfield a few miles west of Seoul. From there, his and other counterintelligence units joined U.S. Army troops and Korean National Police in punishing perceived Communists, including farmers demanding land reform. They raided headquarters of the Farmers Union, Democratic Youth Alliance, and other leftist groups. They searched for and sometimes found evidence of an organized Communist effort to use the failure of the rice collection program to ridicule the United States. Handbills circulated by the South Korea Labor Party accused American soldiers of raping pregnant women "based on their sense of superiority and racial distinction." Sinister motives were seen in the chocolate bars GIs gave to Korean children. Invoking the Opium Wars in China, when Britain crippled the Chinese government by importing large quantities of opium, handbills in Korean said "sweet candy" was part of an American plot "to colonize Korea."

Some recovered documents showed direct North Korean involvement. One message from Pyongyang said the Americans were "making use of Hirohito's residue, and depriving people of their democratic claims and interests." But reports written by American counterintelligence commanders tended to place all the blame for anti-American anger on North Korean "agitation." This was self-serving nonsense. The Korean majority, landless and poor, wanted equality and opportunity—and they did not see it in the policies of the U.S. military command in Seoul.

In September, just as Nichols was getting his feet wet as an army agent, popular agitation gave way to mass violence. Koreans took to the streets to challenge the American occupation in what became known as the Autumn Harvest Uprising. Strikes, marches, and riots erupted in almost every province in the South. A general strike idled a quarter million workers, and crowds of more than sixty thousand gathered in several big cities. The worst bloodshed occurred near Taegu, a city in the southeast, where mobs attacked and occupied the main police station and fought street battles with officers. Forty-four policemen and forty-three civilians were reported killed, many in gruesome ways. Police officers were impaled through the rectum and burned at the stake. Only when U.S. Army tanks arrived did the protesters retreat.

Counterattacks by South Korean police triggered more riots, according to Major Jack B. Reed, commander of army counterintelligence in Korea. "Police methods are brutal," he wrote in a report to Washington. "The Korean people, seeing the police in action during the strike breaking, fall easy prey to agitators." The Americans fought protesters with the help of "right-wing groups [that] volunteered their services." As many as thirty thousand Koreans were imprisoned, including most known members of the South Korean Communist Party and other leftists suspected of being agitators. The bloodshed and mass arrests were another public relations disaster for the Americans—and a gift to Kim Il Sung and Stalin. Hodge told MacArthur that the "Russian propaganda program in North Korea is making tremendous capital . . . and building up the Americans as the most cruel and sadistic imperialists in the entire world."

In the chaos, Nichols smelled opportunity.

"An idea was born in Mr. Nichols' mind" soon after he reported for duty in Korea, according to an air force history of his spy unit (which Nichols helped write). He would create his own team of espionage agents to conduct what he called "positive intelligence." At the time, army counterintelligence agents generally played defense, investigating threats and stopping sabotage. The term "positive intelligence" refers to going on spy offense—infiltrating leftist organizations and sending agents behind enemy lines to find targets and recruit informers. "In those days, no one, in this area, knew or even thought about positive intelligence," Nichols wrote in his autobiography. "We invented it for this area and taught others, as we saw fit, for our own benefit."

Nichols did not personally invent positive intelligence in Korea. After the riots of 1946, General Hodge ordered the entire Korea-based Counter Intelligence Corps to go on offense. But Nichols was singularly aggressive—and uniquely successful—in following Hodge's order to make contact with Korean "political individuals" and extract information from them. Nichols, alone, landed the big fish. He secured the friendship, confidence, and patronage of the one politician who, for better and for worse, would matter most in South Korea.

CHAPTER 2

Rhee and Son

They were an unlikely pair—the porcine young American agent and the
bony old Korean politician.

By the American's account, he first met Syngman Rhee in August
1946, although he does not say where or how. The meeting occurred
when he was fresh from his Tokyo cram course in counterintelligence.
He had no Korean contacts, no influence, and an understandably sketchy
notion of what he was supposed to be doing in Korea. Donald Nichols
had been there barely a month and was just twenty-three.

Rhee, then seventy-one, was the world's most important Korean, in
his own eyes and in the estimation of many Americans. He had lived
most of his life in the United States, where he had scored a stunning
trifecta of elite higher education: a bachelor's degree from George Washington University, a master's in history from Harvard, and a doctorate in
the history of international law from Princeton. His university credentials "evoked awe" among Koreans.

As a politician in exile, Rhee haunted the halls of Congress for four
decades, strutting his Ivy League degrees, lobbying for Korean independence, and winning support from Republicans and Democrats. He also
made many enemies. At the State Department in the mid-1940s, diplomats
viewed him as too old, too stubborn, and too egotistical to be an effective

leader. By 1948, two years after Rhee had returned to Korea, the CIA saw him as an exceptionally risky bet and described him as vain, delusional, and dangerous. "His intellect is a shallow one," a CIA profile said, "and his behavior is often irrational and literally childish." Rhee combined passionate anticommunism with an "unscrupulous" character, the profile concluded, and he would step on "any person or group he felt to be in his way."

When he met Nichols, Rhee had been back in Korea for less than a year and was determined to become president. He wanted to rule the entire Korean Peninsula and crush the regime of Kim Il Sung.

Yet Rhee, for all his septuagenarian prickliness, and Nichols, for all his twentysomething callowness, found favor in each other. In Nichols, Rhee discovered a back door for delivering intelligence that could influence American policy toward Korea. He referred to the young American as "my son Nichols."

In Rhee, Nichols discovered the ultimate inside source—and a shortcut to becoming a very important intelligence asset. He called Rhee "Father."

"I was a good, close, sincere friend of Syngman Rhee from almost the time of his return to Korea from exile until I left in 1957," Nichols bragged in his autobiography. "Because of this friendship and trust, I had complete access to the Republic of Korea government from its highest echelons to the bottom line. His door was open to me twenty-four hours a day, seven days a week. I was one of the people he trusted implicitly, and he had few secrets I did not know. For this reason I was indeed in a position to know what was happening. . . ."

Nichols made certain his superiors knew about his access to the head of state. After the war started, American generals sent reports to Washington that boasted about the singularly powerful source their agent in Seoul had cultivated. In a 1950 cable to air force headquarters, General Stratemeyer, the air force commander in Tokyo, wrote, "President Rhee has recommended Nichols for several South Korean Decorations and has asked for his assignment as personal advisor."

"Mr. Nichols' case was unique," declared a 1953 history of air force intelligence in the Far East. "[He] had developed such friendly personal relations with high ranking Korean personalities that President Syngman Rhee himself requested that he be permitted to remain in Korea."

To enhance his power in Seoul, Nichols would drop Rhee's name whenever he met with his intelligence counterparts in the South Korean government. "If Mr. Nichols had a meeting with Rhee, he always used to tell us that he met with 'Father,'" said Chung Bong-sun, the South Korean air force intelligence officer who worked for Nichols for nearly a decade. "We thought of Mr. Nichols as Syngman Rhee's son, not birth son, but son still."

By boasting about his closeness to Rhee, Nichols secured inordinate attention and influence inside the security apparatus of South Korea. In Seoul's rigidly hierarchical bureaucracy of police, spies, and anti-Communist enforcers, Nichols became a celebrity and a power broker. "For us, the two most famous Americans were Douglas MacArthur and Donald Nichols," said Chung. "Mr. Nichols had our full trust. He was a very famous man. All South Korea ministers knew Mr. Nichols because he was close to President Rhee."

A measure of that trust was Nichols's longtime alliance with Kim "Snake" Chang-ryong, a former Japanese military police officer who became Rhee's right-hand man for anti-Communist vengeance and score settling. The nickname "Snake" supposedly came from MacArthur, who noticed Kim's writhing restlessness. Kim Snake met with Nichols nearly every week in the late 1940s and early 1950s, according to Chung, who described the relationship between the two as extremely close. In the years when he met regularly with Nichols, Kim Snake is believed to have masterminded the executions of thousands of South Koreans suspected of being Communists, according to the findings of a later government inquiry.

"Kim Chang-ryong was a simple guy, an amoral guy—like Nichols," said Kim Dong-choon, a lead investigator for South Korea's Truth and Reconciliation Commission, which in 2005 examined civilian massacres that occurred before and during the Korean War. "Rhee would not work with men he considered to be rivals, and he trusted Nichols and Kim because neither was a political threat."

Nichols passed the loyalty test for more than a decade as his access to the president became the stuff of legend among other American military intelligence agents in South Korea. Lieutenant Colonel Gene Mastrangelo arrived in Seoul five years after Nichols left, but officers there in the Air Force Office of Special Investigations were still talking about him. "Nichols was held in awe. They told me he was the only guy who could walk into Rhee's office unannounced and see the president," said Mastrangelo, who later became deputy director of air force counterintelligence.

It is impossible to document how many times Nichols met with Rhee. The Korean War ripped a gaping hole in the official record of Rhee's rise to power and the early years of his presidency. His appointment books between 1945 and 1950 were destroyed or taken north when the Korean People's Army overran Seoul in June 1950. Biographies of Rhee rarely mention Nichols, though that is hardly surprising because the South Korean military and intelligence establishment has refused to release most records related to Rhee's years in power.

But letters, U.S. government documents, and Rhee's presidential papers show that the bond between the spy and the president was as strong as it was unusual. In a 1949 letter to the American ambassador in Seoul, Rhee personally requested that Nichols be allowed to stay in South Korea as his adviser. The American ambassador in Seoul, John J. Muccio, wrote that Nichols "draws his information primarily from Korean sources. His connections with Korean National Police intelligence officers are especially close, but he also makes full use of intelligence sources of the Korean Army and Navy." A letter from the commander of American forces in Korea said that Rhee was "personally interested" in Nichols, who had won "the maximum in respect and cooperation" from Korean government agencies. The president's wartime appointment book for 1951 shows that he met with Nichols at least five times, sometimes for as long as an hour, and the meetings came on days when Rhee was consulting with the most senior members of his government. On April 29, 1951, for example, Rhee met for half an hour with his foreign minister before meeting for an hour with "Mr. Nichols."

The personal ties Nichols maintained for more than a decade with a foreign head of state have no parallel in the history of U.S. military operations, according to retired air force colonel Michael E. Haas, a former special operations commander who has studied Nichols's career and written several books about special ops during the cold war. Haas said Nichols took advantage of a unique opportunity in prewar Korea: there were no supervisory officers to monitor or limit his contacts with Rhee.

"Incredibly, no one in the U.S. government appears to have asked, 'What the hell is this twenty-three-year-old air force sergeant doing in the role of private confidant to a head of state?'" Haas said. "Inexplicable to this day is that neither General MacArthur's Far East Command, nor the Departments of Defense or State, ever insisted on placing Nichols under the meaningful supervision of a senior intelligence official. It beggars belief that Nichols with his elementary school-only education was left to find his own way in such lethal corridors of power."

Of course, once the Soviet-backed northern invasion forced the United States to care intensely about Korea, no one dared criticize Nichols for being too chummy with South Korea's president. The young spymaster was suddenly indispensable. No other American had his contacts. Nichols later wrote that Rhee, too, was pleased with how their relationship worked out.

"It was not a breach of friendship to use information I garnered from and through my close association with him; Rhee knew I was doing it. He believed it to be in the best interest of his country and mine—indeed, of the world."

Rhee had flown home to Korea on October 16, 1945, after more than three decades of exile in the United States, in an aircraft provided by General MacArthur. The American military occupation was just a month old and already in need of help.

To tame the restive Left-leaning majority, MacArthur and Hodge wanted a brand-name anti-Communist with street credibility. They hoped Rhee could be a steadying force—venerable enough to command respect, absent long enough to rise above petty political rivalries, and Americanized enough to be a useful puppet. Most important for the generals, who had stumbled badly over the question of what to do with the Japanese occupiers and their Korean collaborators, Rhee had anti-Japanese credentials. He had often told American audiences that the Japanese had jailed and tortured him when he was a young man—though it was actually police from the collapsing Korean monarchy who arrested him. Then, as the story went, he emerged from prison unbowed and defiant. He fled Korea rather than collaborate with Japanese colonial authorities.

Born in 1875, Rhee was the second son of a once-noble Korean family that had slid into penury. His mother desperately wanted him to pass a civil service exam, secure a government job, and put bread on the family table. To that end, she pampered and hounded her little boy. When he was six and memorized a book with a thousand Chinese characters, she invited neighbors for a feast. But she also forced him to spend long hours practicing calligraphy. She did not allow him to lift anything heavy or throw stones, fearing nerve damage that might spoil his penmanship.

Rhee never qualified for a civil service job in the corrupt and crumbling Chosun Dynasty, which had ruled Korea for nearly five hundred years. Instead, he enrolled in an American Methodist missionary school, where he excelled in his studies and became a firebrand for democracy. As a twenty-year-old, according to a biographer, he was "impetuous . . . arrogant, heedless, and impatient."

Those personality traits, which persisted undiminished into his eighties, landed Rhee behind bars in 1899. He spent nearly five years in prison. Thanks to an enlightened warden and sympathetic American missionaries, he made brilliant use of the time. He converted to Christianity, read voraciously, and transformed himself into an English-speaking expert on the West. After his release, American missionaries were amazed by his erudition and ambition. They helped him travel to America and to acquire the Ivy League polish that impressed Koreans even more than it did Americans.

Rhee became a lobbyist for Korean independence. In the judgment of historian Bruce Cumings, he also became a parasite: "It seems he was never gainfully employed but supported himself through contributions from other Koreans." Over the next thirty years, he maintained a fiercely loyal coterie of patrons, even as a number of his early contributors came to despise him. They accused him of misusing money, hogging publicity, and being an intransigent pain in the neck. They booted him out as leader of a Korean government in exile, although Rhee continued to insist he would always be the leader of all exiled Koreans. Through it all, he maintained a strong measure of international credibility and held a singular position inside Korea as a legitimate political leader.

He had an instinctive ability to seduce English speakers he thought might be useful to him. "Rhee, far better than any other Korean leader, could take the measure of Americans," Cumings wrote. "He was a master at grabbing the tail and wagging the dog."

This, then, was the politician MacArthur and Hodge hoped would be a force for peace and unity in the American zone. They protected him with bodyguards when he landed at Kimpo airfield and checked him into a suite at the Chosun Hotel in Seoul, where all American dignitaries were put up. He had his own dining room, a conference hall, and the use of a limousine. At a crowded press conference, Hodge enthusiastically reintroduced him to the Korean people. Set loose in the land of his birth, Rhee did not hesitate. He immediately began to wag the dog.

He blamed the United States for allowing the Russians to grab the northern half of Korea and poison it with communism. As American generals would soon learn, the venerable one was just getting started. As the months went by and the American occupation's grip on security continued to falter, Rhee became more obstreperous, more unpredictable, more hostile to U.S. interests. He flew back to Washington to accuse Hodge of being a dictator, noisily insulting the general at press conferences and quietly undermining him at the State Department.

Rhee wanted independence for Korea with no strings attached (except for American money and military hardware) and he wanted to be in charge. To get what he wanted, he was willing to make sweetheart deals with wealthy Koreans who had collaborated with the Japanese and work with the sadistic police force they had trained. While the rich gave him money and the police tortured his enemies, Rhee sheltered them beneath the umbrella of his anti-Japanese reputation. His most powerful political rivals were imprisoned or assassinated. He built mass political support with the help of strong-arm, ultra-Right youth organizations financed by his wealthy backers. These gangs often worked with the U.S. Army's Counter Intelligence Corps, the same outfit Nichols worked for.

The United States soon grew weary of its costly commitments in Korea. The Joint Chiefs of Staff concluded as early as 1947—two years into the U.S. occupation—that Korea was not strategically important enough to justify the cost of troops and bases. The Truman administration decided the following year to withdraw nearly all American troops, give modest economic aid, and hope for the best. As it walked away, the U.S. government wrapped itself in diplomatic double-talk that belied its actions. It said that removal of troops "would in no way constitute a lessening of United States interests" in South Korea. Washington agreed to support UN-supervised elections, which were boycotted by the Left and which Rhee easily won.

Many Americans who witnessed Rhee's rise were depressed and disgusted. Those emotions found their way into a secret CIA assessment of Rhee in early 1948, which described him as a demagogue "bent on autocratic rule" who represented a "small class that virtually monopolizes the native wealth and education of the country."

As president of South Korea, the CIA predicted, Rhee would demand the "ruthless suppression of all non-Rhee" opposition. As for the police force under him, the CIA said it was "inevitably committed to the support of the Right, since it realizes that the successful creation of a Leftist regime in South Korea would mean the massacre of police personnel."

As Rhee assumed the presidency, full-scale guerrilla war spread across much of South Korea. This explosion of violence and killing marked the de facto beginning of war in Korea, many historians have concluded. Tens of thousands of Koreans in the South were already dead—killed by their own government—before the Korean War "officially" began in 1950, with the invasion from the North. Yet the savagery and death toll of this war was largely invisible in the United States in 1948 and 1949—and remains so today. The lack of American interest was a function of who did and did not die. As historian Allan R. Millett discovered, only three Americans were killed in the partisan fight, while estimates of the Korean dead range from thirty thousand to one hundred thousand. Millett has described it as the invisible war that preceded the forgotten war.

The Communist-led insurgency was indeed lethal. It killed more than seven thousand South Korean policemen, soldiers, and paramilitary fighters. But Rhee's forces fought back viciously and disproportionately, often massacring women and children. Some of the fiercest fighting and worst atrocities occurred on the mountainous South Korean island of Cheju, where the guerrilla war began in April 1948. Forces loyal to Rhee razed villages across the island. Of the twenty-five thousand to thirty thousand people who were killed or wounded there, about 85 percent were victims of the police, the military, or vigilante youth groups.

A snapshot of the carnage has emerged from survivor accounts: Rhee's men surrounded the island village of Gyorae before dawn on November 13 and started to burn houses. Soldiers shot villagers trying to escape the fire and threw their bodies into the flames to destroy evidence.

"When soldiers came to burn down my house, I begged them to spare our lives," a villager named Yang Bok-cheon testified. "But the soldier pushed me down and pulled the trigger; the bullet went through my side and made a big hole—about the size of an adult's fist—in my daughter's thigh, who was on my back. Immediately, my son rushed toward me screaming, 'Mom!' Then, the soldier fired a gun at my son. I can still clearly remember soldiers saying to each other, 'The little bastard is not yet dead!' My son's heart protruded through the skin since he was shot on his left chest. They were not human."

This hideous civil war—one that is seldom mentioned and has never become part of America's understanding of Korea—was Nichols's training ground. He traveled to the countryside to watch government executions. He was a regular attendee at torture sessions in Seoul. In the words of John Muccio, the American ambassador in Seoul, Nichols became "especially close" to the Korean National Police, which took the lead in interrogating, torturing, and executing suspected Communists. On at least one occasion, Nichols delivered a truckload of U.S. rifles to the Korean National Police, according to Kim Bok-dong, a translator who worked for Nichols for four years.

"As an active, circulating agent in the villages of South Korea, I witnessed many executions of espionage, sabotage and guerrilla warfare personnel," Nichols wrote in his autobiography. "The people to be executed were brought in by truck, unloaded and stripped of any usable clothing. Then each was tied to a wooden post. A piece of paper with a black dot was pinned to each man's/woman's chest to make a target. Wooden coffins were brought up and placed beside each victim to be executed. With no ceremony, the order began: Ready . . . Aim. . . . !! The people were shot, and their remains placed in the coffins. The rough-hewn coffins were loaded and hauled off to destinations unknown."

Working "in conjunction" with the Korean police, Nichols said he became "an expert interrogator with a real feel for asking the right questions at the right time." During these interrogations, he said he "had to maintain an air of detachment—even approval" as he witnessed various methods of torture. Several U.S. intelligence officers said there was no need for Nichols to bloody his own hands: the Korean National Police had been extensively trained in torture by the Japanese. Nichols often sat in on waterboarding, during which interrogators strapped a suspect to a tilted board, covered his nose and mouth with a cloth, and poured water over the cloth to simulate drowning. After the 9/11 attacks on the United States, the CIA used waterboarding on terror suspects, calling it "enhanced interrogation," even as the State Department described the procedure as "torture." Nichols said waterboarding caused "slow drowning and much pain. The victim told the interrogator anything that he wanted to hear—false or otherwise."

Nichols waited with South Korean torturers while a naked man—

hip-deep in water—stood out of doors in freezing weather until he "told us what we had to know." Nichols observed several naked suspects who were tied down on tables and "burned repeatedly on their testicles with lighted cigarettes." He said he also witnessed a latter-day crucifixion: the suspect was wired to a wooden cross and subjected to electrical shocks until he "began to scream the answers we were seeking."

The capture and execution of senior anti-Communist leaders in the field was often confirmed by cutting off their heads and sending them to Seoul, Nichols wrote. The heads were preserved in gasoline cans. A photograph of Nichols with one of these heads—taken by a U.S. Army Signal Corps photographer—confirms his story. In the photo, Nichols joins several other men on the roof of South Korean army headquarters in Seoul to inspect the head. Other army photos taken that day by the same photographer show the head being pulled out of the bucket and held up by its hair. The head apparently was that of Kim Chi-hoe, a guerrilla leader.

"I have seen these things," Nichols wrote, "and I have survived in spite of the memories." Nichols did not let qualms about the morality of torture disrupt his intelligence work. "In most cases I did not approve of their methods," he wrote, "but I will say that you could obtain whatever information they possessed in short order."

By 1948, Nichols had moved his counterintelligence unit from Kimpo airfield to a separate compound about a mile from the base. There, he and his men had more privacy and flexibility in interrogating suspects, recruiting agents, and entertaining high-level visitors from the South Korean government. Nichols lived in a Japanese-made two-story house; his office was on the first floor and he slept on the second. The U.S. Air Force by then had become a separate service of the military, and the counterintelligence unit Nichols led was absorbed in 1949 into the Air Force Office of Special Investigations, which had been created to root out corruption and mismanagement inside the air force. Nichols, though, had no interest in that mission. As commander of District 8, Office of Special Investigations, he focused on breaking up Communist cells in South Korea and rounding up recent North Korean defectors and refugees for interrogation at his compound. As an "adviser" to the South Korean coast guard, which was funded by the U.S. military, he used its men to seize and interrogate North Koreans who traveled south by boat.

"By this time, our unit was really moving in 'high, very high' South Korean government circles," Nichols said in his book. "By late 1948, we were being visited by high-ranking South Korea government and military officials seeking advice on one matter or another. . . . It became a snow-balling operation. The more we knew—the more we could come to know."

These claims are mostly true, according to Serbando J. Torres, who worked directly for Nichols as his clerk-typist for more than three years, starting in September 1948. In addition to typing thousands of his intelligence reports, Torres lived with his boss in air force quarters and came to regard him as a close friend.

The son of a cannery row laborer, Torres grew up in Monterey, California, where he dropped out of high school to join the Army Air Corps, which sent him to Korea. He was nineteen when Nichols invited him to come live at his compound, where they often ate dinner together and where Torres learned how friendly his boss was with the president of South Korea.

"Nick went over to see Syngman Rhee rather often," Torres recalled. "There was a close relationship there. Nick also became friends with the president's wife [Austrian-born Francesca Donner] and he would talk about both of them. Nick once recommended to Rhee and his wife that there should be a presidential unit citation given to American servicemen in Korea. Rhee and his wife thought it was a good idea and Nick had me write the citation up. After one of his visits to see the president, Nick told us that Rhee wanted him to be his personal air force adviser."

This boast was also true. On June 7, 1949, Rhee wrote an unusual letter to John Muccio, the American ambassador. It said that the South Korean government—"with great concern and sincere interest in more rapidly developing its Air Force"—wanted Nichols (then twenty-six) to serve as the "advisor to the President on Air Affairs."

By that time, nearly all American military personnel had been withdrawn from Korea. Ambassador Muccio thought it over for ten days and then replied in a letter: "Mr. Nichols will be able to advise you on air matters."

But Rhee was not satisfied. The president worried that his young American friend might be transferred elsewhere—a worry that almost certainly was planted in Rhee's mind by Nichols himself. So two months later Rhee wrote another letter to the ambassador.

"I have received information that circumstances have arisen which may cause Mr. Nichols to leave Korea," Rhee wrote. He asked "once again" that Nichols be allowed to stay on in the country and become his personal adviser on air affairs.

There is no record that Nichols asked his superiors in the air force if he could or should take the extraordinary step—as a low-level noncommissioned officer—of becoming a personal adviser to a foreign head of state. He simply did it. In meetings with Rhee, he strongly urged the creation of an air force that would be separate from the South Korean army. To lead it, he recommended a South Korean lieutenant colonel who had become a close friend. Kim Chung Yul was a regular visitor to Nichols's compound, where the two men often walked arm in arm and greeted each other with hugs and kisses.

Nichols's recommendations became government policy when Rhee created the air force and named Kim Chung Yul as its first chief of staff. Kim would go on to become ambassador to the United States and prime minister of South Korea. In his memoir, Nichols describes his role as air force adviser as "one of the most important aspects of my Korean saga. This was an [*sic*] unique operation which I alone negotiated."

As Nichols was advising Rhee to create a separate air force, the American military was insisting that South Korea did not need one. American generals repeatedly told Rhee and many officials in his government that the United States was "in no way committed to support a Korean Air Force with advisors or materiel." They also said that South Korea "was utterly incapable of supporting an air force."

But there is nothing in Nichols's military service record to suggest that he was disciplined for urging Rhee to do precisely what the U.S.

government did not want done. In the late 1940s, no one in the Far East Command in Tokyo seemed to understand how close Nichols was to Rhee. In spite of all the unrest, Korea was still a sideshow. MacArthur and his generals were still not paying attention.

For years, Rhee granted Nichols unusual influence over how the air force operated—in ways both large and small. Nichols made certain that his longtime houseboy, Cho Boo-yi, became a noncommissioned officer in the air force. Nichols sent North Korean defectors to the air force with orders that they should be given commissions as officers. Later on, as Nichols's empire expanded, he took command of hundreds of South Korean air force officers and airmen. They came to work for him at various bases during the war and later at his sprawling compound outside Seoul.

Why would the president of South Korea keep a young, low-ranking American intelligence agent in his back pocket for more than a decade? It is impossible to know for sure. Rhee never publicly explained the relationship. South Korean government documents from that era have been lost or remain secret. Still, there are two likely reasons.

First, Rhee was comfortable working with Americans and expert in manipulating them. Fluent in English, he had been immersed for most of his life in the culture of the United States. Several of his key advisers in Korea were Americans, although they were much older and far better educated than Nichols. Rhee's press adviser and principal hagiographer was Robert T. Oliver, a speech professor at Penn State. Rhee recruited Millard Preston Goodfellow, a former deputy director of the Office of Special Services (OSS), to help buy additional arms. And James H. Hausman, an army lieutenant colonel who was wounded at the Battle of the Bulge, was the single most influential officer in shaping the South Korean army. Rhee also kept in contact with a number of right-wing Republicans in Congress, using them to pressure the State Department.

A more urgent reason for Rhee's friendship with Nichols was the president's hunger for American military hardware—tanks, heavy artillery, and fighter aircraft. Rhee seemed to believe that Nichols could help him get it.

In the summer of 1949, after nearly four years of troubled occupation, the United States pulled the last of its combat troops out of South Korea. Only five hundred American military advisers remained in the country as part of a newly created Korean Military Advisory Group, known as KMAG. After Rhee's personal request—and with the approval of the Far East Air Forces and Ambassador Muccio—Nichols and six of his agents were placed on indefinite duty in Korea and attached to KMAG.

Cynics said the acronym KMAG stood for "Kiss My Ass Good-bye." The joke grew out of South Korea's military weakness compared to the North. For as the Americans withdrew, they decided not to leave behind armor, artillery, or late-model military aircraft. The Truman administration had decided the weapons were needed elsewhere. The president's advisers also worried that Rhee, whose forces had been skirmishing with the North Koreans for months along the thirty-eighth parallel, would use heavy weapons to mount a preemptive invasion.

This was not an idle fear. In the fall of 1949, Rhee wrote a warmongering letter to Robert Oliver, his American press adviser.

"I feel strongly that now is the most psychological moment when we should take an aggressive measure . . . to clean up the rest of them in Pyongyang. We will drive some of Kim Il Sung's men to the mountain region, where we will gradually starve them out. . . ."

In the letter, Rhee asked Oliver to persuade the American public and the U.S. government "to give us all the material backing that we need."

The Soviet Union had by then pulled its own army out of North Korea, but it left behind more than enough armor and artillery to support an invasion. In Pyongyang, Kim Il Sung made no secret of his desire to grab the whole of the Korean Peninsula. In Moscow, he assured Stalin that an invasion could be successful within a few days. As Stalin warmed to the idea of an attack that would embarrass the Americans, he dispatched new shipments of military equipment to North Korea, including scores of late-model military aircraft. He also sent a large contingent of military advisers who helped the North Koreans develop an invasion plan and trained the Korean People's Army to use Soviet equipment and weapons.

Because the Americans had not provided South Korea's army with armor and heavy artillery, Rhee believed (correctly, as it turned out) that in the event of an invasion his country would be unable to defend itself. In late 1949, he begged the White House, State Department, and Congress to reverse course and send him aircraft and other hardware. As Rhee's alarm increased, his police funneled more and more intelligence to Nichols. The reports chronicled the military buildup in North Korea. Rhee's police, army, navy, and air force also brought recent North Korean defectors and refugees to Nichols's compound, where they described the North's feverish and well-supplied preparations for war.

As Rhee clearly intended, Nichols and his men began to churn out reports that documented the muscular rise of the Korean People's Army. They detailed huge shipments of Soviet military hardware, reported on the forced evacuation of civilians from North Korean borders areas where troops were massing, and described concentrations of Soviet-made tanks just north of the thirty-eighth parallel.

Other American intelligence groups based in Korea, including army intelligence and a nascent CIA group, were writing similar reports. But Nichols often had more details, especially about the construction of new military airports and the sudden appearance in North Korea of late-model Russian-made aircraft. His analytical reports were elegant and persuasive, and some were illustrated with excellent maps. In one special report dated February 11, 1950, Nichols explained that new North Korean airfields had been constructed just north of the border in a straight line—a position that made sense only in the event of an offensive strike. If they had been built for defensive purposes, Nichols noted, they would have been positioned throughout the North.

This report caught the eye of General Stratemeyer, commander of Far East Air Forces. He cabled the most alarming excerpts from it directly to the air force chief of staff in Washington:

"Believed significant 'on the scene report' as district commander's judgment and intimate knowledge of situation is excellent. Salient points follow: Ever growing civil unrest and present political situation in Korea tends to assure forthcoming civil war in Korea is inevitable. Air power of north Korea will play important role in overthrow of south Korean Govt.

District commander also advised recently his belief that situation would be too hot for American personnel. . . ."

The cable rang alarm bells among the Joint Chiefs of Staff and at the State Department. A meeting was convened in March at the State Department. Its focus: Who the hell is Donald Nichols and does he know what he is talking about? It was agreed at the meeting "that action should and will be taken to determine what basis there is" for his claim that war is "inevitable."

CHAPTER 3

Muzzling Mr. Nichols

No one of importance in American intelligence cared enough about Donald Nichols or Korea to try to shut him up—until the late spring of 1950. Until then, he had beavered away in obscurity, writing increasingly alarming reports about North Korea's war plans, reports that were either unread or ignored by nearly all the Americans who mattered in Tokyo and Washington.

Nearly every month, his productivity increased, as measured by the ballooning volume of air intelligence information reports he sent monthly to Far East Air Forces headquarters. The civil war that tore South Korea apart in the late 1940s had helped him expand his spying network, as he extracted intelligence from detainees (with the help of Rhee's torturers) and recruited new agents to send into North Korea. In the South Korean government, the few officials whom he could not "win over by sheer friendship and magnetism," he controlled with intimidation, fear, and blackmail.

On his own authority, Nichols traveled to North Korea for what he called a "legal-illegal looky-looky." He disguised himself as an army lieutenant and pretended to be a train commander while transporting supplies from Seoul to American negotiators who were based in Pyongyang in 1947 and claims he occasionally met with Soviet and North Korean officials. As the North Korean military buildup gathered momentum in 1949, he took dangerous low-altitude surveillance flights over North Korea in unarmed, fabric-covered L-4 spotter planes flown by South Korean air force pilots.

At the same time, Nichols attended and photographed executions of South Koreans at the hands of the South Korean National Police and the South Korean army. Thirty-nine "confessed Communists" were secretly killed on the afternoon of April 14, 1950, in the hills about ten miles northeast of Seoul as Nichols took pictures with a Leica he bought at an army PX in Seoul for $174. "No newspaper correspondents were observed and no mention of this particular execution has been noted in the press to date—eleven days afterwards," wrote Lieutenant Colonel Bob E. Edwards, the military attaché at the American embassy in Seoul, in a cable sent to Washington.

The cable included fifteen of Nichols's photographs. The sequence of death, as shown in the photos, was just as he later described it in his memoir: After victims were lined up for roll call, military police used rope to tie them to posts. Open wooden coffins can be seen in the background. Pinned over each victim's heart was a numbered paper target with a large black bull's-eye. After the initial volley from the firing squad, some victims, wounded but not dead, were shot through the head at point-blank range with .45-caliber pistols.

In his cable, Edwards described the scene as "a normal execution as carried out quite frequently in South Korea. . . . The victims were singing the Communist song and giving cheers for the leaders of North Korea when the firing squad opened fire. They faced the squad with a sullen attitude and died bravely."

Nichols dressed for the execution in a business suit, dark tie, and white shirt. An army photograph that day shows him at the front of a cluster of American officers who are watching the killings. He is crouched on his haunches, like a catcher in baseball, snapping photographs.

He had invited Serbando Torres, his clerk, to come along. But Torres said he was "squeamish" and encouraged his air force colleague Sergeant Russell Bauer to go in his place. When Bauer came back to the office in the late afternoon, his uniform was spattered with blood and brain tissue. Torres asked him why. A Korean soldier had used a samurai sword to behead a wounded victim, Bauer replied, noting that it had taken the soldier several whacks before the job was done. The beheading was not included among the photographs that were sent to Washington. Torres said Nichols seemed unaffected by the killings he witnessed. "I don't believe they bothered him," he said.

The trust Nichols established with Rhee meant that he was the first American called when a North Korean fighter pilot defected to the South in a Soviet-made aircraft. In late April 1950, Lieutenant Lee Kun Soon, twenty-four, a flight instructor in the North Korean air force, landed an Ilyushin IL-10 ground attack fighter at an airport in Pusan, at the southern tip of the Korean Peninsula. Nichols hurried to the scene, interrogated the pilot, and persuaded South Korean officials to give the plane to the United States. He also coaxed the pilot into coming to work at his spy base.

These kinds of intelligence scoops thrilled Nichols's supervisors in the Air Force Office of Special Investigations. In twice-yearly officer effectiveness evaluations, they heaped praise on him. "An outstanding investigator and intelligence officer who has demonstrated exceptional ability in securing the trust, confidence and cooperation of Korean military and civil officials," Lieutenant Colonel Spencer W. Raynor wrote in May 1950. Nichols "made himself indispensable" in Korea, another evaluation said. As a spy who aggressively exploits enemy intelligence, Raynor wrote, "Mr. Nichols is the most capable and most outstanding officer I have ever known."

Higher up in the U.S. chain of command, however, Nichols had made an exceptionally powerful enemy—one who would soon try to destroy him.

By stirring up Pentagon and State Department bureaucrats with his report of "inevitable" war in Korea, Nichols had unwittingly challenged the judgment of army Major General Charles A. Willoughby, chief of intelligence for MacArthur.

Five weeks before Nichols predicted a North Korean invasion, Willoughby had sent his own personal prediction to Washington. "Such an act is unlikely," he wrote. A month after Nichols's report of certain war was flagged as "significant" by the Far East Air Forces, Willoughby advised the Pentagon: "It is believed that there will be no civil war in Korea this spring or summer. . . ."

Willoughby was a dangerous man to contradict. Besides being the top intelligence officer in the Far East Command, he was a member of MacArthur's inner circle in the Dai-Ichi Seimei Building in Tokyo. That building was where, as supreme commander, MacArthur took on the airs of a head of state while leading the rebirth of postwar Japan. By 1950, MacArthur was seventy years old and a global legend of wildly contradictory parts. He had been a fearless frontline general in World Wars I and II, earning nearly every conceivable medal for effectiveness and valor, including the Congressional Medal of Honor. His rare gift was for orchestrating spectacular victories without killing large numbers of Americans, as he had done in the war against Japan. Yet MacArthur was much more—and much less—than a battlefield genius. Biographers over the decades have described him as brainy, backstabbing, charming, childish, theatrical, and sly. He was incapable of admitting mistakes. "No more baffling, exasperating soldier ever wore a uniform," William Manchester wrote in his masterful biography *American Caesar.*

MacArthur was also openly insubordinate to Truman, declining a White House invitation after World War II to return to Washington for talks about America's role in the future of the Far East. The general made no effort to hide his presidential ambitions and encouraged Republicans to nominate him for the presidency in 1948. Truman despised him, calling him "Mr. Prima Donna." MacArthur suffered from a character flaw that Manchester diagnosed as "peacockery," a self-blinding mix of arrogance, vanity, and pride. As a five-star general entering his eighth decade of magnificence, MacArthur did not like to be told what he did not already know. Some of his general staff officers were, in the words of columnist Joseph Alsop, "almost wholly simpering and reverential." He rarely met face-to-face with anyone else. As the historian William Stueck put it, MacArthur surrounded himself with men "who would not disturb the dream world of self worship in which he chose to live."

No staff officer was more skilled in giving the great man a soothing bath in his own preconceptions than Charles Willoughby. Starting in the early days of World War II, when he first became MacArthur's chief of intelligence, or G-2, Willoughby was part of the "Bataan Gang," a gaggle of officers who were evacuated with MacArthur from the Philippines in 1942 and stayed with him through the Japanese occupation and into the first year of the Korean War.

Willoughby, fifty-eight in 1950, was born in Germany, and there was much about him that struck his colleagues as insufferably Prussian. He sometimes wore a monocle. His combination of pomposity and affectation generated derisive nicknames: "Sir Charles," "Baron von Willoughby," and "Bonnie Prince Charles." Outside of his flattering audiences with MacArthur, Willoughby could be intimidating, arrogant, and vindictive. He was widely despised.

But he was not a fool. He spoke five languages, including Japanese, and had years of experience in directing sprawling intelligence operations. Because MacArthur did not pay attention to Korea, it was Willoughby—and only Willoughby—who determined what was going on there. In the years before the outbreak of war, he was the chief interpreter of intelligence about North Korea for the Far East Command, the entire U.S. military, the State Department, and the Truman White House. MacArthur affectionately called Willoughby "my pet fascist." The two generals had similar distastes. According to historian Millett, they both looked down their noses at "Democrats, the British, most Asians, Washington agencies in general and the navy in particular, army officers who might be critical of [MacArthur's] infallible judgment, potentially unfriendly representatives of the press, civilian diplomats, and Communists, generously defined." After the war, colleagues would accuse Willoughby of deliberately falsifying intelligence reports to please MacArthur.

Besides arrogance and sycophancy, Willoughby's defining weakness as an intelligence analyst was his reluctance to believe sources he did not directly control, especially reports that relied on the work of Asians. During 1949 and early 1950, Willoughby refused to believe the mushrooming numbers of reports from U.S. military intelligence operatives that showed North Korea's preparations for a large-scale invasion. Some came from Nichols, but many others came from an army intelligence detachment in Seoul called the Korean Liaison Office, which Willoughby himself had established. The American embassy in Seoul and army intelligence advisers wrote similar reports that reached the State Department and the CIA. Almost all of them relied upon the intelligence work of Korean agents, whose judgment Willoughby reflexively discounted.

The reports that came from Nichols were especially suspect, receiving "the lowest possible reliability evaluation." A possible reason was that Nichols and his team of air force agents were "in direct competition" with Willoughby's army spy team.

MacArthur, Willoughby, and the army brass in Washington had a major bureaucratic incentive for discounting the likelihood of war on the Korean Peninsula. Under Truman, who was skeptical of defense spending and did not trust his generals, the military budget kept shrinking. The army was squeezed especially hard. In the second half of the 1940s, its manpower fell from 6 million to 530,000. The army's chief of staff, General Omar N. Bradley, said the cuts had forced the army into a "shockingly deplorable state" of combat readiness. MacArthur complained that he barely had enough soldiers for the occupation of Japan. He viewed the additional cost of supplying, feeding, and training troops in Korea as unnecessary and insupportable. The army argued in 1947 that American troops should leave Korea, and it won the day inside Truman's White House. With its budgetary blinders on, the army did not see the pullout as likely to trigger a Soviet-backed invasion of South Korea. Instead, it insisted that an invasion was merely "possible."

In soft-pedaling the chance of an invasion, the army generals were quite alone. A CIA report had concluded that the "withdrawal of US forces from Korea in the spring of 1949 would probably in time be followed by an invasion." That secret report was supported by the State Department, the navy, and the air force. They joined the CIA in warning the White House that a total pullout was unwise. It would be smarter and safer, they argued, to keep several thousand troops in the country. Yet the army prevailed and nearly all of the troops were withdrawn by the end of 1949.

MacArthur's mule-headed unwillingness to acknowledge the likelihood of an attack from the North was well known in the State Department. "In Tokyo, General MacArthur's intelligence continued in all official assessments down to the outbreak of the war to discount reports and rumors of invasion," the Korean desk officer at the State Department later wrote. He and his staff pulled together the "considerable flow" of reports about new North Korean military units receiving heavy artillery and tanks from the Soviet Union. But the Pentagon and the White House refused to pay attention. As the desk officer explained, they "would only review and adopt the estimates of the Theater Commander," meaning MacArthur—though it was really up to Willoughby.

In Washington, indifference to Korea was understandable. The Truman administration had many hot spots to worry about, especially in Eastern Europe, and the United States had written off Korea as a strategic interest. Busy policy makers had to focus on problems deemed urgent.

In Willoughby's view, scores of reports about an imminent invasion of South Korea never rose to that level. So they were not taken seriously in Tokyo or sent on to Washington with instructions that they be placed in front of officials powerful enough to change a Korea policy that was becoming more delusional and more risky with each passing month.

The report on "inevitable" war that Nichols wrote in Seoul in February 1950 was an exception. This is the report that troubled the Joint Chiefs in Washington in March, the report that the Pentagon bounced back to the Far East Command in Tokyo in April, the report that challenged the judgment of MacArthur, as advised by his chief of intelligence. In May 1950, just two months before the outbreak of war, Willoughby did not attempt to discern the report's accuracy. He went after Nichols and tried to shut him up. When that did not work, he tried to ship him out of Korea. Willoughby also scolded Nichols's commanding officer "for allowing him to submit such information."

Willoughby's offensive began with a word to the American embassy in Seoul.

"It was suggested that Mr. Nichols discontinue reporting information which caused unnecessary alarm," according to a history of Far East Air Forces intelligence. "This, Mr. Nichols refused to agree to do."

In the normal military chain of command, Nichols, then a twenty-seven-year-old chief warrant officer, would follow an order from Willoughby. But by 1950, Nichols had found shelter in a rabbit hole in the command structure. He and his men were officially attached to the Korean Military Advisory Group. KMAG was not under MacArthur's command or Willoughby's; it took orders from the American ambassador in Seoul, John Muccio. Because Willoughby could not sack Nichols, he could only send a letter to Muccio, strongly suggesting that Nichols and his intelligence team be tossed out of Korea.

The actual letter, written on May 9, 1950, is missing. Files at the American embassy were destroyed or lost during the North Korean invasion of Seoul, and Willoughby himself destroyed many intelligence files at the Far East Command, excepting ones he wanted to be seen. He ordered that "all materials other than the copies [he] and General MacArthur took back to the States" be burned in 1951.

But the ambassador's written response to Willoughby, which was classified for sixty-five years, does exist in the archives of the Air Force Historical Research Agency in Montgomery, Alabama. In his letter, Muccio said that Nichols was performing splendidly in Korea and that he remained in the country at the personal request of President Rhee. The letter politely but firmly told Willoughby to buzz off.

American Embassy
Seoul, May 16, 1950

Dear General Willoughby,
        . . . Mr. Nichols' knowledge and friendly relationship to key Korean personalities who have intelligence information

are such that I consider his services most helpful and would consider their loss a serious one. . . .

In my opinion, there is no other American intelligence unit or agency now operating in South Korea which produces a larger volume of useful intelligence material on Communist and subversive activities than does Mr. Nichols' unit. . . .

I do not believe that Mr. Nichols' unit conflicts in any significant way with your own unit here or with CIA activities, and I trust that Mr. Nichols and his unit will continue to function in South Korea in their usual efficient and helpful manner.

Sincerely yours,
John J. Muccio

Nichols, as a result, stayed put. And Willoughby stood by his belief that war was unlikely—a position that did not change until the invasion of South Korea.

As an intelligence agent in his twenties, Nichols had an uncanny ability to find powerful older men who would protect him. Just before the American ambassador shielded him from Willoughby's talons, Nichols had dinner with an air force general who would become his principal wartime patron and defender.

They met at the end of 1949, when Major General Earle E. Partridge flew into Seoul on a post-Christmas hunting junket. Partridge was commander of the Fifth Air Force, the Japan-based command responsible for American air power in the Pacific. Bombers, fighters, and ground-attack aircraft from the Fifth Air Force would soon be drawn into the Korean War. But at the time, Partridge knew next to nothing about Korea, even though he had been in command in the Pacific region for nearly eighteen months. He had no contingency plan to deploy aircraft there. He had not been privy to any of the early warnings from Nichols and other intelligence sources about North Korea's preparations for an invasion.

A primary reason for his ignorance was that Willoughby did not widely circulate those alarming reports to most senior officers in the Far East Command. Willoughby's intelligence guidance suggested that the Fifth Air Force should prepare for a flare-up of violence in the Philippines and, to that end, Partridge had sent his best intelligence officers to Manila.

The general had come to Korea for sport: to shoot game birds on Cheju. The fighting between Communist guerrillas and Rhee's forces that had decimated human beings on the island had benefited pheasants, which thrived in abandoned farmlands.

On the night before and the night after his successful hunt, Partridge dined in Seoul. The guests at these two dinners gave him what he later described as his first introduction to South Korea. He encountered "all the ones necessary to know in the top of that government." At the first dinner, he met Ambassador Muccio, the head of the South Korean air force, and Nichols. At the second, he met Rhee. Nichols must have made a good first impression: in the year that followed, Partridge would single out the young chief warrant officer as the most valuable intelligence man in the Far East.

Partridge was then nearing fifty and perhaps saw something of his younger self in Nichols. Neither of them owed their rise to economic privilege or family connections. While the general's childhood was less squalid than that of Nichols, it was similarly scarred. Without money for college and without a mother (who died when he was fifteen), he had joined the army at eighteen and his first war was unglamorous, digging ditches in France during World War I. Partridge had managed to bootstrap himself into a remarkable military career, winning an appointment to West Point, becoming perhaps the best aerial machine gunner and bomb dropper in the Army Air Corps, and helping to lead the bombing of North Africa, Sicily, and Germany during World War II. Partridge was "incautious with his own life." Flying in a one-seat propeller-driven fighter aircraft—and ignoring antiaircraft fire—he routinely accompanied bomber groups on missions over Germany. En route, he critiqued the formations and made his own assessments of bomb damage. In the last year of the war in Europe, he was promoted to major general, given command of the Third Bomb Division, and led bombing campaigns that created firestorms in German cities like Hamburg, killing tens of thousands of civilians.

Like Nichols, Partridge had no patience with "any rule that stood in the way of a good idea." To get more bang from each mission, he ordered his men to pack B-17 bombers with two thousand more pounds of bombs than they were authorized to carry. And while he said that he personally believed that bombing civilian populations was "useless, useless, foolishness," he never hesitated to follow orders. "If the powers say bomb the city," he said, "you bomb the city." During the war in Korea, Nichols and his agents would be the general's primary source of targeting information as the Fifth Air Force bombed every city in the North.

In appearance and manner, Partridge was nothing like Nichols. Reed thin and carefully dressed, he was soft-spoken and self-effacing. Like many generals of his era, he lived like an aristocrat, golfing, playing squash, and shooting birds at every opportunity. But he did not put on airs. He judged junior officers by their performance rather than their pedigree. A character appraisal by his boss in the Far East Air Forces, General Stratemeyer, said Partridge was "not bound by convention or past concepts but retains an open mind and is willing to consider and try out new methods. . . ."

Nichols was a case in point. Partridge was not put off by his youth, his lack of education, his sometimes bumptious aggression, his struggles to control his weight, or his refusal to wear a proper uniform. Partridge never mentioned these issues in the twenty-eight references he made to Nichols in his diary and oral histories. Instead, he celebrated Nichols's quirks: "He had his own code, that is, one not approved by MacArthur's intelligence people. Of course, in this respect, he was illegal as a three dollar bill . . . but he could do anything. . . . Just an incredible man."

Bombing campaigns in North Africa and Europe during World War II had taught Partridge to take special care of his spies.

"I learned—it took me just one day—that you can't do anything without the complete support and confidence of your intelligence section," he later said. "[B]ecause when you arrive in theater, you know zero about what's going on."

When North Korea invaded, Partridge indeed knew little about the Korean Peninsula. Nichols quickly brought him up to speed. In return—and to keep the intelligence flowing—Partridge decided to create a special spy unit for Nichols and give him funding for his own intelligence base. Under the general's wing, Nichols found shelter from the Willoughbys of the U.S. intelligence community: those in the army and the CIA who attempted to control, reel in, or otherwise nibble at the empire that Nichols was just beginning to build. Partridge also invited Nichols to come along with him to shoot birds.

Undeterred by Willoughby, Nichols wrote scores of reports during the first six months of 1950 about North Korea's preparations for an invasion. In the late spring, Nichols told air force headquarters in Tokyo of an intercepted message from Moscow to Pyongyang that said Stalin had approved of an attack on South Korea. Three days before the attack, Nichols wrote that thirty truckloads of North Korean troops were on the move "for the purpose of preparing to invade South Korea."

Nichols later claimed that he wrote a "major report" in early June that nailed the timing of the invasion. He said he predicted it would begin between June 25 and June 28, 1950. It occurred on June 25. "Some ass at General MacArthur's Headquarters in Tokyo and/or Washington didn't believe what was being reported. . . . Or was too stupid to credit it," he wrote in his autobiography.

This prescient report, if it exists, has not yet surfaced in the National Archives or in those of the air force. It may have been destroyed when Willoughby ordered the burning of intelligence records of the Far East Command, or Nichols might not have written it at all. There is reason to be suspicious. During his years in Korea, Nichols exaggerated his accomplishments. Some military historians have concluded that while Nichols did excellent work in chronicling North Korean preparations for war, he was no better than army intelligence or the CIA in finding hard evidence of an imminent attack.

Partridge believed otherwise, insisting that Nichols sent a precise invasion date to MacArthur's headquarters—where it was intentionally ignored and destroyed.

"My one-man army told them there was going to be a war," Partridge said in his oral history. "He had put operators behind the border. He knew what was going on, and he watched them build up their units and supplies. . . . Then he went up to an offshore island where with a telescope he could get a look along the border. He said, 'The war will start within a week.' He then sent this message to Tokyo, and it was suppressed by somebody."

Besides starting a war, the invasion triggered decades of second-guessing and finger-pointing in Washington about who was to blame for ignoring the Soviet-backed buildup inside North Korea. The verdict of history is that there was indeed a major intelligence failure. The invasion genuinely surprised American political and military leaders in Washington, as well as the American public. They had not been told what Nichols and other U.S. intelligence operatives had been telling Willoughby for many months.

Truman was embarrassed and angered by the failure of the CIA to give him a clear warning of war. He fired the agency's director, Roscoe H. Hillenkoetter, named a new director in the summer of 1950, and a far-reaching reorganization of CIA operations soon followed. A congressional committee asked MacArthur why he and his staff officers did not know about the strength of North Korea's military buildup:

"I don't see how it would have been humanly possible for any men or group of men to predict such an attack as that, any more than you could predict such an attack as took place at Pearl Harbor," MacArthur replied, not mentioning, of course, the intelligence information that his own intelligence chief had known about and ignored.

Willoughby responded to criticism by saying he had forwarded hundreds of intelligence reports to the Pentagon that detailed what North Korea and the Soviets were planning. He neglected to admit that he had consistently undermined these reports, giving them low evaluations for credibility and thereby guaranteeing that they would not be taken seriously in Washington. He also neglected to say that he had tried to destroy the career of a young air force intelligence agent who had been particularly insistent—and accurate—in predicting the war.

Willoughby, though, was nothing if not flexible.

As MacArthur scrambled to turn back North Korea's invasion, Willoughby changed his approach to the problem of Donald Nichols. Instead of trying to banish him from the Korean Peninsula, Willoughby demanded that Nichols come work for army intelligence.

PART II
WAR SPY

CHAPTER 4
Dark Star

The Korean People's Army began firing artillery across the thirty-eighth parallel at 4:00 a.m. on Sunday, June 25, 1950. Two hours later, North Korea's blitzkrieg began. Soviet-made T-34 tanks led about 90,000 troops south across the border. The eighty tanks in the first assault were all but unstoppable. Mortars, artillery shells, and bazooka rockets bounced off their thick, sharply angled armor. By 9:00 a.m., the first South Korean town, Kaesong, had fallen. North Korean soldiers also came by sea, wading ashore on the east side of the peninsula from a ragged armada of junks and small boats.

Donald Nichols called Far East Air Forces headquarters in Tokyo at 9:45 that morning and struggled, over a scratchy phone line, to make himself understood. Several times, his agitation turned to anger. He spent nearly all day on the phone, trying to explain the seriousness of what was happening.

General Partridge was out early Sunday, shotgun in hand. He was shooting skeet in Japan and having a fine time of it. In his diary that night, before any mention of the invasion, he wrote that he had hit 116 out of 125 clay targets. It was not until late morning, when he returned to his quarters at Nagoya Air Field, where the Fifth Air Force was based, that he learned about the attack.

Like nearly everyone else in Japan, Partridge had not been expecting trouble in Korea. So instead of rushing to Tokyo, about an hour away by plane, he telephoned General Jarred Crabb, deputy chief of staff for operations at air force headquarters there, and discussed the only contingency plan that had been made for Korea—evacuating American citizens. Partridge told Crabb to get started with preparations. Then, with his wife, Katy, and daughter, Kay, the general went out for an afternoon round of golf.

Asked years later if he had understood the seriousness of the invasion, Partridge said he had not. Willoughby's intelligence shop had kept him in the dark about North Korea's preparations for war. "Had I known what Nichols had said previously, which was suppressed, I would have known instantly that we were in for deep trouble."

MacArthur was not initially alarmed, either. "This is probably only a reconnaissance-in-force," he said at a briefing on Sunday night. "If Washington only will not hobble me, I can handle it with one arm tied behind my back."

Nichols knew better. With Seoul just thirty-five miles south of the thirty-eighth parallel, he knew the Korean People's Army would take it—soon. He ordered his men to remove five file cabinets from his office in a rented house on the outskirts of the capital. They emptied them on the ground and burned all the files, which included names, addresses, and reports from agents who were on Nichols's payroll in North and South Korea. "It took most of Sunday to destroy all that stuff," said Serbando Torres, the army clerk who would stay by Nichols's side for much of the war.

Nichols's prediction was again accurate. Within twenty-four hours of the invasion, Seoul was doomed. Three divisions of the South Korean army had been broken. Its soldiers were on the run, fleeing toward the Han, a broad river on the southern edge of the capital, as North Korean tanks and infantry gave chase. In Tokyo, MacArthur began to grasp the scale of the disaster. "Our estimate," he told the Joint Chiefs of Staff in a teleconference, "is that complete collapse is imminent."

In Washington, as the news sank in, the Truman administration saw much more than just the invasion of an inconsequential Asian country. It saw global communism on the march and the black arts of Stalin at work. At a meeting at Blair House, Truman's temporary residence while the White House was being renovated, generals, cabinet members, and the president himself spoke of "raw aggression" and voiced "moral outrage." In their great-power pique, Truman and his advisers did not see the invasion as a consequence of decisions that they had made about the Korean Peninsula. They had defined it as strategically unimportant and had withdrawn the army from South Korea. By leaving behind no armor, no artillery, and no modern military aircraft, they had made South Korea a sitting duck, just as Rhee had feared.

The attack did not provoke introspection in Washington. Instead, it was viewed as a test of national character, one that demanded action. "We've got to stop the sons of bitches no matter what," Truman told his secretary of state. Two days after the invasion, the White House pushed the United Nations Security Council to authorize the use of force. The Soviet Union could not veto the resolution because its representative skipped the meeting. In less than a week, Truman approved the use of ground forces.

Americans welcomed the rush to war. In the cold war summer of 1950, the Red Scare was real. Commies, it seemed, were everywhere. Five months before the invasion, U.S. senator Joseph McCarthy of Wisconsin had produced a piece of paper that he said listed the names of 205 Communist Party members who were then working and making policy decisions at the State Department. Screenwriters, directors, and actors had been subpoenaed to testify about their Communist links. While most Americans knew nothing about the Korean Peninsula, they believed, for a few intoxicating months, that it was worth fighting for. It made sense to most Americans that the Reds then gobbling up Korea would soon devour the United States, unless they were stopped. A week after the invasion, 81 percent of those polled by Gallup shared Truman's gut reaction to "the sons of bitches." In Congress, word that Truman had committed air and sea forces triggered "spontaneous applause." Nearly every American newspaper supported the use of force. The editorial cartoonist for the Scripps Howard chain was told to go easy drawing caricatures of Truman because it would be bad for "the morale of our readers to picture the commander-in-chief as a grinning nincompoop." With the president pounding his drum as the press cheered and the public followed along, American generals in the Far East Command suddenly had to fight a war they had not anticipated in a place they did not know or understand. A useful symbol of their collective cluelessness when it came to Korea was the round of golf that Partridge, a vastly experienced wartime commander, decided to play after learning about the invasion.

On the second day of the war, after Partridge flew to Tokyo and met with other air force officers, he was overwhelmed by the scale of what he called an "intelligence failure in the field." None of them knew that Nichols, who worked for the air force, had been predicting war. The next day, MacArthur ordered the Fifth Air Force to hit the North Koreans "with every resource at our disposal." In response, Partridge incautiously promised to have a bombing "mission operating against the North Korean forces before dark." That mission was aborted when Partridge discovered that his intelligence operation was incapable of finding targets and "completely disorganized." In his diary that night, Partridge wrote that he had never seen such incompetence in wartime and that it "must be corrected."

The correction would be Donald Nichols.

His four years of anonymous spadework in Korea were about to pay handsome dividends—for the air force, the American war effort, and Nichols himself. Making use of his unrivaled access to South Korean politicians, generals, and spies, he began providing the air force with bomb targets and annotated maps. By mid-July, the Far East Air Forces appointed him as its special representative with authority to gather intelligence across the battlefield. By mid-August, the army and the air force began squabbling over who needed his services most. The invasion revealed Nichols as a natural warrior. As other Americans panicked, Nichols calmly destroyed records and guarded the identity of his agents. The American embassy, by contrast, left its personnel files on five thousand Korean employees unprotected—and available to the North Korean army.

Nichols would win numerous awards for valor and receive lavish praise from senior commanders, one of whom called him "a legend to the South Korean people." The invasion also revealed his darker side. A week after the invasion, he watched South Korean police participate in the mass killing of thousands of civilians and became part of a cover-up that lasted for more than half a century.

As for his close friend President Rhee, the invasion was an opportunity to consolidate power. Truman's resolute military response to the attack gave Rhee hope that the Americans would finally abandon the notion of a divided Korea. Rhee expected the United States to lead a war that would extirpate Communists in the North and bring the entire peninsula under his control. To that end, just three weeks into the war, he wrote to Truman:

> The time has come to cut out once and for all the cancer of imperialist aggression, the malignant growth artificially grown within the bosom of our country by the world communists. The Government and the people of the Republic of Korea consider this is the time to unify Korea, and for anything less than unification to come out of these great sacrifices of Koreans and their powerful allies would be unthinkable.... Daily I pray for the joint success of our arms, for clear skies so that the planes of the United States Airforce may search out and destroy the enemy, and for the earliest possible arrival of sufficient men and material so that we can turn to the offensive, break through the hard crust of enemy forces and start the victorious march north.

As North Korean artillery began to strike the outskirts of Seoul, Nichols helped Americans evacuate to Japan. With a white sheet tied to his jeep,

he drove back and forth across the tarmac at Kimpo airfield, signaling
when it was safe for air force pilots to land in their C-47 transport planes.
As Nichols remembered it, "all other U.S. intelligence units immediately
sought safety in Japan." Three of his agents also evacuated.

Nichols stayed.

"I was a loner," he wrote in his autobiography. "In a disorderly advance to the rear, the loner follows the withdrawal leaving a path of
destruction of millions of dollars of aircraft and other supplies. . . . I appointed myself the job of destroying what others had left behind: buildings which contained classified material, aircraft, vehicles, communications
equipment. . . . I used gasoline, hand grenades and small arms to do most
of the destroying."

But Nichols was not a loner. Serbando Torres stayed with him, risk-
ing his life and winning a Bronze Star. "If he was the only American,"
asked Torres, "where the hell was I?" Torres did not see Nichols destroy
anything in Seoul other than his office files.

Anxiety turned to mass hysteria in the streets of Seoul on Tuesday,
the third day of the war. Rhee and senior ministers in his government
fled south by train. Ambassador Muccio and his remaining staff evacuated in a convoy later that morning. Some South Korean military leaders
had fallen back to Suwon, a city twenty-one miles to the south, to organize an effort (which failed) to stop the North Korean army before it
could cross the Han River.

Nichols and Torres also fled to Suwon on Tuesday morning, but American officers there immediately ordered them back to Seoul. They returned in separate jeeps, with Nichols in the lead. An air force history of
Nichols's spy unit, which Nichols wrote, says the two men spent the re-
mainder of Tuesday destroying radio equipment and a C-54 transport
plane at Kimpo airfield. Torres said that account is fiction.

"We just waited around," he said. "We never went near Kimpo [ten
miles outside the city] and we didn't destroy anything. We drove to
American dependent housing, which was deserted, and bedded down
for the night. Around two in the morning, we were told that the North

Korean army was just outside the gates of Seoul. We said we better ske-daddle."

Back in their jeeps at 3:00 a.m. on day four of the war, they drove toward the Han River, inching through streets choked with panicked families fleeing by truck, bicycle, oxcart, and on foot. In Seoul, there was only one highway bridge over the half-mile-wide river. Nichols and Tor-res had not heard the explosion that earlier in the night destroyed part of the bridge.

The South Korean army, without announcing it to Seoul citizens, had planted 3,600 pounds of TNT on the southern side of the bridge. Intended to stop North Korean tanks, the explosion was disastrously ill timed, killing between 500 and 1,000 civilians and soldiers who were crossing it while trapping 30,000 South Korean soldiers on the north side of the river.

Nichols and Torres abandoned their jeeps near the Han River and walked in darkness toward the damaged bridge, where they could see shattered vehicles and mangled bodies. In his autobiography, Nichols said he was surrounded by "blood, guts, and powder." In a night of chaos and panic, he described himself as singularly heroic.

"I was the only American there at the time, all others had evacuated. I stayed there as long as I could—until the enemy was within small arms firing range. I obtained a small boat, permitted others to get in, jumped in the water, held on to the back of the boat and kicked like hell in an effort to get to the other side in as short order as possible. The boat was loaded so heavily that the top edge was only two or three inches above water level—had anyone sneezed or moved the boat would have turned over. In those days CIC (Counter Intelligence Corps) agents carried a metal badge, much like one carried by our policemen, this was used as a means of identification. I lost mine while crossing the river. . . ."

Nichols overstated his heroism once again. He was not the only American on the wrong side of the river that night. In addition to Torres, there were at least thirty others from the KMAG advisory group—and four American journalists—who were also trying to flee Seoul.

As Torres recalled the night, there was no enemy fire in the vicinity of the bridge, only the anguished cries of Koreans desperate to cross the river. Torres fired his carbine into the air to get the attention of South Korean army engineers in a small boat out in the middle of the Han. They quickly came to the riverbank when they heard the two Americans shouting in English and in Korean. Within minutes, the boat picked them up, together with Nichols's dog, Brownie, a mutt that would stay with him throughout the war. Frantic Korean civilians pushed and shoved, fighting with one another to get aboard, and several of them fell into the Han. But the boat was never dangerously overloaded and Nichols did not jump in the water or kick like hell to propel it across the river; the boat had an outboard motor. The crossing was quick and uneventful. Nichols did not get wet, although he did lose his CIC badge. Within a few hours of their escape, Seoul fell to Kim Il Sung's invading army.

To Torres, Nichols's version of the river crossing was amusingly self-glorifying, but it got the most important thing right. "Nick wasn't afraid of a damn thing," he said. "He was so fearless in that war you could say he was crazy."

From the south side of the river, Nichols and Torres hitched a ride to Suwon, where American commanders were scrambling to find bomb targets. After meeting with his contacts in Rhee's security apparatus, Nichols came up with three targets in Seoul—the main railway station where troops from the North were concentrating, a motor pool where thirty North Korean tanks were supposedly parked, and a seized radio transmitter already broadcasting North Korean propaganda. Nichols annotated the targets on Korean maps of the city and sent them by plane to the Far East Air Forces headquarters in Tokyo. The next morning, two U.S. B-29s bombed Seoul's railway station, where a large number of North Korean troops were reported killed and wounded. "The most ground information we ever had" in the early days of the war was "a map of Seoul and the location of the North Koreans in Seoul as sent by Mr. Nichols," said Lieutenant Colonel O'Wighton D. Simpson, deputy for intelligence at the Fifth Air Force.

Nichols's self-aggrandizement does not negate his superb performance in the first months of the war. General Stratemeyer, head of Far East Air Forces, quickly promoted him from lieutenant to captain and wrote in his diary that Nichols had "performed the impossible."

Five days into the war, on June 30, American and South Korean forces retreated south from Suwon. Enemy tanks rolled in on July 2. In the intervening days, Nichols snuck back into Suwon with a unit of South Koreans and destroyed American planes left behind at the airfield. Two weeks later, in the first of the fifty airborne reconnaissance missions he participated in during the war, Nichols volunteered to fly at low altitude in an unarmed reconnaissance aircraft over Pyongyang, where he spotted eighteen Soviet fighter planes. His intelligence led to "a highly successful strike" for which he was awarded the Air Medal and the Distinguished Flying Cross. Two days after that he saved the life of the deputy chief of staff of the Korean air force, whose jeep had careered off a road and flipped over in a swamp. Nichols was awarded the Soldier's Medal for heroism not involving actual combat with the enemy. About a month into the war, in the southern town of Taegu, Nichols was wounded and won a Purple Heart after leading a patrol of South Korean soldiers who stopped a larger North Korean unit trying to infiltrate Taegu airfield.

In early August 1950, with the North Koreans relentlessly pushing south and the Americans in disarray on the ground, Nichols went after big game—Russian-made T-34 tanks. The U.S. military viewed these World War II–era tanks as North Korea's most lethal weapon, saying they were "largely instrumental for the many casualties and setbacks suffered" in the first weeks of war. The North Korean invasion was led by 150 T-34s, and through July, American and South Korean forces struggled to stop them, often dying in the process. Standard 2.36-inch bazookas were useless against them, as was cannon fire from American light tanks. Air attacks had also failed to stop the tanks.

Nichols learned on August 3 that two T-34s had been disabled behind enemy lines. An air force citation says that he rushed there with four Korean assistants:

Fully aware of the extreme danger involved, he advanced beyond the front lines, crawling through intense cross fire. Reaching the disabled tanks, Captain Nichols discovered that enemy tank crews and other enemy troops were less than 40 feet distant. Despite the threat of imminent discovery, and equipped only with a pair of pliers and a screwdriver, Captain Nichols removed all nomenclature plates, vital operation parts, technical manuals, the complete radio, and several 85 millimeter shells. He further determined by evaluation the vulnerable points where the tank could successfully be attacked. Although removal of this equipment necessitated several arduous trips of nine hours' duration under increasingly hazardous conditions, Captain Nichols continued, unmindful of his personal safety. When one of his assistants was wounded by mortar fire, Captain Nichols, at the risk of his life, evacuated him to friendly lines.

Nichols won the Silver Star, America's third-highest military honor, for "conspicuous gallantry" in obtaining "essential" intelligence for the war effort. The weakness found in the rear armor of the tank—an opening for a vent that cooled the engine—was soon exploited by air force fighter jets, which began killing T-34s. Nichols claimed in his autobiography that his tank salvage mission "caused a change in the war. . . . The morale of our troops went up and instead of retreating, we started—for a change—to stand our own ground."

Nichols, again, overstated the impact of his work. When the U.S. Army shipped in larger tanks and more powerful rocket launchers in the late summer and fall of 1950, it also destroyed plenty of Soviet tanks. Yet the importance of the T-34 salvage mission was undeniable: air force attacks with rockets and napalm became a highly effective way of destroying T-34s.

There is a question, though, about what Nichols actually did on the ground during the tank mission. He seems to have exaggerated his personal bravery. Like several of the other "impossible" missions Nichols received medals for in the initial weeks of the war, the tank operation had few independent eyewitnesses. The citation for his Silver Star seems to be based on accounts that he alone provided; the wording echoes his autobiography. There is, however, an independent version of what happened during that mission. It comes from a highly reputable, high-ranking South Korean officer who was on the scene. Yoon Il-gyun was assigned to work for Nichols in the early summer of 1950 when he was a major in the intelligence section of the South Korean air force. He would later become a general and director of the Korean Central Intelligence Agency, now called the National Intelligence Service. In a memoir published five decades after the war, Yoon wrote that Nichols never climbed into the T-34. Instead, he and Nichols waited at a safe distance from the damaged tank as two Korean volunteers camouflaged themselves, crawled to the T-34, and climbed inside.

"They were reading documents inside the tank and getting changed into North Korean uniforms and having a cigarette. I was astonished by their courage to be able to grab everything inside that tank. . . . Based on an analysis of our obtained information, a conclusion was made that napalm would be effective."

Yoon discussed what happened during the tank mission in an interview for this book in Seoul in 2015, when he was ninety. It was "understandable," he said, that Nichols's Silver Star citation would be exaggerated, because that was standard procedure during the war. He explained that American officers involved in planning a mission were always honored for its success, regardless of what they did on the ground. Throughout his time in Korea, Nichols's craving for ribbons, honors, and medals did not go unnoticed by the U.S. Air Force. An evaluation of his effectiveness as an officer in 1955 found that his "desire to have his performance recognized by decoration" soured his standing among his own men. Seven years after he was pushed out of the air force, he requested the complete text of all his awards and decorations. In his will, he insisted to his heirs that his medals "cannot ever be sold, destroyed, traded or given away under any circumstances other than in case of an extreme emergency."

Even so, Yoon said he believed Nichols fully deserved his medal and that the tank mission was a tide-shifting event in the war.

The first weeks of the North Korean invasion were among the most catastrophic in the history of the U.S. military. Some infantry units were gripped with "bug out fever," as GIs ran for their lives at the first sign of an attack. Many were poorly armed, ill trained, overweight, and overwhelmed. "I saw young Americans turn in battle or throw down their arms, cursing their government for what they thought was embroilment in a hopeless cause," wrote Marguerite Higgins in the *New York Herald Tribune*.

For those who fought, the numbers of dead, wounded, and missing soared on all sides. By August 1, American losses had risen above 6,000. In the South Korean army, a staggering 70,000 men were missing. North Korea, too, paid an enormous cost for the ground that it gained, losing 58,000 men in the first five weeks of the war. The North's army, initially dismissed by MacArthur as likely to run at the mere sight of American soldiers, earned a reputation for toughness, discipline, and cruelty. They handcuffed American prisoners of war and shot them in the head. As grim details about the fighting became known in the United States, the initial flush of patriotic fervor turned to dread.

The huge losses on all sides during the invasion summer—captured in newspaper dispatches and detailed over the years in books—have long framed Western understanding of the Korean War. Yet there is another story of cruelty and killing that took place in Korea that summer, one that the United States and South Korea covered up for more than half a century.

The government of Syngman Rhee used the invasion as an excuse to slaughter—in just a few weeks—tens of thousands of South Korean civilians, including women and children, who it suspected were Communists or who happened to be in jail when war broke out. They died because

Rhee and others in his government feared they might join or help the Korean People's Army. The massacres were conducted by South Korean police and army forces—often as American servicemen watched, taking photographs, and sometimes writing reports. MacArthur was informed of these "deeply disturbing" executions, but viewed them as "an internal matter" for the South Korean government and took no action.

In the first week of July, Nichols witnessed and photographed one of the largest of these killings, near the city of Taejon. He was a party to the cover-up that grew out of it, making no attempt to alert his commanders, write a report about it, or send his photographs to Far East Air Forces headquarters. He waited thirty-one years—until publication of his autobiography—before describing South Korea's role in an "unforgettable massacre." Yet even then he knowingly misstated where it occurred so that his book would not challenge official U.S. versions of what happened near Taejon.

"Trucks loaded with the condemned arrived," he wrote. "Their hands were already tied behind them. They were hastily pushed into a line along the edge of the newly opened grave. They were quickly shot in the head and pushed into the grave. An efficient group of personnel followed; their [.]45[-caliber] pistols could hardly miss the fatal head shots from 2-3 feet away of the ones who were still kicking. . . .

"The worst part about this whole affair was that I learned later that not all the people killed were communists. The Koreans weren't taking any chances, and didn't have the time or transportation to move the prisoners South. So, rather than leave them behind for the enemy, they emptied all jails in Suwon and surrounding areas and did away with them. . . ."

Although he specifically cited Suwon in his autobiography, the atrocity Nichols witnessed did not occur there. It occurred about seventy miles south of Suwon in a valley near the town of Taejon, to which American forces, including Nichols and Torres, had fled by the first week of July. Nichols himself confirmed this in a handwritten letter that described "the 1800 I witnessed SK forces executing in valley outside Taejon."

The location of the killing is crucially important because the U.S. government publicly denied early press accounts of a South Korean massacre near Taejon in early July, calling them a "fabrication." Later in the war, after the bodies of several thousand South Korean civilians were found there in shallow pits, the U.S. Army blamed all the killings in Taejon on North Korean forces. That false claim found its way into the official army history of the Korean War, which was published in 1992 by the army's Center of Military History. At Taejon, the history says, "American troops soon discovered that the North Koreans had perpetrated one of the greatest mass killings of the entire Korean War."

Nichols said he was the only foreigner at the July massacre, but this, too, was false. Documents and photographs show that other American intelligence and military officers witnessed the killing. On-the-ground reports from the CIA and army intelligence said the South Korean government ordered and carried out the executions as an act of revenge ordered by the "top level" of Syngman Rhee's government. These chilling reports, though, were stamped "secret" in Washington in 1950. They were then filed away in government archives, where they stayed hidden for more than four decades. To maintain the cover-up, the South Korean government intimidated families of massacre victims around Taejon; for decades, they were afraid to talk. It was not until 2005, fifty-five years after the massacre, that an investigation into the incident was allowed as part of the government's Truth and Reconciliation Commission. At that time, South Korean policemen acknowledged killing civilians in Taejon. "Even at point blank range some were not killed outright," said Yi Chun-yong, then a prison guard. "I shot those who were still alive and squirming." Yi did not regret killing convicted Communists, but said that there were many who were killed who had nothing to do with North Korea or with communism. "I wonder," he said, "what kind of people led our nation who allowed them to be executed as well."

The Truth and Reconciliation Commission found that senior officials in the South Korean government had approved the killings, that American officers witnessed it, and that Rhee was probably aware of it.

Though Nichols chose not to, a number of other American officers did report mass killings by South Korean forces in the summer of 1950, and their graphic descriptions compelled American generals and diplomats to complain to Rhee. On August 10, army sergeant Frank Pierce, a military police investigator for the First Calvary Division, watched South Korean police kill about three hundred civilians, including some women and at least one girl of about twelve. The method was similar to what Nichols witnessed: police with rifles fired one shot into the back of the heads of victims who had been lined up along the lip of a shallow canyon.

"It was noted in several of the shootings that due to poor aim of the weapon, the prisoner was not killed instantly, but it was necessary for several other shots to be fired," Pierce wrote. "[I]n some cases the mercy shot was not administered, and at about three hours after the executions were completed, some of the condemned persons were still alive and moaning. The cries could be heard coming from somewhere in the mass of bodies piled in the canyon. . . .

"Extreme cruelty was noted from the Military Policemen to the condemned persons such as striking them on the head with gun butts and kicking them for no reason. The Commanding Officer of the execution group stated that the prisoners were killed as they were 'spies.' No other information was given."

Two weeks after this report was written, Ambassador Muccio met with Syngman Rhee, told him about the "irregularities," and received the president's promise that he would do "everything possible" to stop them from happening again. Though the pace slowed after the summer of 1950, civilian killings continued.

In his autobiography, Nichols wrote that it was "atrocious" to watch the executions. He said he tried to stop them, but "gave up when I saw I was wasting my time. . . . Sometimes I think I'd rather have gone with the dead and gotten it over with quick and easy—then I wouldn't have these terrible nightmares."

Much as his memories—mass executions, torture, and severed heads—might have haunted him, Nichols remained silent. He had a career-based motive to do so. He surely knew that if Rhee and his senior security men suspected him of passing on such information to the U.S. command, then his special access to the president could disappear.

On the day he witnessed the massacre at Taejon, he casually mentioned it to Torres.

"He told me they were slaughtering all these people, but it didn't seem to bother him that much," Torres said. "At the time, if he had wanted a report done, I would have typed it up. But I don't think he wanted it known."

CHAPTER 5
Code Break Bully

By early August 1950, North Korea had taken nearly 90 percent of South Korea's territory. Bedraggled American and South Korean forces had fled to the southern end of the peninsula, where they clung to a patch of land that was barely fifty miles wide and a hundred miles long. The port of Pusan, the sole major city not yet controlled by Kim Il Sung, was at the southern end of this toehold, which became known as the Pusan Perimeter. It was there that Lieutenant General Walton "Johnnie" Walker, commander of the Eighth Army and the senior American commander in Korea, announced that U.S. forces would stand or die.

Walker was a short, pudgy, plainspoken Texan whom the press often likened to a bulldog. During World War II, while leading an armored corps across France and Germany, he earned a hard-charging reputation not unlike that of his famous mentor, General George S. Patton. But by the summer of 1950, Walker was sixty. Some generals in Tokyo and Washington believed he had lost a step. MacArthur had flown into the Pusan Perimeter on July 27 and told Walker that withdrawal was no longer an acceptable strategy. The upshot of that visit was the most eloquent statement ever attributed to Johnnie Walker:

"There will be no more retreating. There is no line behind us to which we can retreat. Every unit must counterattack to keep the enemy off balance. There will be no Dunkirk, there will be no Bataan, a retreat to Pusan would be one of the greatest butcheries in history. We must fight until the end. Capture by these people is worse than death itself. We will fight as a team. If some of us must die, we will die fighting together."

Walker's rhetorical flourishes played well in newspapers back in the States. But many GIs inside the Pusan Perimeter heard it as an absurdity— a Kafkaesque command to "stay and die where you are." Under Walker's leadership, the soldiers had staggered south in July, absorbing one humiliating defeat after another. Thousands of them were sick with dysentery and respiratory infections. Bad food, bad water, and lack of sleep had caused battle fatigue that left many unable to control their fear and unwilling to fight. They did not understand why they were in Korea. They certainly did not see why they should be willing to die, as Walker said they must, to defend the little bit of it that was left. In *This Kind of War*, historian T. R. Fehrenbach described Walker's infantrymen as "exhausted, dispirited, and bitter."

Donald Nichols was there, too, having fled south from Taejon in mid-July before North Koreans took it with tanks and infantry. He and Torres set up an intelligence office in a two-story house in a residential neighborhood of Taegu, a refugee-swollen town of four hundred thousand people located roughly in the center of the Pusan Perimeter. Because roads and rail lines came together in Taegu, it had been chosen as the temporary seat of the South Korean government and as Korean headquarters for the Eighth Army and the Fifth Air Force.

There were frequent outbreaks of fighting to the north and west of the city. Nearly every night, as Torres recalled, he and Nichols heard the thud and whistle of artillery shells and saw flashes from explosions. Like Walker's infantrymen, Nichols had been forced to retreat south again and again. Yet he was anything but exhausted, dispirited, or bitter. His war had been exhilarating, winning him praise, medals, and promotion. Now, in Taegu, he had a new trick up his sleeve: a team of code breakers who would cement his status as an invaluable spymaster.

Among the hundreds of North Korean defectors Nichols had interrogated before the outbreak of war, there had been one who fled the North with stolen codebooks from the Korean People's Army. His name was Cho Yong Il, and Nichols's discovery of him would prove to be a key to halting the North Korean offensive. Cho had been a private in the Japanese army and a merchant seaman with the Soviet navy. Until he defected from North Korea in 1949, he was a radio operator and cryptographer for Kim Il Sung.

Before the war, when Nichols first learned of Cho's expertise as a North Korean cryptographer, he arranged for Cho to meet his friend Kim Chung Yul, chief of staff of the South Korean air force, which Nichols had recently helped create and over which he exercised considerable influence. "Nick was always thinking ahead," Torres said. "He told the South Koreans to hang on to this guy. He also told Cho to train a team of cryptographers."

By anticipating a need for code breakers in Korea, Nichols was light-years ahead of the rest of the American intelligence community. The cryptographic resources of the United States—such as they were—had ignored North Korea. The secretary of defense, Louis Johnson, issued a top secret order in 1949 that created the Armed Forces Security Agency (AFSA), which would evolve into the National Security Agency, today's global data-vacuuming leviathan. But when North Korea invaded in 1950, the agency's code-breaking capacity was hobbled by budget cuts and warped by a near-exclusive focus on the Soviet Union. The agency had one self-taught Korean linguist, no Korean typewriters, and no Korean dictionaries. Under Johnson's order, each branch of the military was supposed to create a unit for "tactical" code breaking in the field. But these, too, were poorly funded, understaffed, and had no expertise in the Korean language. They also feuded endlessly with one another. When it came to cryptography and Korea, the Americans were helpless.

As instructed by Nichols, the South Korean air force commissioned Cho Yong Il as a second lieutenant and put him in command of a radio intercept station on the outskirts of Seoul. His unit started work on June 1, 1950, which gave them three weeks on the job before North Korea seized the capital.

Though Cho had to abandon much of his equipment, he made it safely to Taegu in early July, where he and his men set up five radio positions and began monitoring them with three receivers. His unit could intercept and understand North Korean army radio messages because the North, in what would prove to be a disastrous blunder, had not bothered to change its rudimentary radio codes. Cho's stolen codebooks allowed his team of cryptographers to decipher everything they could hear.

By this time, Nichols had set up his shop in Taegu, where he made himself the chief provider of targets for the Fifth Air Force. He was delighted to learn that Cho was decrypting North Korean radio codes—so delighted that he commandeered the lieutenant and his entire code-break team. "I was ordered by Mr. Nichols to move our equipment and members to his house," Cho said. "This I could not refuse."

Cho and his code breakers moved into a high-walled residence directly across the street from the building where Nichols lived and worked with Torres. Beginning on July 17, 1950, more than two thousand intercepted and decoded messages were hand carried to Nichols's house, where interpreters translated them into English. They arrived at all hours of the day and night. Whatever the time, Nichols had given standing orders for either Torres or Sergeant Russ Bauer to type them up immediately and jump in a jeep to deliver the intel.

"It was top priority and I delivered the messages to General Walker's Eighth Army and to General Partridge's Fifth Air Force," Torres said, referring to army and air force headquarters in Taegu. "We had the feeling we were doing really important work. Of course, we were saving our butts, too. Those North Koreans were right outside our back door."

These intercepted radio messages allowed the air force to find and pound North Korean tanks, supply lines, artillery installations, and troop concentrations, which impressed Partridge and confirmed his faith in Nichols's "genius." Generals Walker and Partridge began working closely together inside the perimeter. Partridge himself piloted a single-engine, two-seat T-6 surveillance plane that took Walker out on battlefield surveys. It was relatively safe because the Fifth Air Force had total air supremacy.

Having tapped a vein of intelligence that pleased the two most powerful American generals in Korea, Nichols pushed aggressively for more code breakers, more linguists, and more radios. He persuaded the South Korean navy to move sixteen of its cryptologists into the building across the street from his quarters, where they worked at the same table with Cho's men. Nichols also joined forces with South Korean code breakers working with Walker's Eighth Army.

After building his code-break fiefdom, Nichols ferociously guarded it. He did not want other American spy agencies horning in and stealing his glory. The first outfit to try was the Air Force Security Service, the cryptology arm of the air force that was separate from and, in theory, superior to Nichols's seat-of-the-pants code-break team. In late July, it sent First Lieutenant Edward Murray from Japan to Taegu to find local linguists and set up a radio intercept unit in a mission code-named "Project Willy." Murray arrived in a transport aircraft and brought along a trailer full of new radio equipment.

Nichols refused to cooperate with Murray in any way, declining to lend him a single linguist. As a result, Murray "didn't have the Korean personnel to get any results," said Lieutenant Colonel O'Wighton D. Simpson. "It became obvious that Mr. Nichols, who was an independent operator, I might add, was the best source."

Two weeks after Murray arrived in Korea, Partridge ordered him back to Japan. As for Murray's equipment—Nichols kept it all.

"The breathless nature of Nichols's coup left [Murray] spinning," said a top secret history published in 1995 by the National Security Agency. "Murray's mission became entangled in one of the most bizarre incidents in the history of American cryptology." Back in Japan, Murray complained bitterly about Nichols and "a severe jurisdictional battle ensued, encompassing command organizations in the United States, Japan, and Korea."

Murray won—or so he thought. He returned to Taegu on August 12 armed with "a letter of authority" from air force general Charles Y. Banfill, deputy for intelligence with the Far East Air Forces. "Lt. Murray is proceeding to Korea to assume overall direction of Project Willy," said a message that summarized his new and expanded authority. "[Nichols] is being relieved of this function with all equipment, personnel, and documents to become Murray's responsibility and he will direct all activity."

Nichols, on his own authority, decided that the orders were insufficiently explicit. He was "still unwilling to relinquish control," according to the NSA history. Five days later, the Fifth Air Force again ordered Murray out of Korea.

This time, though, Nichols threw Murray a bone, allowing him to depart with North Korean codebooks and technical information, which he used in Japan to set up a code-break team. Two years after Murray's double dose of humiliation, the Air Force Security Service commissioned a study to find out what had happened and why. It concluded that the early code-breaking history of Korea was a "struggle for empire" that Nichols won; he made himself a "king" and sold his fellow Americans "right down the river."

———————

Nichols picked the perfect moment to become the king of code breaking.

The Pusan Perimeter, more than any other area the Americans had tried to defend in Korea, was defensible. It had natural barriers against invaders: rugged mountains to the north; a major river, the Naktong, to the west; and everywhere else, the sea, which was controlled by the U.S. Navy.

West Point–trained infantry and armor commanders knew how to fight in such a place, with clear battle lines, allies at their flanks, and reserves in the rear. They also had a major logistical edge. Inside the perimeter there was a modern and relatively well-maintained network of roads and railways, a legacy of Japanese colonial rule that meant they could quickly move troops, ammunition, and other supplies to where they were needed most. As important, the American war machine was finally beginning to hum. In the late summer and fall of 1950, more well-trained soldiers and marines, tanks, and artillery arrived at Pusan with each passing week. As South Korea's only deep-water port, Pusan could accommodate thirty oceangoing ships at a time.

There was even a psychological advantage to being trapped: it concentrated the mind. "Bug out fever" abated because for an infantryman, the only real choice was to dig in and prepare to fight or die. When Walker said there would be no more retreat, one regimental commander noticed a change in the behavior of his men: "a greater amount of earth came out with each shovelful." In a prophetic editorial in late July, the *New York Times* said a turning point in the war was at hand. "For five weeks, we have been trading space for time," the *Times* said. "The space is running out for us. The time is running out for our enemies."

As the Americans resupplied, the Korean People's Army struggled to keep its supply lines from collapsing. American control of the air and sea all but stopped the North's efforts to move large shipments of food, fuel, and ammunition. Mechanical and maintenance problems, along with napalm air strikes made more deadly by the intelligence discoveries of Nichols and his team, had slashed the number of battle-ready T-34 tanks from 150 to about 40. Lacking doctors, drugs, and medical facilities, injured North Korean soldiers began to die of treatable wounds.

Although combatants on both sides were unaware of it, a fundamental shift had taken place. The number of troops on the ground had swung to the advantage of the Americans and the South Koreans. By August, North Korea's 70,000 troops faced a combined American and South Korean force of 92,000 soldiers and marines. The imbalance would soon get much worse for North Korea. MacArthur was getting ready for a massive counterattack. At Inchon, about thirty miles west of Seoul, he was preparing an amphibious landing that on September 15 would insert 70,000 American troops into the middle of the peninsula, where they could cut supply lines to North Korean forces besieging the Pusan Perimeter.

General Walker knew he did not have to hold the line forever—just long enough. When the North Koreans tried to punch a hole in the Pusan

Perimeter, Walker had to be ready to fill the hole and punch back. As he admitted in early August, if the North were to focus all its forces, create a single gaping hole in the line, and then drive "straight and hard for Pusan," he could not stop them.

No such punch ever came.

North Korea squandered its greatest advantage. It ignored a fundamental battlefield tactic of concentrating power. The failure was typical of Kim Il Sung. He was a sloppy war planner and an incompetent battlefield tactician. His only real experience as a commander had been leading a few hundred guerrillas—armed with knives and rifles—in hit-and-run strikes against Japanese police in the 1930s. He had bragged to Stalin that the war in South Korea would be won in a few days, but he did not know how to sustain an armored invasion force for a longer fight and his subordinates were afraid to question his judgment. In his hurry to invade South Korea by the end of June, Kim declined to wait for eighty-nine additional T-34s that Stalin would send him in July and August. They would have doubled the number of tanks in his initial invasion, allowed Kim to attack with three armored divisions instead of just one, and increased his chances of a crushing victory in the Pusan Perimeter. His generals, as they faced the perimeter, chose to divide their ten armored divisions and strike from four locations. It diluted their strength, giving Walker a fighting chance.

Moving his men on trains, borrowing men from one regiment and lending them to another, and hustling newly arrived weapons and fresh troops to where they were most needed, Walker managed—just barely—to beat back the Korean People's Army. The Pusan Perimeter held. American and South Korean forces withstood a half dozen major assaults. Walker's reputation was rehabilitated. The Fifth Air Force knew where to strike behind enemy lines and did so with more than fifteen thousand sorties between late June and mid-September. U.S. napalm and bombing attacks caused catastrophic shortages of ammunition. After the success of MacArthur's Inchon landing, some North Korean divisions lost 80 percent of their soldiers.

"Walker lived in crisis," wrote historian Fehrenbach. "His command decision had to be a never-ending series of robbing Peter to pay Paul. . . . He had to guess where the greatest peril lay, and guess correctly, for in war there is no prize for being almost right."

In fact, thanks to Nichols's code-break operation, Walker did not need to guess.

The Americans had "perfect intelligence," recalled James K. Woolnough, then a junior commander in the Eighth Army in Taegu. "They knew exactly where each platoon of North Koreans were [sic] going, and they'd move to meet it. . . . This was amazing, utterly amazing."

Walker had "what every military commander around the world secretly dreams about, near complete and real-time access to the plans and intentions of the enemy forces he faced," wrote intelligence historian Matthew Aid.

Some of this intelligence came from Americans working desperately hard in Japan and the United States. The U.S. government might have been cryptographically clueless on the day of the invasion, but it quickly recovered. Using listening stations in Japan, American code breakers in Tokyo and Arlington, Virginia, discovered that the North Korean military communicated with easily breakable radio codes—and sometimes with no codes at all. Within a month, Americans knew everything the North Korean military was planning. Still, nearly two thirds of what they intercepted could not be turned into useful intelligence. For outside of Taegu, the Americans were crippled by a severe shortage of Korean translators. Another problem was getting intelligence to Walker in time for him to use it.

While Nichols did not have the analytical talent or the equipment that was available in the United States and Japan, he and his large stable of Korean code breakers and linguists were far better positioned inside the war zone. They had speedy access to Walker and Partridge, via a short ride in Torres's jeep. The decoded information that Nichols produced was also speedily circulated in Taegu because it was not "so over-classified that it was unusable," according to officers at Fifth Air Force intelligence, which relied almost exclusively on Nichols for bombing information.

When code breakers in Virginia learned in late August that North Korea was about to launch a major attack west of Taegu, there "appears to have been no mechanism" for their decoded information to reach Walker, according to the CIA's Center for the Study of Intelligence. It said the general probably relied on intelligence reports from the team assembled by Nichols.

Walker, though, never had a chance to explain exactly how much he depended on Nichols in Taegu. He was killed on December 23, 1950, when his jeep collided with a South Korean army truck. The general had always insisted that his driver go fast on crowded roads and he often stood up in his jeep, chest thrust out, steadying himself by holding on to a grab bar.

Before Walker's death, however, he made it clear that Nichols had helped save the Eighth Army, personally commending him for "his untiring efforts in procuring timely and invaluable information." The South Korean government also gave Nichols credit for helping to save the Pusan Perimeter. By order of President Rhee, Nichols received the country's second-highest military honor for valor, citing as the primary reason his work in obtaining and decoding enemy messages.

Partridge and his boss, General Stratemeyer, began pushing aggressively in the summer of 1950 for Nichols to be promoted—and not just because of his code-break triumph. Nichols had begun to play such a pivotal role in the war that his low rank raised awkward and embarrassing questions for the Far East Air Forces: Why is the best intelligence officer in the region a lowly chief warrant officer? Why is this twenty-seven-year-old so important that he can snub and humiliate other officers? Don't you have West Point–trained officers who are more capable than this middle-school dropout? By promoting Nichols, in just a few weeks, from chief warrant officer to lieutenant and then to captain, generals Partridge and Stratemeyer were rushing to keep up with the de facto authority that Nichols had grabbed amid the anarchy of the war's first three months.

Even before U.S. forces broke out of the Pusan Perimeter, Partridge was giving Nichols new responsibilities. In early August, he asked Nichols to locate and map airfields, supply dumps, and other enemy targets that could be bombed by the Fifth Air Force. With the help of South Korean intelligence officers, Nichols found forty-eight agents, plucking them out of the South Korean army, air force, and police and sending them for a week's training in Japan. They were parachuted behind North Korean lines on August 23.

"One Korean agent had the misfortune to break both of his legs in striking them on the horizontal stabilizer of the C-47 from which he parachuted," said an air force history. "He was nevertheless able to convince a North Korean farmer to defect to the South and to carry him to safety. . . . Not only did the injured agent return safely, but he brought the important information of the whereabouts of an enemy fuel dump."

This heartening story, however, is not at all typical of what happened to agents Nichols recruited and sent north. Most of his agents did not return from that first mission and the pattern would recur again and again. "Nobody expected them to return alive," said Kim Bok-dong, a translator who worked for Nichols in 1950. "It was as if they were being sent to be killed."

Several of the agents who beat the odds and managed to slip through North Korean territory were later killed by friendly fire as they tried to cross battle lines. Nichols would later tell his agents to "discard all their clothing and approach with their hands in the air," which he claimed reduced losses. But the number of lives lost in parachute drops would remain staggering throughout the war. The toll stains the memory that many South Korean war veterans have of Nichols.

"Nichols was very focused, but he sacrificed too many Koreans to accomplish his mission," said Lee Kang-hwa, a retired general in the South Korean air force who fought in the war and knew Nichols. "It is very unfortunate that a lot of Koreans were sent to die."

Nichols was not the only American sending South Koreans to near-certain death. CIA operations during the war were "not only ineffective but probably morally reprehensible in that the number of lives lost and the amount of time and treasure expended was enormously disproportionate to attainments there from," an agency review concluded years after the war.

In the panicked summer of 1950, however, the losses were acceptable, at least to the Americans. The deaths certainly did nothing to hurt Nichols's reputation among air force and army generals in Korea and in Tokyo. A measure of his rising status was the changed behavior of his prewar nemesis, General Willoughby. In April, Willoughby wanted Nichols out of Korea; by August, he wanted Nichols working exclusively for him.

In mid-September, Willoughby was "about to absorb" Nichols and his code-break team, a possibility that horrified Partridge. "I strenuously oppose this move," Partridge wrote in his diary. In the final months of 1950, Partridge referred five times in his diary to his turf war with Willoughby over Nichols. Panicked about what he should do to keep his best agent, Partridge even sought Nichols's advice. Telling Partridge exactly what the general wanted to hear, Nichols said he was an air force man and wanted to remain an air force man. He seems to have used the tussle between the army and the air force to increase his own power. Nichols was "concerned especially with the Air Force's side of the picture, while the others [were] concerned with the Army's side," Partridge wrote in his diary. "For this and other reasons, I am going to continue to oppose the absorption of Nichols' unit."

Nichols wagered that he would have more resources and less supervision under Partridge than under Willoughby. It was a canny bet. Within six months, Nichols would take command of a special operations unit created especially for him (although the term "special operations" was not yet used in the U.S. military). He would also begin building spy bases on islands around North Korea. Willoughby, meanwhile, would soon be banished from the Far East Command and spend much of the rest of his life sidestepping responsibility for his errors in judgment in Korea.

CHAPTER 6

Any Means Necessary

For a couple of months in the autumn of 1950, the war seemed won. North Korea all but disappeared as a state as Kim Il Sung slunk away to hide in a bunker near the Chinese border. Freshly promoted, Captain Donald Nichols found himself poking around in the Great Leader's abandoned residence in Pyongyang.

After the victory at Inchon and the breakout from the Pusan Perimeter, South Korean and American forces pushed north to the North Korean capital and then to the Yalu River, which marked North Korea's border with China. The North Korean army had collapsed, losing as many as 50,000 soldiers and nearly all of its Soviet-supplied tanks and armor. The Soviet ambassador in North Korea told Stalin that Kim Il Sung was confused, hopeless, and lost. Before fleeing Pyongyang, Kim sent an urgent cable to Stalin.

"We consider it necessary to report to you about extremely unfavorable conditions for us," he said. "The enemy's air force, possessing about one thousand planes of various kinds, is not encountering any resistance from our side, and has full control in the air. It conducts bombing at the front and in the rear daily, around the clock."

By October, the Fifth Air Force had so thoroughly bombed North

Korea's major cities that it complained of "a scarcity of strategic targets" and sent home some B-29s and their crews. Thirty thousand tons of high explosives had been dropped with "devastating effects," said the bombing commander, Major General Emmett "Rosie" O'Donnell, in an autumn assessment of his work. "We came out prepared to burn down the cities in Northern Korea, to completely knock out their industrial potential, and to raise havoc with their transportation system," he said. "All these things have been done."

Nichols hopscotched north with the victors, rushing to pull his spy network back together in Seoul and seed agents across the rubble of North Korea. Flying with Partridge, he returned to Kimpo airfield on September 19. A month later, he was in Pyongyang, searching Kim Il Sung's house and offices. He and his men found seventy thousand documents produced by the North Korean air force that showed the location of previously unknown enemy airfields and supply dumps—all of which were soon bombed. In early November, Nichols moved his code-break team— still staffed by South Koreans and run by Cho, the North Korean defector— forty miles north of Pyongyang to Sinanju airfield. There, Cho and his men tried to intercept Chinese radio messages. But China was far more careful than North Korea, staying off the radio, unless it was to broadcast disinformation.

The Chinese People's Army was secretly moving into North Korea, traveling at night, using back roads and tracks in the forest. U.S. aircraft could not see these troops and code breakers could not track them. For the American forces that had surged into northern Korea, the bloodiest and most terrifying battles of the war were soon to come. There would be another round of intelligence failures, battlefield humiliations, and ignominious retreats. Just as MacArthur and Willoughby failed to expect a North Korean invasion in June, they failed to see the Chinese coming in October. And this time Nichols rang no alarms. He was as clueless as the CIA, which said on October 12 that "there are no convincing indications of an actual Chinese Communist intention to resort to full-scale intervention in Korea" and "such action is not probable in 1950."

About the time Truman was reading these assurances, more than

30,000 Chinese troops were crossing the Yalu River southward into North Korea. Another 150,000 crossed over by the end of October. In a preview of what was to come, the Chinese engaged South Korean and American forces on October 25, bloodying them with mortars, Katyusha rocket artillery, and small arms. During this fight, the Americans and South Koreans captured and interrogated twenty-five Chinese soldiers who proved to be talkative. They told army and CIA interrogators that an offensive was under way and that many thousands of Chinese troops were already inside North Korea.

"CIA officers in Korea had the temerity to cable Washington with the results of interrogations of the Chinese prisoners," writes the intelligence historian Matthew Aid. The cables upset Willoughby, who reacted to the CIA agents in October much as he had reacted to Nichols earlier that year—by punishing the messenger. From Tokyo, Willoughby ordered that CIA personnel be kept away from army POW cages containing Chinese soldiers. The worrisome news about the Chinese incursion, though, did get through to Washington. The agency told Truman in the first week of November that nearly 750,000 Chinese soldiers were near the Korean border and about half of them could soon start "sustained ground operations in Korea."

At MacArthur's headquarters in the Dai-Ichi Building in Tokyo, the new evidence did not change minds. MacArthur told the Eighth Army to push all the way to the Chinese border, predicting it would be the last offensive of the war. He said he would "get the boys home by Christmas."

America's failure to grasp the mortal danger posed by the Chinese buildup was "one of the greatest, most persistent enigmas of the Korean War," wrote Max Hastings, a military historian. He said that MacArthur and Willoughby "absolutely declined" to heed clear warnings of battlefield catastrophe. "They had created a fantasy world for themselves, in which events would march in accordance with a divine providence directed from the Dai-Ichi building. The conduct of the drive to the Yalu reflected a contempt for intelligence, for the cardinal principles of military prudence, seldom matched in twentieth-century warfare." Matthew B. Ridgway, the general who would replace MacArthur in 1951, said that the Far East Command "knew the facts, but they were poorly evaluated. . . . It was probably in good part because of MacArthur's personality. If he did not want to believe something, he wouldn't."

Mao had begun warning MacArthur in late September, soon after the Inchon invasion. His government had tried to use diplomatic back channels to inform South Korea and the United States that if their troops pushed north of the thirty-eighth parallel, China would fight. The warning had nothing to do with affection for or loyalty to Kim Il Sung. Mao did not like the North Korean leader, believing him to be headstrong, doctrinaire, and a "number-one pain in the butt." Still, Mao could not accept MacArthur's demand for North Korea's complete surrender and was unnerved by the prospect of an American-backed united Korea on his eastern border.

To lead the fight against the Americans, Mao selected his most trusted general, Peng Dehuai, a hero of Communist China's long civil war. General Peng met with Kim Il Sung, quickly sized him up as an "extremely childish" military mind, and elbowed him out of way. The Great Leader soon became a bystander in the war he had started. Under Peng, the counteroffensive would be a Chinese operation, assisted by what was left of the North Korean army, with air support from the Soviet Union. The Chinese People's Army, with 300,000 troops in North Korea, attacked in earnest on November 25, overwhelming Walker's Eighth Army on the west side of the peninsula. The ill-prepared Americans fell back from the border and abandoned Pyongyang, suffering 11,000 casualties as they fled 120 miles south to the thirty-eighth parallel. It was the longest retreat in American military history. In a cable to Truman, MacArthur said, "We now face an entirely new war."

In the mountains on the east side of the peninsula, the American defeat was only slightly less awful. As a Siberian cold front drove temperatures to −35 degrees Fahrenheit, the Chinese tried to trap and destroy the First Marine Division and the Army X Corps near a man-made high-country lake called the Chosin Reservoir. Thanks to superb marine leadership and gutsy fighting, Americans escaped the trap without catastrophic losses. But it was a major defeat and Peng's forces would soon take back all of North Korea and more.

Shortly before Chinese troops chased Americans out of Pyongyang, Nichols stole portraits of Stalin, Mao, and Kim Il Sung from the Great Leader's office. From behind Kim's desk, he took "a huge, red, revolving, overstuffed chair."

The Chinese attack, along with the willful failure of MacArthur and Willoughby to see it coming, again revealed gross incompetence in the intelligence operations of the Far East Command. Complaints about Willoughby increased. After an army briefing in December, Ambassador Muccio grumbled to General Walker (who would die in a week's time in his jeep) that "since long before the war started" there has been a "major battle between the various agencies" that collect intelligence. Muccio blamed it on Willoughby. A week later, Willoughby himself acknowledged the organizational chaos. He told the Far East Air Forces commander, General Stratemeyer, that the CIA, army intelligence, "and Captain Nichols should all get on the same team."

It would never happen. Partridge wanted Nichols to play exclusively for his team, the Fifth Air Force. After the Chinese entered the war, Partridge needed Nichols, his targeting information, and his unrivaled network of Korean contacts more than ever.

The Chinese offensive humiliated MacArthur—and made him vengeful. He demanded that the gloves be taken off the American bombing campaign, which had already devastated population centers in North Korea. MacArthur wanted U.S. bombs to "destroy every means of communication and every installation, factory, city, and village" in North Korea. He ordered the air force to create "a desert" between United Nations lines and the Chinese border. Before the Chinese intervention, the air force dropped only conventional explosives when it bombed North Korean cities and towns. But after the Chinese made him look like an old fool, MacArthur approved the use of incendiary chemical compounds like napalm. North Korean cities that had already been knocked to pieces by the first round of bombing were soon engulfed in flames. "In blind desperation," war correspondent Homer Bigart wrote, "we tried to burn with napalm every town and village that might hide enemy troops and equipment along the mockingly empty roads coming down from Manchuria."

In addition to needing Nichols to help carry out this "fire job," the air force was desperate for his assistance in locating and rescuing the crews of downed aircraft, particularly B-29s. These big bombers and many other American planes were being picked off in the late autumn of 1950 at an alarming rate by a new Soviet-made fighter jet, the bat-winged, blazingly fast MiG-15. When it first appeared in the skies over the Yalu River—a patch of Chinese and North Korean airspace that soon became known as "MiG Alley"—the Americans had no aircraft that could compete with it. The MiG-15 climbed faster, flew higher, and was armed with bigger guns. Its 37-millimeter cannon fired a high-explosive, half-pound projectile that had a range of up to a mile. A MiG-15 pilot could squeeze off eighty rounds in less than five seconds. The fighter was nightmarishly effective against lumbering American bombers of the World War II era.

By late November, about 400 MiG-15s took control of the skies over MiG Alley, chasing off U.S. bombers, protecting supply routes for China's ground troops, and vexing the Far East Air Forces. The United States had no choice but to escalate the air war, rushing its best fighter jets, the F-86 Sabres, from the United States to Korea. The Sabres were the only American aircraft that could compete with MiGs. As the first all-jet air war got under way, MiG-15 fighter pilots were almost always Russian. They were Stalin's best, imported from air bases near Moscow. Stalin ordered them to pretend to be Chinese. They wore Chinese flight suits and carried documents with fake Chinese names. Stalin even ordered them to speak Chinese on the radio when they flew over MiG Alley. It was an order they did not have the language skills to obey.

So they spoke Russian on the radio as they shot down American aircraft, killing American pilots and crew members. When this information reached the White House, Truman chose not to tell the American people. He did not want to arouse populist sentiment in the United States for a larger war against the Soviet Union. Following Truman's lead, the Pentagon lied about the all-jet air war, saying that the MiGs were being flown by pilots from China, which "almost overnight" had become a major air power. American fighter pilots were threatened with dismissal from the war zone if they mentioned a word about the air war with Russia. For many years after the war ended, American pilots remained silent about whom they had fought.

_____

As 1951 began, Seoul fell for the second time to Communist forces. More U.S. aircraft were being shot down, which necessitated risky rescue missions behind enemy lines. By February, the Americans were avoiding air combat in MiG Alley.

It all added up to an urgent need for more and better spying, a need that could be met only by Donald Nichols. That, at least, is how Partridge saw it. So in the first week of January he went to his boss, General Stratemeyer, to discuss how to repackage Nichols, by giving him less administrative work and more power in the field. By then, Nichols was back in Taegu, where Fifth Air Force headquarters had again been forced to relocate and where he was spending half his time on paperwork.

After the meeting with Stratemeyer, Partridge wrote in his diary that Nichols needed "some sort of independent status where he can use his talent for organization and for dealing with the Korean people." Two days later, Partridge and Nichols played "hooky" from the war. Along with a small number of officers, they flew to Cheju Island to shoot birds. The hunt was a success, killing more than fifty fowl. Partridge does not say so in his diary, but it is likely he used his time with Nichols to brainstorm about a new kind of spy outfit, one designed specifically for Nichols.

Its name was opaque: Special Activities Unit #1. After four months, it was changed to something even more opaque: Detachment 2 of the 6004th Air Intelligence Service Squadron (AISS). In Korea, many airmen called it "Nick's Outfit" or simply "NICK." South Koreans called it "NEKO." Whatever the name, nothing like it had existed before in the air force.

Nichols was given open-ended authority to gather intelligence and conduct sabotage, demolition, and guerrilla operations behind enemy lines. The orders creating his unit explicitly limited his "administrative burden." While Nichols was empowered to lead covert missions, other air force officers were ordered to shuffle his papers. In a highly unusual organizational move, Nichols no longer had to communicate through the normal air force chain of command. Instead of dealing with majors or colonels, he reported directly to General Partridge. In military jargon, it is called stovepiping, and it is intended to move sensitive information directly to a commander without being delayed or diluted. The decision to stovepipe showed how much Partridge and the Fifth Air Force needed Nichols—and how free Nichols was to wage a secret war.

The first fifty-six men assigned to his unit came from the South Korean air force. The transfer was arranged by Partridge with General Kim Chung Yul, the air force chief of staff who owed his job to Nichols and who probably had no choice in the matter. The South Korean air force would soon be sending hundreds more of its officers and men to work—and die—for NICK.

The sudden emergence of NICK among the competing U.S. intelligence operators in the Far East did not go down well with the CIA, which was beginning a period of global expansion and pushing to play a more important role in Korea. When Frank Wisner, chief of covert operations for the agency and a man with a volatile temper, visited Tokyo and heard that Nichols was commanding his own guerrilla army, "all hell broke loose," according to Ed Evanhoe, a former army intelligence officer in Korea. "Wisner demanded to know what the air force thought it was doing forming air force-led partisan units. . . ." The CIA pushed MacArthur to issue a direct order to the air force to "stop all efforts" aimed at developing an independent guerrilla force. The words "sabotage" and "demolition" were deleted from Nichols's mission directive. He was instructed to cooperate with the CIA and army intelligence. None of this, however, did much to rein in his power.

One reason was the end of MacArthur in the Far East. The famous general was famously sacked on April 11, 1951. "I fired him because he wouldn't respect the authority of the President," Truman explained years later. "I didn't fire him because he was a dumb son of a bitch, although he was, but that's not against the law for generals." The firing also removed Willoughby from the Far East Command, sending him back to the United States, where he faced pointed questions about his competence.

With MacArthur and Willoughby gone, Nichols could give Partridge and the Fifth Air Force exactly what they wanted; indeed, more than they could have hoped for. A week after MacArthur was fired, Nichols led a team of Koreans that wrested "information of inestimable value from the very grasp of the enemy." He brought back parts, photographs, and technical specifications of the MiG-15. Along with the T-34 tank salvage operation for which Nichols won a Silver Star, the MiG operation was one of the most important intelligence achievements of the Korean War. But, as with the tank mission, during which Nichols might or might not have climbed inside a tank, there are two versions of what Nichols actually did during the MiG mission. In one version, he dodged bullets on the ground; in the second, he supervised the operation from the relative safety of a nearby air force cargo plane.

In the version that is exhaustively detailed in air force citations, in Partridge's diary, in Nichols's memoir, and in air force–authorized stories that appeared in American magazines, Nichols appears as a man of action with ice water in his veins. He "coolly and efficiently photographed" the jet's fuselage. To get at engineering secrets inside, he dismantled the MiG with hand grenades. He alone dragged the MiG's horizontal stabilizer back to a waiting helicopter.

"We were being shot at by small arms fire, heavy machine guns and flak all the way in and out, the rotor blades of the copter were hit," Nichols wrote in his autobiography. "I never saw so much flak in my life. It was constantly around us from the time we hit land on the way in until we left land on the return trip. Upon arriving at the target area we found it under guard, I ordered the copter pilots to land a short distance from the downed aircraft. A few fast exchanges of fire ran the guards off. The only other encounter we had while on the ground was to keep our pilots from taking off and leaving us."

The second version comes from Yoon Il-gyun, who worked for Nichols during the war, who later became director of South Korea's central intelligence agency, and who, as described earlier, also said that Nichols did not personally salvage a T-34 tank in 1950.

As Yoon tells the story: Nichols organized and managed the MiG mission. In the weeks before a crashed MiG was spotted for salvage, he trained Yoon and seven other South Korean air force agents in parachute jumping. He taught them how to remove key parts from the jet, using hand grenades, if necessary, to blow apart sections of the aircraft that could not be quickly disassembled. He drilled them on swiftly transferring parts to a helicopter under simulated combat conditions. When a crashed MiG-15 was located in April behind enemy lines near the Chong-chon River, Nichols, Yoon, and the other Koreans boarded a C-119 Flying Boxcar cargo plane to fly over the crash site. As Yoon and the other Koreans parachuted down to the crash site, Nichols stayed behind in the plane "to command the operation."

Asked why Nichols and the U.S. Air Force would exaggerate Nichols's role in the mission, Yoon explained—once again—that it was routine during the war to "put all the achievements on one person." Yoon said he never held it against Nichols. Quite the contrary, Yoon was one of several senior South Korean intelligence officials who invited Nichols back to South Korea in 1987 to celebrate his wartime spying triumphs. At a dinner during that visit, Yoon presented Nichols with a plaque thanking him for service that "led to the frustration and demoralization of the enemy."

The MiG salvage mission in April 1951 did much more than frustrate the enemy. It changed American assumptions about Russian backwardness in aerospace engineering. It demonstrated that the Soviets were keeping up with—and in some cases exceeding—Western innovations in jet-engine design, while "general workmanship appears comparable to practices used in the US and Great Britain." The information Nichols found also triggered design changes in America's comparable fighter, the F-86 Sabre. As the war dragged on, those changes gave the Sabre the capacity to outmaneuver and shoot down large numbers of MiGs. The Pentagon would also accelerate investment in fighter-jet development.

The mission also electrified generals in the Far East Air Forces, especially Partridge, and boosted Nichols's career. "This morning I went out to Nichols's establishment to look at the parts of the MiG aircraft which he had recovered yesterday," Partridge wrote in his diary. "He did a wonderful job and I am going to see that he is decorated for it. . . . It was a wonderful piece of work."

Partridge made good on his promise. Nichols won the Distinguished Service Cross, which is awarded for "extraordinary heroism" during combat and is the nation's second-highest military honor. Partridge also rewarded Nichols by giving him more power, authorizing him to collect intelligence "by any means necessary." Nichols now had his own secret army and he interpreted his orders as a "legal license to murder."

As his powers expanded throughout the spring and summer of 1951, Nichols remained in close touch with Syngman Rhee, meeting personally with the South Korean leader at least five times. On April 29, during a Sunday afternoon conversation with Rhee, Nichols passed on political gossip he had just heard from his commanding generals about the coming South Korean presidential race.

At the time, Rhee was publicly claiming he would not run for reelection in 1952, and American generals, including Partridge and army general James Van Fleet, commander of the Eighth Army, were eager to influence who the next president might be. On Saturday, the day before he talked to Rhee, Nichols joined Partridge and Van Fleet for a "discussion of the Korean political situation," Partridge wrote in his diary.

In his meeting with Rhee the following day, Nichols reported that "the whole [U.S. military headquarters] and everybody is talking about nothing but the next election. . . . ," said a letter written by Rhee's wife, Francesca Donner. She described Nichols in the letter as her husband's "very helpful" adviser and informant.

Rhee soon changed his mind about retiring. To secure another term, he declared martial law and rammed through constitutional amendments that changed the way presidents were chosen in South Korea. No longer would the National Assembly, whose support Rhee had lost, select the country's leader. Instead, there was a direct popular vote in 1952, which Rhee handily won.

─────────

As Nichols's authority expanded, so did his power to recruit young men. He needed hundreds of them to go behind enemy lines. But he also wanted a select few to visit him in the evenings in his private quarters, according to three South Korean veterans who worked for him in the 1950s. They said Nichols found these young men in the South Korean air force and army.

"Young, good-looking airmen were invited into Mr. Nichols's room and sometimes two of them visited him at the same time," said Chung Bong-sun, the retired air force colonel who worked closely for Nichols as an intelligence officer.

"Mr. Nichols sent a plane to get one airman who worked for me," said Chung. "I asked him later, 'What did you do?' He told me he went to Mr. Nichols's place and had good food and fun. He said Mr. Nichols hugged and kissed him."

It was widely rumored among Koreans who worked in Nichols's unit that he had "some kind of sexual issue," said Kim In-ho in an interview at his home in Seoul in 2015, when Kim was eighty-nine. Kim said he worked in the South Korean air force without rank for five years, during which time he was assigned to Nichols's unit, where he helped train agents. Kim said that five or six young and good-looking soldiers visited the base regularly to see Nichols and it was rumored that they "took turns giving him hand jobs." Kim said he never spoke to the soldiers involved.

In South Korea in the 1950s, heterosexual contact between American servicemen and prostitutes was rampant, cheap, and widely tolerated by the U.S. military command. As a result, in the desperately poor years during and after the war, the majority of the nation's prostitutes lived near military bases. But homosexual contact of any kind was a serious offense on any American base, as well as a cultural taboo.

Exacerbated by cold war fears of "subversives," homophobia peaked in the armed forces in the 1950s. The Pentagon distributed a memo in 1949 that unified and toughened regulations for all branches of the military. It said that there could be no "rehabilitation" of homosexuals or lesbians, that they were not permitted to serve in any capacity, and that "prompt separation of known homosexuals from the Armed Forces is mandatory." It also urged careful investigation of suspected homosexuals.

Yet what went on for years in Nichols's quarters did not damage his command authority or his reputation as an officer. There is no hint of concern regarding his sexuality in his twice-yearly officer efficiency reports, which were written by his immediate superior officer. Those reports, during the war years, judged his conformance to air force standards of conduct to be "superior." In his autobiography, Nichols said nothing about the young airmen brought to him in the evenings.

As for the South Korean officers who worked with Nichols, they looked the other way. Nichols was a close friend of President Rhee—far too powerful and well connected to question. He had also won the loyalty of South Koreans who worked with him. "He was a very trusted man," said Chung, adding that he personally trusted Nichols more than any other American.

"He acted like a king during the war, but he was also an incredible spy," said Kim In-ho. "He lay the foundation for espionage in South Korea. Without him, we would have lost the war."

In his autobiography, Nichols goes on at length about how he personally trained the young men he sent behind enemy lines. When he opened a parachute school in Taegu during the first year of the war, some of these men refused to jump. So he led by example, even though he had never had any training in parachute jumping. By war's end, Nichols had jumped from nine different aircraft and helicopters on training and spy missions. The cumulative impact damaged his knees, forcing him, when he was in his fifties, to wear metal braces on both legs.

"Without questioning the men as to why they didn't jump, I took the chute off a man about my size, put it on, and told everyone to get back on the plane," Nichols wrote. "I then told them that I had never jumped before, which I hadn't, but that I was going to as soon as the plane got airborne and went over the [drop zone] and that everyone else had better jump or they were going to have to account to me personally why not, after the plane landed."

After the young men learned to parachute, Nichols sent them on suicide missions.

"There is no sense in going into the feeling one gets when he sends a person on a mission knowing well—in many cases—that he will not return," Nichols wrote. "I don't believe I'm capable of explaining this feeling; all I can say is that it is terrible and one can never forget. However, some fool has to do this ugly job."

Nichols chose not to mention in his autobiography that a small group of Koreans—apparently alarmed at the high rate of death and disappearance among agents being sent behind enemy lines—physically attacked him late one night in the early spring of 1951. Details of the attack are sketchy, but it is clear that it occurred. "It was a kind of riot so big that it was difficult to put down," said Serbando Torres, who was in a nearby building on the night of the attack. "Nick did not go in detail about why it happened, other than to say it was a disturbance."

Kim Gye-son, who claims to have worked for Nichols's unit in the 1950s, described the attack in testimony posted on a Korean War blog. He said six angry agents burst into Nichols's quarters intending to kill him. Nichols responded with gunfire, according to the post, and shot three agents to death at the scene. The other three were court-martialed.

A notable participant in the incident was Lee Kun Soon, the North Korean pilot who defected to South Korea in a Soviet aircraft in 1950 and whom Nichols then hired. On the night of the attack, Nichols shot Lee twice but did not kill him. In his account of what happened, Lee said it was all "a misunderstanding" amplified by alcohol.

"Nichols must have thought it was a serious matter," Lee said in an account published in 1965 in a South Korean air force collection of war memories. "Maybe he thought we were there to hurt him. Later, he testified that he shot me out of self-defense because he didn't want things to get complicated."

Remarkably, the late-night shootout does not warrant any mention in Nichols's service record—a telling indicator of his near-total autonomy as a military officer and spymaster. His officer efficiency report for the first six months of 1951, written by a colonel who was supposedly supervising his performance, says only that Nichols performed during that period in ways that were "audacious yet level-headed" and "spirited but tactful."

By the spring of 1951, no one seems to have been supervising or reviewing the day-to-day activities of his unit. His orders were to report directly to Partridge, the general who was running the entire air war in Korea. Only the general was responsible for "direct control" of what Nichols did.

In addition to the gunfight in his quarters, there were a number of bizarre and violent episodes involving Nichols that never appeared in his military service record or in air force histories of his spy units—at least, not in those that have been declassified. Nichols had the authority to send individuals on flights over North Korea and drop them behind enemy lines—and he appears to have used it to punish those who angered him.

"When we were in Taegu on the first retreat in 1950, there was an incident that upset Mr. Nichols," recalled Chung, the South Korean air force intelligence officer. He said that two young South Korean generals who were friends of Nichols—one of them was Lieutenant General Chang Sung-hwan, who became air force chief of staff in the 1960s and died in 2015—were arrested in a bar by a South Korean military policeman. "The MP interrogated them and hung them upside down by a rope," Chung said. "When Mr. Nichols found out about this, he put the MP on a plane and dropped him off in a parachute over North Korean territory. I never saw the MP again."

The MP's disappearance was not an exceptional event, according to Lee Kun Soon, the North Korean defector whom Nichols shot during the 1951 attack on his office. Lee said Nichols had a reputation that terrified many Koreans. "He was headstrong. He didn't care for human rights,"

Lee said. "When he didn't like someone's face, he put that person in a parachute and sent him off to North Korea."

Nichols went along on some of these flights. Jack A. Sariego, who served as an airman second class under Nichols during the war, said he accompanied Nichols on an L-4 observation plane that took a North Korean colonel, a prisoner of war, out for a flight over the Han River. When the plane reached an altitude of thirty-five hundred feet, the North Korean officer, who was not wearing a parachute, was pushed out. He was last seen splashing into the river.

"Nick was livid!" Sariego wrote in an e-mail. "He decided to take the captured Colonel on a Joy Flight."

The colonel had been suspected of killing several young Chinese soldiers who were prisoners of war and also worked as houseboys for air force officers.

In his autobiography, Nichols described several of the "methods" he developed to eliminate "dangerous or untrustworthy agents." These included "bail him out [of an aircraft] in a paper-packed chute; dump him off the back of a boat, in the nude, at high speed; give him false information plants—and let the enemy do it for you."

There were no regulations governing his "cloak and dagger" work, which Nichols said he "played by ear." Citing an order from his commanding general, Nichols said Partridge gave him a "blank check." One letter from Partridge written nearly two years after the Korean War ended does support Nichols's contention that the air force gave him a free hand: "The work that you are doing is quite unusual and to be productive must at times be carried out along lines which you deem appropriate regardless of what the regulations would say about the matter—if there were any regulations. . . ."

Donald Nichols (infant on left) with his three older brothers, William, Judson, and Walter, in Hackensack, New Jersey, in the late summer of 1923.

Courtesy of Diana Carlin.

Myra Nichols abandoned her husband and four sons when Donald was seven. Before leaving the family, she was known to bathe naked in the kitchen sink and be intimate with suitors in the living room. Because of his mother, Donald later said he hated women.

Courtesy of Diana Carlin.

His wife gone, Walter Nichols Sr. moved to Florida with his sons in 1933. He struggled to find work during the Great Depression and never got over Myra. Still pining for her, he died in 1940, at fifty-three. "He died of loneliness, nothing else," Donald said.

Courtesy of Diana Carlin.

Nichols quit school in seventh grade to scrounge scrap metal, which he sold to help his family eat. At seventeen, he joined the army for the "big pay day" of twenty-one dollars a month and served as a mechanic in India during World War II. As a child, he often went to bed hungry—and later blamed his upbringing for his "psychopathic" yearning for sweets and his long struggle with obesity.

Courtesy of Lindsay Morgan.

South Korean president Syngman Rhee, America's chosen puppet to lead the fledgling nation, soon proved a troublemaker. The CIA saw him as vain and delusional; the U.S. Army had a plan to topple him. Despite his refusal to fall in line—not to mention committing gross human rights abuses—he stayed in power for a dozen years and became a very close friend of a young spy named Donald Nichols.

Library of Congress.

Nichols (center) arrived in Korea in 1946, four years before the Soviet-backed North Korean invasion. He had time to learn Korean and cement ties with Rhee before war broke out. In a civil conflict fought inside South Korea—a fight the American public largely ignored—Nichols worked closely with Rhee's security forces as they savagely suppressed South Koreans believed to be Communists.

Courtesy of Lindsay Morgan.

Nichols had a gift for finding older men who would advance his career and cover his back. No American did that more than Air Force general Earle E. Partridge. During the Korean War, Nichols reported directly to Partridge, who described his protégé as "the most amazing and unusual man" he'd met in the service.

U.S. Air Force.

President Harry S. Truman (right) with John J. Muccio, U.S. ambassador to South Korea, and General Douglas MacArthur in 1950. Muccio praised Nichols as the best spy in Korea and blocked efforts by MacArthur's staff to have him reassigned. Six months after this photo was taken, Truman fired MacArthur.

Courtesy of Harry S. Truman Library.

Major General Charles A. Willoughby was MacArthur's worshipful chief of intelligence. He sheltered MacArthur from unwanted news, including richly detailed reports from Nichols that war in Korea was imminent. Before the war, Willoughby tried to silence Nichols; after it started, he tried to hire him.

The Associated Press.

Lieutenant General Walton "Johnnie" Walker commanded the Eighth Army when it was caged inside the Pusan Perimeter at the southern tip of the Korean peninsula. A team of Korean cryptographers working for Nichols broke North Korean army battle codes, giving Walker advance notice of enemy attacks and helping the Eighth Army break out of the perimeter.

U.S. Army.

This previously unpublished photo, taken on the roof of South Korean army headquarters in Seoul in 1949, shows Nichols (far left), along with unidentified U.S. and South Korean officials, inspecting a human head in a bucket. Severed heads of Communist guerrilla leaders were often sent to Seoul to show progress in the civil war, Nichols wrote. "I have seen these things," he said. "I have survived in spite of the memories."

Frank Winslow for the U.S. Army.

Nichols (far right) at the execution of thirty-nine alleged South Korean "Communists" on April 19, 1950, two months before the start of the Korean War. To aid the firing squad, South Korean military police tied victims to stakes and pinned targets to their chests. Bodies were then "hauled away to destinations unknown," Nichols wrote.

Frank Winslow for the U.S. Army.

Using a new Leica purchased at the PX in Seoul, Nichols documented the secret execution. Fifteen of his photos were included in a classified cable to Washington. It was "a normal execution as carried out quite frequently in South Korea," an embassy official wrote.

National Archives.

Soon after the war began, Nichols witnessed what he called an "unforgettable massacre" by South Korean forces of thousands of civilians, including women and children. But he did not tell his commanders or write a report about it—perhaps because of his closeness to Syngman Rhee. Nichols waited thirty-one years before mentioning the atrocity in his memoir—and then knowingly misstated where it occurred so that his book would not challenge the official U.S. Army version of the Taejon massacre, which falsely blamed North Korea.

National Archives.

Serbando J. Torres, an air force clerk, was Nichols's closest aide for three years and often shared quarters with him. He said his boss was "so fearless" in the Korean War that "you could say he was crazy." He also said Nichols "dreamed up a lot of baloney."

Courtesy of Serbando J. Torres.

Nichols loved dogs. In Korea, he had a snarling pack of mutts for protection from North Korean assassins. At his spy base outside Seoul, his dogs sometimes ate with him in the officers' mess and occasionally bit other air force officers.

Courtesy of Lindsay Morgan.

The relationship between Nichols (far right) and General Partridge (second from right), commander of the Fifth Air Force, served both men well. Nichols provided the general with thousands of bomb targets inside North Korea—and Partridge rewarded his "one man war" with promotions, medals, and extraordinary autonomy.

U.S. Air Force.

Nichols taught himself how to parachute out of airplanes. Then he trained hundreds of Korean agents to do it and sent them on suicide missions over North Korea. "Some fool has to do this ugly job," he said, referring to himself.

Courtesy of Lindsay Morgan.

Nichols was a colossus among the Koreans, standing six feet two inches and weighing as much as 260 pounds. "No Korean could match his height or fatness," said one of his Korean intelligence officers. Nichols was also known for inviting handsome young South Korean airmen to his quarters for dinner and sexual encounters.

U.S. Air Force.

After the North Korean invasion, the U.S. Air Force authorized Nichols to create and command a covert unit known as NICK. He recruited agents from prisons and refugee camps. In this photo from Taegu, South Korea, he inspects a parachute unit training for deployment behind enemy lines.

Courtesy of Serbando J. Torres.

When the Korean War ended, Nichols stayed on as a spymaster in South Korea for four more years. He continued to train Korean spies, as in this 1957 photo of a training march. He also remained close to President Rhee.

U.S. Air Force.

For Nichols, life after Korea was a maddening mess. In late 1957, he was confined to the psychiatric ward of a military hospital in Florida, where air force doctors gave him electroshock treatment. Forced into medical retirement, he said he became "a misfit wherever I went." In the mid-1960s, he fled to Mexico after being accused of sexually abusing a boy in Florida. He lived in Guadalajara with his son, Donnie, and his dogs for about a year before his older brother Judson convinced him to return to Florida, where he was acquitted.

Courtesy of Diana Carlin.

Nichols with Judson (left) in the 1960s. After the war, Judson welcomed his brother into his home, where Donald stored hundreds of thousands of dollars in cash—loot smuggled home from Korea—in the family freezer.

Courtesy of Diana Carlin.

S, HERO OF KOREAN WAR
                A.I.S.S. US AIR FORCE

When he was sixty-four, Nichols returned for the first and only time to Seoul, where his old spy comrades gave him a hero's welcome. His visit received much favorable coverage in the South Korean press. When he returned home to Florida, he was again charged with sexually abusing boys.

Courtesy of Lee Beom-gu.

During the war, Nichols won a tableful of medals from the United States and South Korea. They include the Distinguished Service Cross and the Silver Star, the second- and third-highest American honors for valor.

Blaine Harden

NICHOLS

DONALD
18 FEB. 1923
2 JUNE 1992

KIM HWA
6 DEC. 1931
18 FEB. 1953

THANKS FOR STOPPING AS YOU PASS BY
AS YOU ARE NOW SO ONCE WAS I

Nichols died in 1992 in the psych ward of a VA hospital in Alabama. His burial plot in Florida is marked by a headstone that shows the spymaster's sleight of hand. It bears the name of a woman named Kim Hwa, who he claimed was his wife during the Korean War, and the mother of Donnie. It is unlikely he married her or that her remains were buried alongside Nichols's.

Blaine Harden

CHAPTER 7

Empire of Islands

War stopped rolling up and down the Korean Peninsula in the late spring of 1951. To a substantial degree, it was because President Truman had finally found a general whose ego did not prevent him from commanding the limited war that the White House wanted to fight.

General Matthew Ridgway was fifteen years younger than MacArthur, far less vain, far more focused. He singlehandedly changed the war by firing incompetent senior officers, restoring the morale of the Eighth Army, and breaking the momentum of the Chinese army. A brainy battlefield tactician who led airborne troops in the D-day invasion, Ridgway deployed artillery with savage efficiency and slaughtered wave upon wave of Chinese infantry. "The ground situation is excellent," Partridge noted in his diary. "We are killing Chinese by the tens of thousands and no enemy can take this punishment for long."

Unlike MacArthur, Ridgway was willing to accept the reality of a divided peninsula. He turned a humiliating retreat into a sustainable stalemate. His forces pushed the Chinese and the North Koreans north of the thirty-eighth parallel. By summer of 1951, the war was more or less back where it started. As fitful peace talks began, combatants on all sides dug in for what would be two more years of fighting. On the ground, it came to resemble the trench warfare of World War I. In the air, all-jet dogfights raged over MiG Alley. Elsewhere, American B-29s continued to pulverize North Korea with bombs.

It was during this standoff, as the American public grew weary of the war and stopped paying close attention to it, that Donald Nichols spread his spymaster wings. It was the most magnificent season of his life. He became a name brand among American spooks jockeying for power, funding, and clandestine glory. There was army intelligence. There was the CIA. There was NICK.

In February 1951, the intelligence unit created for Nichols—Special Activities Unit #1—did not yet amount to much. It was just him and three air force sergeants, plus a handful of Koreans on loan from the South Korean air force. He ran it from a temporary office in a temporary base in Taegu, where Americans had fled during the Chinese offensive. But by the end of 1952, Nichols commanded a sprawling spy empire— Detachment 2, 6004th Air Intelligence Service Squadron—with fifty subdetachments. Seven of his bases were in South Korea along the thirty-eighth parallel. The rest were "north of the bomb line" on small, close-in islands along the east and west coasts of North Korea. Reporting to Nichols were 52 U.S. Air Force officers and airmen. More important, he controlled more than 900 Korean agents and fighters, including 178 Korean air force officers and enlisted men. A history of Detachment 2, which appears to have been written to please Nichols, describes his outfit as "an organization of tremendous proportions" that far exceeded the dreams he had upon arrival in Korea in 1946.

Nichols, the seventh-grade dropout, became an educator. He built schools to teach interrogation techniques, parachute jumping, and agent survival skills. He presided over the writing of an interrogation handbook, which focused on identifying targets to bomb in North Korea. He created a map project, which allowed interpreters to pinpoint target coordinates. To communicate with his expanding operation, he built a radio network. To move men between islands, he assembled a small navy, begging, scrounging, and stealing vessels that ranged from skiffs to sailboats to a ship for landing tanks. Several of his boats were rebuilt wrecks dug out of mud in the Han River. Others were stolen from Chinese fishermen near the North Korean border with China. A few were purchased or built to order with air force funds.

For errands, Nichols kept a helicopter at his headquarters. For money, he hired a Korean counterfeiter and bought a printing press. In tall cabinets behind his office desk, he stored bundles of cash, both counterfeit and real. In premission meetings with agents, he liked to reach back, grab a bundle or two of cash out of a cabinet, and toss them in the air. If agents caught the money before it hit the floor, he laughed and sometimes threw more.

The frozen front lines of a stalemated war were precisely what enabled Nichols to build an empire. His interrogators promptly moved into the large, semipermanent camps constructed by UN forces for refugees and prisoners of war. They grilled thousands of North Koreans, seeking fresh intelligence for bombing missions. Then they selected able-bodied young men and forced them to return to North Korea on spying missions.

Nichols's archipelago of occupied islands, which formed a kind of horseshoe around North Korea and was defended by UN air and naval forces, simplified the logistics and reduced the risks of infiltrating and extricating agents. At night, in groups of two or three, they went ashore in small boats or crossed mudflats on foot at low tide. The islands, which were also used by army intelligence outfits and the CIA, served as collecting stations for North Koreans on the run. They were screened by island-based NICK agents, and if deemed useful as potential spies, they were transported to Seoul for training.

It took Nichols months of trial and error to figure out what types of missions he could pull off without losing most of the agents he sent off to North Korea.

In the spring of 1951, with a blank check from Partridge for covert ops, Nichols tried his hand at commando-style sabotage. He trained fifteen South Koreans as guerrillas. He taught them how to blow up bridges and outfitted them with Korean People's Army uniforms, complete with forged identification cards, counterfeit currency, and PPSh submachine guns, a Russian-made weapon that Stalin shipped by the tens of thousands into North Korea.

Nichols put together an ambitious mission for his guerrillas. After parachuting into North Korea at dawn on June 1, their orders were to find and blow up two railroad bridges. Between the bridges, Nichols hoped, they would trap an enemy train, which would be an easy target for fighter-bombers of the Fifth Air Force. The fifteen were then to locate what was left of a nearby crashed MiG-15. (This was the same MiG carcass that Nichols's team had partially salvaged on April 17, in the mission that he might or might not have participated in on the ground.) If his agents spotted remaining useful parts of the jet, "they were to put them on ox carts and proceed to the west. There, they were to steal a boat and sail to the island of Cho-do," where Nichols had a base.

This ambitious plan failed before it began. Chinese troops captured Nichols's agents as they parachuted in. They were interrogated and presumably executed, except for one who escaped. Yet this failure did not stop Nichols from organizing an even more complicated operation on enemy turf.

On July 20, he went after the wreckage of another MiG-15 that had crashed in coastal mud flats off the west coast of North Korea. In aerial photographs, the fuselage of this downed fighter appeared substantially less damaged than the one that went down and caught fire in April. The air force hoped to recover an unburned, undamaged instrument panel for analysts at the Air Technical Intelligence Center at Wright-Patterson Air Force Base in Dayton, Ohio.

To fetch it, Nichols organized a multinational, interservice salvage operation involving an army landing ship equipped with a salvage crane, a British Royal Navy destroyer for fire support, fighter planes from a British aircraft carrier to provide low cover, and Fifth Air Force fighters to ward off MiG-15 attacks. The army landing ship's arrival was timed to a thirty-foot tide that lifted the ship high off the mudflat to allow its crane to grab the crashed jet's fuselage.

Remarkably, it worked. Thanks to Nichols, for the first time in the war, American aircraft experts were able to examine the intact cockpit and instruments of a Russian fighter jet that was shooting down American pilots and airmen. The avionics of the enemy's best aircraft were now in U.S. hands.

By the summer of 1951, under air force regulations, it was long past time for Nichols to go home. He had been based in Korea for five consecutive years, rarely taking home leave or vacation. Moreover, he faced a reset of his senior bosses. In May, General Stratemeyer suffered a major heart attack and retired. In July, General Partridge returned to the States, where he took a new job in Baltimore, Maryland, as director of the Air Research and Development Command. On his way out of Korea, he invited Nichols and Torres to join him, telling them that the work at the research base would be interesting and safe. In Baltimore, Partridge focused on improving the performance of the F-86 Sabre jets that were dueling with MiG-15s.

"We were expecting Nick to come with us, but he changed his mind," said Torres, who jumped at the chance to get out of Korea. "I think Nick realized that if he had come to Baltimore, he would have just been another junior officer. In Korea, he was the commander of his own intelligence unit."

Nearly every year, Nichols had to write to his immediate supervisor and justify his continued deployment in Korea. In those letters, he always played his ace: he was a close personal friend of President Rhee and an associate of other powerful men who controlled South Korea. He was much too valuable to be sent home.

"I am aware that current regulations do not provide for an additional extension of overseas duty without return to the [United States]," he wrote in 1950. "But I believe that I can contribute much more to the Armed Forces if retained in my present capacity. Since my assignment to Korea in June 1946 I have developed sources of information on a level which enables me to furnish a continuous and increasing flow of intelligence reports which are of considerable interest to commanders concerned."

Every year his commanders overruled regulations and approved his stay. In late 1951, when his request was approved, his bosses added a sweetener, promoting him to major. A month earlier, his operation had been expanded again, as the Fifth Air Force authorized "the establishment and building of an organization large enough to capitalize on the tremendous opportunities existing in the intelligence collection field." These "tremendous opportunities" were the coastal islands on the east and west coasts of North Korea. Nichols steadily gained access to more of these islands in 1951 and 1952, each time opening another NICK subbase.

It had become almost impossible to move agents back and forth across the dug-in front lines of the mainland war, and spies who parachuted into North Korea were almost always caught and killed. So the islands, by default, became preferred conduits "for infiltration and exfiltration of friendly agents." This meant, in addition to building and staffing his island bases, Nichols needed to recruit more North Koreans who were willing to return home to spy—or who could be pressured into doing so.

One North Korean whom Nichols forced to become a spy was Kim Ji-eok.

He was nineteen in the second year of the war and living on a farm about ten miles west of Pyongyang. To avoid conscription into the Korean People's Army, he had found a job with the state railways, but there was little work because so many tracks had been destroyed by American bombs. When the government forced Kim Ji-eok to do farm labor instead, he feared the bombs and napalm that had destroyed 75 percent of Pyongyang and continued to fall in and around the capital. He thought his chances of surviving the war would be better if he could sneak south and find his aunt and uncle in Seoul. He hired a guide who promised to lead him through the front lines, but on a pitch-black night near the front in April 1952, the guide became lost and then disappeared. Kim walked on alone. At daybreak, he found himself on the west coast, where mudflats led toward small, rocky islands.

An American patrol boat spotted him and took him to nearby Yongmae Island. Kim believed he was lucky. "I thought the Americans would set me free," he said. "I was expecting to meet my uncle."

Instead, they handed him over to South Korean airmen who worked for Nichols. They fed him salty soup and kept him in a house with ten others who had fled North Korea. One by one, each was interrogated about why he wanted to live in South Korea and what he knew about North Korean military bases, particularly air bases, flight patterns, and airplane hangars. Apparently satisfied that he was not a spy, Nichols's men transported Kim to Inchon by boat and then by truck to Seoul, where he was dropped off at a former girls' school in a downtown neighborhood called Anguk-dong. Nichols had taken over the two-story, nineteen-room building and made it his headquarters.

Kim's interrogation continued there. He was ordered to detail the location of military bases near his home. He worked with mapmakers to draw diagrams of his home and the surrounding neighborhood. "I did not know about any military installations," Kim said. "I was so disappointed because I had heard so many good things about South Korea and because I had paid all the money I had for a guide."

His interrogator had news for Kim that was even more distressing.

"He told me I must go back home. He wanted me to find Mirim Airport [a military airfield near Pyongyang] and get information about it," Kim said. "He also told me that if I didn't go back, he would send me to prison. If I completed the mission, he promised I could join the South Korean air force. That was something I wanted. I believed that if I became an airman, I might be able to bring my family to Seoul."

After Kim agreed to return, he received two weeks of training. Then he and two other North Korean defectors who had become reluctant spies were taken by boat back to the west coast of North Korea. Walking at night to avoid the Americans' daytime bombing attacks, they traveled eighty-five miles over twenty days to the outskirts of Pyongyang.

"We were ordered to find the hangar at Mirim airfield and learn the type and number of aircraft," Kim said. "Of course, it was impossible. We couldn't get near the airfield and the two guys in my group ran off. I wanted to stay alive. But I also wanted to go back to South Korea and join the air force."

Kim said he made no attempt to spy on the airfield and focused instead on finding a more reliable guide to lead him safely back to South Korea. He found a woman who owned a rice-cake shop in Pyongyang, and she helped him return to the west coast, where he again walked across mud-flats to an island controlled by the Americans. He turned himself in as a returning spy.

"I was nervous that something bad was going to happen to me," he said. "The investigators kept asking about the hangar at Mirim airfield—and I couldn't answer."

For reasons that Kim did not understand, the South Koreans who worked for Nichols selected him for more spy training and transported him back to Nichols's headquarters in Seoul. There he had a brief but unforgettable audience with the commander.

"Nichols was really fat, with a huge, bulging belly. The Koreans called him 'Neko, Neko.' In his office there were all these yellow dogs and they barked at me. I didn't even sit down. There was an American pilot in the office. I learned he was going to take me to a training camp. For the trip, Nichols gave the pilot a bundle of money. I don't know how much it was. Nichols did not talk to me."

After two short flights and a boat journey, Kim arrived on Jebu, a west coast island where the South Korean air force operated a training camp. Most of the sixty trainees were volunteers from South Korea who would become noncommissioned officers in the air force. The rest were North Koreans or young men who did not belong to any military orga-nization.

Kim had become an agent-in-training for a future parachute drop over North Korea. His group of press-ganged spies, called Class C, was given American military uniforms without insignia, a pair of American-made military boots, and C rations, the U.S. military meals intended for soldiers far from mess halls or field kitchens. But they were paid nothing and had no rank, serial number, or identity card. "Officially, we did not exist," Kim said.

From May until September 1952, his training consisted mostly of running, often with a parachute strapped to his back. He learned how to fold the parachute quickly and how to mark coordinates on a map. Once during training, he smiled while saluting and was severely beaten by Koreans who worked for Nichols. When he reported that he had a stomachache, the Koreans again beat him.

By September, Kim's fellow Class C spies began leaving the island. They did not say good-bye or graduate. Every few days, a few of them simply disappeared. Kim suspected they had been selected for missions in the North. Rumors spread in the camp that South Korean instructors pushed terrified agents out of airplanes.

"I decided my best chance of living would be to escape," Kim said.

With several others, he walked away at night across mudflats to the mainland. They found their way to the headquarters of the South Korean air force outside Seoul and, rather improbably, were allowed to tell their stories to General Kim Chung Yul, the air force chief of staff who had won his job with Nichols's help. The general allowed the men to join the air force.

Kim Ji-eok survived the war by working in a military hospital. After eight years in the air force, he found a job at a noodle restaurant owned by his aunt in Seoul—and that is where he was still working in 2015 when he told his story, at age eighty-two.

"People call Nichols a hero, but I'm not so sure," said Kim. "If he had sent me back again to North Korea, it would have been the end of my life."

In *Apocalypse Now*, Robert Duvall as Lieutenant Colonel William "Bill" Kilgore famously calls in a sortie of air force jets to firebomb the enemy.

"I love the smell of napalm in the morning," he tells his men as a coastal jungle explodes in flames that reek of gasoline. "Smells like . . . victory."

The movie, of course, is about Vietnam, where Americans dropped a staggering 388,000 tons of napalm between 1963 and 1973. The colonel's deranged speech—together with a Pulitzer Prize–winning photograph of terrified Vietnamese children running from a napalmed village—secured napalm's infamy in the annals of modern warfare. While Colonel Kilgore was a satiric fiction, there was nothing fictitious about the U.S. military's twentieth-century love affair with the sticky, long-burning gel that melts human flesh. It was invented at Harvard in the early 1940s, and American bomb planners quickly sent it to war. About 20,000 tons were dropped on Germany. A napalm attack over Tokyo one night in March 1945 created a firestorm that killed about a hundred thousand people and turned fifteen miles of the city to ash. Bomber pilots recalled the smell of "roasted human flesh."

Yet the U.S. military did not fully appreciate napalm until it dropped 32,000 tons of it on the Korean Peninsula between 1950 and 1953. "Napalm was one of the 'discoveries' of the Korean War," wrote J. M. Spaight, a British airpower expert in the 1950s. "[I]t was in Korea that its effectiveness as a stopping weapon was fully demonstrated. . . . But for [napalm] the United Nations force might have been bundled neck and crop out of Korea. . . ."

A decade before Vietnam, Donald Nichols smelled victory in napalm's flames. "Napalm Bombs have the greatest psychological effect on the people of North Korea, due to the lasting burning effect it has on whatever it comes in contact with," he wrote in an air intelligence information report.

Nichols's song of praise was part of an American military chorus in Korea, where operations analysts for the Fifth Air Force "heartily endorsed napalm as the best single antipersonnel weapon" in the war. The Far East Air Forces listed napalm as its "first choice weapon against troops." The Twenty-seventh Fighter Escort Wing, a U.S. unit that attacked Chinese troops in 1951, said napalm was its "primary weapon." General Ridgway dispatched B-29s with napalm over Pyongyang on January 3 and 5, 1951, "with the goal of burning the city to the ground." Altogether, the United States dropped nearly twice as much napalm on Korea as it did on Japan in 1945.

In the early days of the war in Korea, when American soldiers were outgunned and fleeing south, napalm was the great equalizer. Even a near miss could generate enough heat to ignite fuel inside a T-34 tank. When Chinese forces surged south and attacked in human waves, napalm killed thousands and terrified many more. But the bulk of the napalm that the Americans dropped in the war was used strategically rather than tactically, which means it was used to set fire to cities, towns, and villages across North Korea.

As the war progressed, the American definition of what constituted a reasonable military target in North Korea kept expanding. At first, Truman believed that attacks on targets that were not "purely military" could provoke a larger war with the Soviet Union. The White House resisted an early air force proposal to do a "fire job"—using napalm—on North Korea's five major industrial centers. But after the Chinese intervention, American restraint disappeared and the fire job began in November 1950. It continued throughout the rest of the war. Bombing targets, for napalm and conventional bombs, included nearly every man-made structure in North Korea, as well as most human or animal activities that could conceivably be interpreted from a war plane as suspicious.

"During recent days we have been carrying out attacks above the bomb line on any activities which might have military significance," Partridge wrote in his dairy in mid-December 1950. "For example, we have been attacking all males who are carrying arms or who are moving about in a manner which indicates that they are [a] potential enemy. We are attacking any transportation and carts, animals capable of acting as beasts of burden. . . . Lately we have received through friendly sources, information that some of these attacks have been on people who were in some cases South Korean and in other cases, were entirely innocent. This is a matter of extreme regret, but I do not know how to direct selective attacks without giving the enemy sanctuary over a wide area."

As the target list expanded, so did the use of napalm. One reason was the satisfaction pilots felt after dropping it. "When you've hit a village and have seen it go up in flames, you know you've accomplished something," one pilot said. American fulfillment in using napalm in Korea sometimes exceeded its military utility, according to an air force survey of prisoners of war. The prisoners said that while they feared napalm, the most effective weapons were fragmentation bombs. "The Fifth Air Force's preference for napalm as an antipersonnel weapon may not have been completely realistic," the survey found.

By the summer of 1951, with the war stalemated, the Far East Air Forces had more bombers and more napalm than it had targets. The imbalance forced Nichols to rethink what it meant to be a special operations commander. There would be no more code breaking, sabotage attempts, or salvage operations. His orders were to collect "information suitable for air target selection," assess bomb damage, and determine the "psychological effects of air power on the enemy."

To that end, Nichols told his men to interrogate as many defectors and prisoners of war as possible. He recruited agents by the hundreds, and his training schools taught them how to slip into North Korea on foot, by boat, and by parachute. They were told to travel to their home regions, where they knew the lay of the land and had friends. After finding and mapping targets worth bombing, they were to slip away, preferably by walking across mudflats to an island where Nichols had a base. As Nichols's operation moved into high gear in late 1951 and 1952, an acceptable loss rate for agents—caught and killed or simply bugging out—appears to have been 40 percent.

Nichols also killed his own spies if he believed they were double agents loyal to North Korea. To smoke them out, he orchestrated elaborate cons. One particularly theatrical operation occurred when Nichols was building his island empire, according to George T. Gregory, an air force major who served as an executive officer under Nichols. As Gregory tells the story, Nichols was aboard one of his boats, transporting agents to the mainland, when "blinding beams of searchlights suddenly bathed them in white.

"They were boarded and forced to line up with their hands behind their heads by the grim-looking men in North Korean navy uniforms," Gregory wrote. "The North Koreans advised their captives that they were taking the 'white foreigner' [Nichols] with them, but would blow the ship and its crew of vile, traitorous South Koreans—American puppets—out of the water. Nichols was being led towards the enemy ship when one of the crewmen began screaming that he was a North Korean agent."

Nichols had found his mole.

"The dummy Communist vessel, complete with North Korean Navy markings, sailor uniforms and Soviet guns, was planned and carried out by Nichols in its entirety," Gregory wrote.

Between 1951 and the end of 1952, Nichols doubled his production of air intelligence information reports, as the monthly total jumped from five hundred to about a thousand. "The increasing flow of reports made it necessary to work American personnel and indigenous translators and draftsmen in headquarters on frequent occasion at night and holidays," according to a history of his unit.

The official air force history of the war describes Nichols as the "most important single collector" of air intelligence for the tactical bombing of North Korea. His reports pinpointed hand-grenade factories, freshly dug caves, radio stations, parking lots, food warehouses, ammunition dumps, print shops, a paper factory, a zinc factory, locomotives, Russian officer quarters, Chinese troop concentrations, and an underground clothing factory dug into the side of a mountain. Many reports included finely detailed maps. In a report on an airfield in downtown Pyongyang, there were maps and drawings of electrical transformer stations, water supply lines, and an aircraft repair shop disguised among village huts.

Bomb planners in Tokyo relied on Nichols's reports. His targets were bombed with explosives or burned with napalm or both. In the final year of the war, when the air force was running low on targets, Nichols was called upon to help destroy a giant hydroelectric dam on the Yalu River. The Suiho Dam had been bombed several times but stubbornly continued to produce electricity. Nichols conceived of a plan to use covert agents who had grown up near the dam, and they were parachuted in as sleeper agents. Their mission was to find employment at the dam, establish trust, and use their inside access to produce "proper maps and annotated photos" for bombing attacks that would cripple the dam. At war's end, the agents were apparently still establishing trust—or, more likely, dead. The dam survived.

American bombs and napalm destroyed more of North Korea, in relation to its resources, than all the combined air attacks on Japan during World War II, including the atom bombs that hit Hiroshima and Nagasaki. That was the conclusion of the Far East Air Forces. The air force also believed that air attacks tipped the balance, forcing a crippled, traumatized enemy to the peace table. "We are pretty sure now that the Communists wanted peace, not because of a two-year stalemate on the ground, but to get airpower off their back," General Otto P. Weyland, commander of the Far East Air Forces, said in 1954.

The air force was so proud of its performance that it institutionalized the lessons learned in Korea and used them a decade later in Southeast Asia, where it carpet bombed and napalmed insurgents in Vietnam—and failed spectacularly to win the war. There were many who analyzed the bombing of North Korea and concluded that the air force had learned the wrong lessons. They found overwhelming evidence that bombing failed to stop "the forward movement of supplies" to North Korean and Chinese fighters.

Even Nichols, who won accolades for his success in identifying bomb targets, was among those who doubted the utility of the air-delivered devastation. "To a certain extent you could say we wasted our bombs on the roads, bridges, railroads, tunnels, etc.," Nichols wrote in his autobiography. "The enemy made a fool of us."

The enemy did so by transporting fuel, ammunition, and food in the same way that ants transport food to their colonies—in small quantities distributed among a large number of disciplined and highly motivated individuals. The North Koreans used an A-frame: a kind of backpack on stilts that was strapped to a man's shoulders and had two wooden support sticks that dragged behind on the ground. With this primitive rucksack, Koreans could lug loads weighing up to 150 pounds.

"I saw teams of hundreds and hundreds all equipped with their frames," Nichols wrote. "These teams worked by night and slept by day . . . they usually dispersed themselves under trees and in and around mountains. Through this means the front line [Chinese] troops were well served and we could do very little about it; after all, our planes couldn't strafe every man in North Korea."

In the end, American bombs did not stop the war; Stalin did, by dying. After the dictator's death on March 5, 1953, no one who mattered in the Soviet Union wanted to prolong the expensive bloodshed in Korea. Within days, the Soviet leadership moved to work with the Chinese and seek "the soonest possible conclusion" to the war. Peace talks with the Americans suddenly turned serious.

Stalin's death was also a turning point for Nichols. His island empire stopped growing. By late May, the air force ordered him to remove his agents from islands off the east and west coasts of North Korea. By late July, the major combatants in the Korean War had signed an armistice. The thirty-eighth parallel was again the internationally accepted dividing line between the two Koreas and fighting stopped. Nichols would stay on in Korea, remain in command of a spy base, and continue to meet regularly with Syngman Rhee. But his spy career—and, as it would turn out, his life—had peaked. He was thirty.

CHAPTER 8

Famous in Pyongyang

As the war wound down, Donald Nichols found himself exposed. North Koreans who read state-controlled newspapers and listened to state radio knew who he was and what he did for a living. He worried then—and for the rest of his life—about assassination. "He thought somebody was after him," according to a nephew who lived with him in Florida after the war. "He was always paranoid."

Nichols had good reason to worry. He learned before the war that his name was on a North Korean list of American spies. During the war, he was mentioned in propaganda radio broadcasts from Pyongyang and Beijing. The bounty for killing him, depending on who told the story, ranged from $7.50 to $200,000. Nichols claimed in his autobiography that three attempts were made on his life; but two South Korean intelligence officers who served with him throughout the war remember only one, and that would-be assassin was caught and killed well before he could get to Nichols. After the war, in a one-of-a-kind show trial in Pyongyang, Nichols was named as a spymaster in an American-backed plot to overthrow Kim Il Sung.

A transcript of the trial, printed in the *Rodong Sinmun*, the official party newspaper, mentioned him by name at least eleven times. Testimony identified him as a U.S. Air Force intelligence officer who worked for the Far East Command, who sabotaged and murdered Communists inside South Korea, and who infiltrated agents into high positions in North Korea in an effort to cause armed riots and topple the government.

There was, of course, considerable truth in these charges.

The show trial was a Kim Il Sung production that tried to blame his country's dire postwar predicament on a dozen "anti-party traitors." It also whipped up hatred of the United States, which was accused at the trial of secretly starting the war and masterminding an espionage plot—with Nichols as a principal plotter—that encouraged the twelve traitors to overthrow Kim.

Kim Il Sung needed a diversion. His invasion of South Korea had achieved nothing, killed millions, and turned North Korea into a smoldering, starving ruin. His performance as a military leader had been inept and humiliating. He squandered early battlefield advantages by failing to resupply his invading army. Disastrously, he ignored warnings that the United States was planning a counterattack by sea at Inchon, which led to the destruction of most of his army. When Chinese forces rushed in to save his skin, Kim had to surrender control of the war to a Chinese general who called the Great Leader a fool and treated him like a child.

The trial rewrote this embarrassing history by spinning a largely fictional narrative that cast Kim as a commander who outsmarted backstabbing Korean comrades and scheming Yankees. Evidence at the trial purported to show that America sneakily started the war and that North Korea won it, thanks to Kim's brilliant generalship and his uncanny skill in catching traitors. As one of Kim's hagiographers summarized his achievements: "To have successfully fought U.S. imperialism, the strongest enemy, while spy cliques were entrenched in the Party and carrying out their intrigues! How great is Comrade Kim Il Sung!"

Publicized slavishly by state media and covered by a small contingent of foreign correspondents, the trial replicated the hollow pageantry of Soviet show trials of the 1930s. It was carefully rehearsed, lethal in its consequences, and unintentionally risible, part Stalinism, part *Saturday Night Live*.

"I am a running dog of American imperialism," said Yi Kang Guk, a defendant who had worked in North Korea's ministry of trade. "I thank you for giving me an opportunity to die after making my confession."

Each defense lawyer declared that his client had been proven guilty. Every defendant confessed enthusiastically to treason, admitted to being an American spy, and embraced the fairness of his sentence while welcoming the confiscation of his property. The court found everyone guilty on all charges presented, with ten men sentenced to death and two to long prison terms.

"I am grateful for having been provided with an advocate and for the opportunity to speak freely during the four days of the trial," said Yi Sung Yop, the former North Korean minister of justice who was accused of masterminding the planned coup against the Great Leader. "Whatever punishment I am given by the trial, I will accept with gratitude. Had I two lives, to take them both would have been too little."

Historians who have examined transcripts of the trial believe that the absurd confessions were the likely result of torture, blackmail, and false pretrial promises. Much of the testimony was wildly implausible. A case in point was the claim that Harold Noble, an American diplomat, met in Seoul with one defendant on June 26, 1950, the day after the North Korean invasion. Noble supposedly told defendant Yi Sung Yop about the secret U.S. plan for the amphibious invasion at Inchon. It was an impossible claim because Noble was not in Seoul that day; he was on vacation in Tokyo. And on June 26, the United States was still struggling to understand news about the invasion; Americans had no plan then for a counterattack at Inchon. "The evidence presented in the trial documents is hardly convincing," concluded Dae-Sook Suh, the most widely respected of Kim's biographers.

Yet the trial made a case against Nichols that appears to have been based on deep North Korean knowledge of his career as spy. All twelve defendants in the trial were longtime Communists from the southern half of the peninsula. Before moving north to join the government of Kim

Il Sung, they were leaders of the South Korean Workers' Party, which was one of Nichols's primary targets for infiltration, sabotage, arrests, and executions.

Paek Hyong-bok, one of the accused traitors and a former South Korean police investigator, testified that he had taken orders and three thousand American dollars from Nichols. The orders, Paek said, led to the arrest and murder of a hundred officials in the South Korean Workers' Party. While the numbers are probably exaggerated, the gist of the accusation rings true. By his own admission as well as abundant documentary and photographic evidence, Nichols worked for years with South Korean police to dismantle and destroy South Korean Communist organizations, particularly the Workers' Party. In his memoir, Nichols wrote that he had planted "a small number of agents" in the party hierarchy by 1947 and that they helped him sabotage its operations and arrest senior members: "During 1948 and 1949, we broke up numerous commy cells in S.K."

All of this raises an obvious question. Because Nichols, an active-duty air force intelligence commander based in Seoul, was accused by name of being an American spymaster and a murderer during an internationally publicized trial that had no precedent in North Korea, why wasn't the accusation publicized by members of the large international press corps then in Seoul?

Based on available archival evidence, none did, at least in the English-speaking world. Nichols's links to spying in North Korea were never mentioned in major American newspapers—at the time or ever.

There are four likely reasons. First, Nichols excelled at being a nobody in Seoul. Throughout his time in Korea, he kept away from parties and dinners that might attract journalists; his name meant nothing to them. Second, even if reporters had asked questions, press officers in the air force would have refused to discuss intelligence operations. Third, reporters had little to no direct access to Nichols, who lived on a closed and secret base outside the city. Finally, and probably most important, Kim Il Sung's show trial was ludicrous on so many levels that few Westerners took it seriously enough to try to distinguish facts from farce.

Despite his notoriety in Pyongyang, Nichols's name did not bubble up in scholarly Western accounts of the trial until two decades after the war. Even then, when his name appeared in a respected two-volume academic history titled *Communism in Korea*, eminent historians Robert Scalapino and Chong-Sik Lee seemed unaware of the pivotal intelligence role Nichols played in the Korean War. During the show trial, they wrote, it was "impossible to separate truth and half-truth from total falsity in the myriad of charges. . . ."

Nichols's personal life in Korea was even murkier than his life as a spy. According to his military service record, he worked too much to even have a personal life. In his first seven and half years in Korea, Nichols took less than thirty days' leave, wrote Colonel Eugene G. Cook. "Such devotion to duty, to his unit, and to his mission is unparalleled. During this time he was on duty 24 hours a day, 7 days a week."

In his autobiography, Nichols wrote that he did find time to fall in love, get married, and have a son, but the details he offers in the book do not entirely make sense or are contradicted by other witnesses. Available evidence suggests he may have invented a wife and a biological child—years after leaving Korea.

He wrote that his Korean wife, Kim In Hwa, died while giving birth to Donald Nichols II on February 18, 1953. Yet if he had a wife then and if she died on that date while giving birth to his first and only child, it would have been a ghastly and unforgettable coincidence. For Nichols was born on February 18. In his autobiography he does not note that he lost a wife and gained a son on his own birthday. It is an improbable omission—a signal that he probably was fabricating a story.

Nichols was mostly vague about his family in his book, writing that "there is much that could be said about In Hwa; our marriage, her death. However, I elect to keep those secrets to myself." No government records of his marriage, his son's birth, or his wife's death could be located in Seoul, Taegu, or Inchon. Even if they once existed, many records of that era have been lost or destroyed, and South Korean privacy laws make it all but impossible to attempt a record search.

Nichols's extended family was never certain that Nichols was the birth father of Donald "Donnie" Nichols II, who was sent from Seoul to Florida to live with one of Nichols's brothers in 1955. "We all thought that boy was adopted," said Nichols's nephew Donald H. Nichols, who was a teenager when the boy came to Florida. "Donnie was part Caucasian, but did not look anything like my uncle Don, not in the big ears, or the big nose, not in any facial features. If he was my uncle's son, not many of his genes passed through."

For many years, Nichols told government agencies and his family that Donnie was adopted. In a petition of naturalization that he filled out in Miami, Nichols wrote that he was the boy's "adoptive parent." He told the same thing to air force doctors in 1957. In occasional conversations with his brother Judson's family in the 1960s, he sometimes hinted that he was the boy's father. Those hints would gel over time into a firm claim that Donnie was his "blood son." Still, in a letter to his air force friend Torres that he wrote more than a decade after returning to the United States, Nichols referred to Donnie as one of "3 adopted Korean children" he brought home after the war.

As for Nichols's marriage in Korea, even less is clear. His book, most of which is written in tough-guy prose, is uncharacteristically saccharine in describing his wife and recounting his marriage.

"I was privileged to know her only three years before she left for Heaven. . . . Even in the midst of war, terror, hunger and uncertainty, we were happy. She gave me everything. . . . [I]n 1951, I had held my wife's hand while I told her of the beauties of Florida where I would be taking her as soon as we were successful in freeing her people and her homeland. She was seven years my junior—I loved her dearly. Her physical beauty, outstanding as it was, did not compare with the spiritual and moral qualities contained within that soul which would never live to see the United States. . . .

"If I could write prayers, I would write one of thankfulness for the brief period during which I was privileged to know and enjoy the exquisite presence and love of my beloved wife. Then I would write another of thankfulness that because of her astute and noble dedication to womanhood and motherhood, she somehow saved our son, Donald."

Nichols never explained where or how he met Kim In Hwa. He does say that she was born and raised near Seoul, that the wedding was "one of the proudest moments of [his] life," and that his bride was nineteen when they were married on January 12, 1951.

That wedding date, however, is highly unlikely. The war was then at a fever pitch, with Chinese forces advancing across Korea and the Joint Chiefs of Staff announcing that it might not be possible to hold the peninsula indefinitely. Having taken Seoul a week earlier, the Chinese drove UN forces out of Inchon on the day of Nichols's purported wedding. In a bloody infantry engagement with the Chinese in the city of Hoengsong, about seventy miles east of Seoul, the Eighth Army suffered more than two thousand casualties.

In the preceding weeks, the entire command structure of the U.S. military in Korea, including Nichols and Torres, had been forced to retreat south, back to the city of Taegu. There, Nichols and his men were under intense pressure to find more and better bombing targets to help the army stop the Chinese. During that time, Nichols lived in an intelligence compound just outside Taegu, together with a small group of American and South Korean officers and airmen. Torres recalls the tension and intense workload of the period, but remembers nothing about his boss getting married.

"Nick never mentioned anything about it to anybody, as far as I know," Torres said. "He slept at the compound every night. We never saw him with a woman and if he spoke about women, he said he didn't like them. The part of his book about marriage is pure fantasy."

When Nichols returned to Florida in 1957, he told air force doctors he had "never been married." In conversations with his family and a letter to Torres, he did not mention a marriage and did not describe himself as a widower. Donald H. Nichols, the nephew who briefly lived with Nichols after the war, is certain that his uncle was gay.

"Uncle Don was a closeted homosexual in a macho world," he said. "In those days, he was what we all called a 'confirmed bachelor.' Not once did he mention women. Even when we were around pretty girls in a store, he didn't look at them. In the family we thought his mother had screwed him up so much that he never had a normal relationship."

A niece, Diana Carlin, who lived with Nichols in the late 1950s and again in the mid-1960s, said he never brought women to the house. "He had some men friends over, but they were the kind of men who made my mother uncomfortable. They were not the kind of people you find in our church."

Staying in the closet would not have been unusual for a proud ex–air force officer. And a fictional marriage—especially one that ended years ago in a distant war zone with the death of a saintly woman—could have been helpful to Nichols. It would explain why he was a single father. If Nichols did invent his marriage, it would not surprise relatives who knew him after the war. "My uncle was quite special and you never quite trusted him," said his nephew Donald H. Nichols. "A faked marriage? The guy was always up to something."

Seven weeks after the armistice was signed, Nichols revealed how deeply his spy operation had penetrated the command structure of the North Korean military.

His disclosure of sources and methods occurred in his quarters at Oryu-dong, his sprawling hillside compound about forty minutes by jeep from downtown Seoul. Nichols had moved his spy base there in early 1953 to get away from the crowded city and have more elbow room for training agents and interrogating North Koreans. The base at Oryu-dong was fronted by an orphanage and a local police station. It had a parade ground, a tailor's shop, a photo shop, and a headquarters building. Airmen and officers lived in Quonset huts on opposite sides of the mess hall. Nichols lived alone in separate and more spacious quarters halfway up the side of the low mountain valley.

It was there that Nichols told some of his secrets to a fighter pilot named No Kum Sok, a senior lieutenant in the North Korean air force. Hours earlier, Lieutenant No, twenty years old, had defected to South Korea in a MiG-15. In photographs taken that day, September 21, 1953, No wore a rakish leather flight jacket and looked like someone who might be chosen to play a fighter pilot in a movie. He was lean and handsome, with high cheekbones, bright eyes, and thick black hair. Nichols was not photographed that day, but it is safe to assume that, as always, he bore no resemblance to a cinema spy. His beefy frame was packed into a dark green uniform with no markings. The pilot from North Korea thought Nichols dressed like the high-ranking Soviet officers he had known in China, where foreigners were not allowed to wear insignia on their uniforms.

The conversation between the American spy and the North Korean fighter pilot took place after No Kum Sok had pulled off one of the most celebrated thefts of the cold war. Shortly after nine on a clear and crisp Monday morning, No had taken off from Sunan airfield near Pyongyang in a battle-ready MiG-15 bearing the markings of the North Korean air force. Seventeen minutes later, he had landed in South Korea at Kimpo airfield, then the busiest U.S. military air base on the Korean Peninsula. He landed the wrong way on an active runway and nearly crashed head-on into an American Sabre jet that was landing at the same moment from the opposite direction. The terrified American fighter pilot shouted over the radio, "There is somebody landing the wrong way! It's a goddamn MiG!"

The pilot's shout reverberated around the world. RED MIG-15 BROUGHT TO SEOUL said a banner front-page headline in the *Washington Post*. Similar headlines appeared on the front pages of nearly all the major newspapers, except those in China, the Soviet Union, and North Korea. The news embarrassed and infuriated Kim Il Sung, who happened to be in

Moscow begging for financial assistance. The defection handed the United States a sensational and unexpected propaganda victory, along with a late-model and long-coveted piece of advanced Soviet aerospace technology.

After the MiG had safely come to a stop on the tarmac, and after the air force determined that its pilot wanted to defect, No was driven in a jeep to the office of the commander of the Fifth Air Force, Lieutenant General Samuel E. Anderson. Because Anderson spoke no Korean, he and No waited together in an uncomfortable silence.

It took Nichols twenty minutes to get there. He jumped in the helicopter he kept on standby at his nearby spy base, flew to Kimpo, and burst into Anderson's office. Without saluting the general, Nichols spoke excitedly to No in Korean. After ten minutes, Nichols announced, "Let's go to my place." They boarded his helicopter, flew back to his compound, and hurried to his private office.

There, No was alarmed by a growling greeting party of ten mixed-breed dogs, including several large huskies. On Nichols's order the dogs calmed down and wagged their tails. No remembered, too, the office refrigerator, which contained nothing but large bottles of Coca-Cola. Nichols suggested they each drink a bottle. No had never tasted a sugary American soft drink before, but as soon as he tried it, he found he loved ice-cold Coke. Years later, he would buy stock in the company.

Nichols encouraged No to take a seat in the large swivel chair behind his desk. This may have been the chair Nichols stole from Kim Il Sung's office in Pyongyang during the first year of the war. The pilot declined, believing that the American should sit in his own chair to conduct his duties.

Nichols then got down to business. He asked if No knew other MiG pilots who might want to defect in a fighter jet. When No said that he did know one, Nichols strongly urged him to write that pilot a letter.

"How will you deliver the letter?" No asked.

Nichols assured him that he had his ways. No immediately wrote a letter to his best friend and fellow pilot, Kun Soo Sung. Many years later,

No learned that Kun, along with four other air force comrades and commanders, was executed soon after his defection. He never learned if his letter was intercepted or played any role in the executions. Nichols also asked if No was acquainted with General Lee Whal, vice-commander of the North Korean air force. No was stunned by the question. That very morning, he and the general had exchanged pleasantries on the tarmac before No took off in the MiG. No explained this to Nichols, who clapped his hands in delight.

"General Lee is my friend," Nichols told the pilot. "I wrote him two letters."

During their chat, No was still flushed with adrenaline from his risky defection and did not fully grasp who Nichols was. But the pilot later realized he had read about the American spymaster named Nichols before his escape. In the spring of 1953, Nichols's name had appeared in a secret Workers' Party report that No, as a party member, had access to. The report, as No recalled, detailed accusations against Nichols that would later be made public in the postwar show trial of the twelve North Korean traitors.

Nichols's comments about being in contact with the vice-commander of North Korea's air force were of particular interest because No had wondered for years about the general's loyalty. For a top North Korean official, Lee Whal had an unusual background. He was the son of a wealthy landowner who had prospered in Korea under Japanese occupation and served as a military pilot for the Japanese during World War II. The North Korean regime did not normally trust individuals with such tainted backgrounds. Kim Il Sung ordered them killed. General Lee had apparently been given a special dispensation because he volunteered to train pilots in North Korea and donated his own property as facilities for pilot housing and education.

No had firsthand experience that led him to suspect that General Lee was an American spy. On two occasions during the air war over MiG Alley, No had been part of fighter formations that were ambushed by U.S. Sabre jets whose pilots seemed to know precisely when North Korean air force MiGs were arriving and at what altitude. In No's recollection, the first ambush occurred on January 25, 1952, when General Lee ordered sixteen MiG-15s—including one piloted by No—to fly at low altitude from their base at Dandong, in northeast China, into North Korean airspace. They were attacked immediately from above by American fighters, which shot down three MiGs. The second ambush occurred fourteen months later, on March 21, 1953, when sixteen MiG pilots—including No—took off from a base in Tonghua, China. The lead North Korean pilot in that formation contacted General Lee by radio during the mission, reporting that he and other pilots could see a huge cloud of vapor trails on the near horizon. Lee responded from the control tower, saying the vapor trails were probably from Russian or Chinese aircraft—and not to worry. Sabre jets soon attacked, shooting down two MiGs.

"I had a strong belief at the time that General Lee Whal purposely guided our flights to the waiting American planes," No said years later. The general's possible links to Nichols and American military intelligence were apparently never made public.

On the day of his escape from North Korea, the young pilot did not have the presence of mind to discuss all this with Nichols. Instead, No tried to be as cooperative as possible. When Nichols asked him to pose for propaganda photographs with the MiG-15, No did so, and news agencies flashed the pictures around the world. When a team of air force interrogators flew in from Tokyo, No answered nineteen hours of questions over two days, talking to the point of exhaustion.

For the United States, No's defection was a key intelligence windfall of the Korean War era. He delivered the first combat-ready MiG-15 that could be test flown. The air force rushed two of its best test pilots—Major Chuck Yeager (the first man to fly faster than the speed of sound) and Tom Collins (holder of a world speed record in a Sabre)—to the Far East to fly No's plane. As important, No proved to be a uniquely valuable and well-informed eyewitness. During intensive interrogation—six hours a day, five days a week, for nearly half a year—he added rich new detail to U.S. suspicions about the Soviet Union's involvement in the Korean War.

The defection was also a grace note in Nichols's life as a spy. It showcased his analytical skills—as well as his heart.

Nichols personally wrote the first report about No's defection. Finished in three days, fifty-five pages long, and kept secret for sixty years, it was a bravura piece of intelligence work. It shrewdly assessed the value of the secrets spilled by the fighter pilot and put them into a broader geopolitical context. The report used precise language, photographs, and drawings to fill substantial holes in American understanding of the conduct of China and the Soviet Union in the Korean War, as well as Kim Il Sung's plans for postwar confrontation with the United States and South Korea. It won commendations for Nichols for "prompt, exacting action" from General Otto Weyland, commander of Far East Air Forces. In Nichols's military service record, his group commander praised the report as an example of Nichols's "foresight, initiative, willingness to accept responsibility, and his ability to improvise."

The Americans were eager to show off their prize defector, so eager that they scheduled a press conference for No on his second day in South Korea. Fortunately for No, he had another meeting with Nichols before he went in front of the press.

"I was thinking of going to the United States but did not know who to ask about it," No recalled. "Then, before I could even bring it up, Nichols met with me and emphasized that I would have a great future and good opportunities if I demanded to go to America. He specifically told me not to join the South Korean air force and to go to college in the United States."

Nichols gave No enough confidence to declare at the press conference that he wanted to live in the United States and study at a university— a declaration that appealed to the American press corps, which showcased his educational aspirations on front pages across the United States. Within a year, it came to pass. Agents from the CIA enrolled No as a freshman at the University of Delaware, where he earned a degree in engineering. He would become an American citizen, change his name to Kenneth Rowe, raise a family that spoke mostly English at home, and have a long career as a university professor and aerospace engineer with a top-secret security clearance.

Many years later, in retirement and living in Daytona Beach, Florida,

Kenneth Rowe credited the spy he drank Coke with for giving him guidance that changed the trajectory of his life. "By telling me to go to America," he said, "Nichols sealed my fate."

When the United States, the Soviet Union, and China negotiated an end to fighting in Korea, Nichols's most important intelligence source in South Korea, Syngman Rhee, fell into a near-paralyzing funk. The South Korean leader wanted, more than ever, to unify the peninsula under his control and put a stake through the heart of his nemesis, Kim Il Sung. The only way to do that, he believed, was with war. It was infuriating to Rhee that the new American president, Dwight Eisenhower, had accepted the permanent existence of a sovereign North Korea under Kim's leadership. "You can't cooperate with smallpox," Rhee whined.

Without a war, Rhee worried that he would lose his leverage with the United States. He feared the Korean people would view him as weak. He threatened, rather emptily, to fight on alone against China and North Korea. He organized mass rallies, demanding unification by force, and refused to accept the idea of peaceful coexistence with North Korea. His government staged a "spontaneous" protest by five hundred young schoolgirls who marched through the streets of Seoul in pigtails, waving white handkerchiefs, weeping, and screaming at the United States: "You are murdering our country. Why are you murdering our country?"

When such histrionics failed to change American policy, Rhee tried to sabotage the emerging peace deal. On June 18, 1953, he released about twenty-five thousand North Korean prisoners of war from camps in South Korea. At that point in the armistice talks, Kim Il Sung's negotiators had been demanding the return of all North Korean prisoners of war to North Korean territory. By releasing them in the South, Rhee hoped that the Communists would accuse the Americans of bad faith and break off negotiations.

China and North Korea, however, were eager to end the war, and although they complained about the prisoner release, they did not walk away from the armistice deal. Rhee did succeed in infuriating the Pentagon, the State Department, and Eisenhower. More than ever, they came to see the elderly Korean leader as ungrateful, irritating, and dangerous. General Mark Clark, commander of the Far East Command, lamented having to wrestle with both Communists and Rhee in the peace talks, but said the "biggest trouble came from Rhee." Secretary of State John Foster Dulles told Rhee that American GIs had paid a high price in "blood and suffering" to save South Korea—and that Rhee had no right to waste their sacrifice by trying to torpedo the peace talks.

But it was Eisenhower who delivered the most sustained scolding when Rhee visited the White House on July 27, 1954.

"[W]hen you say that we should deliberately plunge into war, let me tell you that if war comes, it will be horrible," the president said. "Atomic war will destroy civilization. It will destroy our cities. There will be millions of people dead. . . . If the Kremlin and Washington ever lock up in a war, the results are too horrible to contemplate."

Rhee was neither intimidated nor chastened. The day after his combative meeting with Eisenhower, addressing a joint session of Congress, he advocated a new war to unite the Korean Peninsula. He suggested that South Korea should join forces with Taiwan to attack China—with support from the U.S. Navy and Air Force.

Fearing that Rhee would act on these ideas, the U.S. military command in South Korea developed a secret contingency plan to impose martial law and arrest Rhee should he become completely unmanageable. Called Operation Everready, it had first been proposed in 1952, when Rhee had imposed martial law to intimidate political rivals, and was revisited in 1953, when he tried to sabotage the armistice.

American officials, though, could not find a popular anti-Communist to replace Rhee, and they feared that a coup would spark resentment in South Korea. So Washington concluded it had no choice but to appease "the stubborn old fellow," as Eisenhower privately called Rhee. In return for Rhee's reluctant pledge not to start another war, the United States gave him massive economic aid, a mutual defense treaty, and modern weapons.

The end of the war did little to weaken the symbiotic relationship between Nichols and Rhee. They saw each other regularly, according to air force records. Rhee's government, in a postwar assessment of American spies in Korea, singled out Nichols for praise. It claimed he produced more accurate intelligence reports and trained better agents than the army or the CIA. For Rhee, the American spymaster remained a reliable backchannel to the U.S. military. For Nichols, the president, his generals, and his legions of Korean-speaking spies continued to be important sources of intelligence about North and South Korea. The air force was well aware of Nichols's unique relationship with Rhee and approved of it—until higher-ups in the U.S. government changed their minds.

PART III

RUINED SPY

CHAPTER 9
Sacked

After the war, Donald Nichols continued—for nearly four more years—to operate as an intelligence prince. His authority, autonomy, and the budget of his secret base in Korea were protected and funded by General Partridge, who returned in April 1954 to take command of the Far East Air Forces in Tokyo. Partridge pulled strings for his war-tested spy in Korea and in the United States.

Nichols had returned to the States in early 1954 to take what he thought would be a brief vacation, as well as to attend a parachute instruction course at Fort Benning, Georgia. But while he was back, he was ordered to report for permanent assignment in Washington as an aide to the deputy chief of staff for operations in the air force directorate of intelligence. Nichols had no intention of sitting behind a Pentagon desk and pushing paper. Korea was the only place he felt respected and important. So when he heard that Partridge was returning to the Far East, Nichols wrote him and asked if they could speak by phone. He asked Partridge to bring him back—and the general was astoundingly quick to oblige. Three days after Nichols wrote his letter, Partridge sent a memorandum to his friend General Emmett O'Donnell, the former bomb commander in Korea who had recently become deputy chief of personnel at air force headquarters in Washington. "Although Nichols has been in

Washington only a short time after completion of a tour in the Far East," Partridge wrote, "he desires this reassignment [to Korea] and I feel it is in the best interest of the Air Force to have him reassigned again. . . ."

After an absence of only three months, Nichols again took command of his spy base near Seoul. Partridge again had his back. If junior air force officers at the base complained about Nichols's management style, as they often did, according to his military service record, Partridge took care of it.

"I have the utmost confidence in your integrity as well as your ability, and you should know that you operate with my full understanding and support," Partridge wrote to Nichols in the spring of 1955. His letter was in response to a personnel problem Nichols had with one of his former officers. While the exact nature of that officer's complaint about Nichols was not spelled out, the general called the complainer a "loser" and encouraged Nichols to run his outfit as he saw fit.

The Korean armistice had created a ragged peace and a demand for services that Partridge believed only Nichols could provide. The air war flared up in 1954–55, with brief but sensational engagements between American and Chinese fighter jets. North Korean ground fire shot down two air force planes, killing three American pilots and leaving a fourth missing in action. Cold war anxiety about the intentions of China, the Soviet Union, and North Korea, combined with State Department and White House anxiety about Rhee's bellicose behavior, generated a substantial American appetite for spying north of the thirty-eighth parallel and inside Rhee's government. Nichols's men interrogated defectors and recruited agents for secret missions inside North Korea. They dispatched boats to deliver and retrieve spies and trained intelligence officers for the South Korean government. As a history of Nichols's unit put it: "Although the operating of the Detachment will be somewhat hampered by the ceasefire agreement, its mission remains unchanged. It is contemplated that a continuing effort shall be exerted to uncover any and all intelligence information that would prove of value to the U.N. forces should hostilities commence again in Korea."

The air force reorganized its intelligence operation in Korea after the war. It eliminated Detachment 2, the special covert unit created for Nichols, as well as two other detachments of the 6004th Air Intelligence Service Squadron—and folded them into the 6006th intelligence squadron, which also had covert responsibilities. Nichols survived the shake-up better than anyone. He was named commander of the 6006th squadron. While the Pentagon was cutting budgets across the board in Korea, Nichols's unit continued to receive relatively generous funding. "It may be stated that the 6006th Air Intelligence Service Squadron was in better shape than it ever has been at any other time in its history," Nichols wrote in 1955.

Part of the reason was Partridge's position as commander of Far East Air Forces. The other part was Nichols's performance. He continued to reel in high-value, headline-generating North Korean defectors who revealed secrets about Kim Il Sung's regime, which was rebuilding rapidly. When a North Korean air force pilot and his navigator escaped south in a Soviet-made Yak-18 trainer aircraft and landed at a South Korean air base on June 21, 1955, Nichols elbowed in and took control of the defection. He persuaded the South Korean air force, which had taken "technical custody" of the defectors and their aircraft, to hand over "actual custody" to him. Then Nichols took the North Koreans and their plane back to his base "for the purpose of expediting exploitation" of inside information about air power in the North. Within a week, Nichols began sending fresh intelligence and possible target data to air force regional headquarters in Tokyo.

A few weeks before that intelligence coup, Partridge visited Nichols's base, where the two wartime friends were photographed together for a final time. It was the general's farewell visit. He had been promoted, this time to commander in chief of the North American Air Defense Command in Colorado Springs, Colorado. A year after Partridge's departure, Nichols received what would be his last positive evaluation as an intelligence officer.

"Major Nichols should be promoted to Lt. Colonel ahead of his contemporaries," it began. "He is an outstanding officer possessing great ability to accomplish tasks under difficult and unusual circumstances."

The July 1956 report went on to enumerate his character strengths and intelligence achievements. Among them were maintaining contact with key military and civilian leaders in South Korea, especially President Rhee, and predicting the outcome of South Korean elections more accurately than other U.S. intelligence agencies and diplomats. The report said Nichols "inspires" his commanders. It quoted General Laurence S. Kuter, the new chief of Far East Air Forces, who attended an intelligence briefing Nichols gave in Korea and was deeply impressed: "Nick is the type of man I would like to have come to rescue me if I were shot down in enemy territory."

Colonel Frank L. Dunn, the Tokyo-based commander of the 6002nd Air Intelligence Group and Nichols's immediate commander, concluded the report: "Major Nichols is loyal, an aggressive individual who is outstandingly able to further US Air Force objectives under any conditions in which he may be assigned. He is particularly well suited to continue in intelligence activities and should be so assigned wherever his services are needed. He is an invaluable man."

Twelve months later, the "invaluable man" was sacked. Colonel Dunn, who had recommended in 1956 that Nichols be promoted, demanded in 1957 that he be relieved of his duties, removed from Korea, and sent back to the United States—never again to serve in a position "involving command of USAF personnel."

"During the past year official complaints have been leveled, letters have been written to Senators, and many allegations have been made against Major Nichols," Dunn wrote in an officer efficiency report dated June 24, 1957. It mentioned "sworn testimony" that confirmed "unusual and abnormal conduct as a commander. . . .

"Investigations, both formal and informal, inspections and staff visits have confirmed certain of the allegations, complaints and unfavorable reports. The relief and rotation of Major Nichols as commander is the minimum action considered appropriate under the circumstances."

This was the first "derogatory report" of Nichols's seventeen-year military career. Strangely, though, all of the specific criticisms of Nichols in the report were for behavior that his commanding officers had known about and tolerated for a decade.

"He appears in formation in front of his troops in fatigue uniform without any insignia. . . . He has allowed himself to gain weight up to approximately 260 pounds. . . . He barks orders to his officers and men; yet, his dogs have bitten airmen, congregate in his headquarters building and office during official visits, and eat in the mess hall at the same time as officers. . . . Men in his organization in sworn testimony state they never knew his rank except for the 'Donald Nichols' which he signed on official papers. . . . He maintains 'Prussian' type discipline in his squadron area; yet, as escort for Korean military officials in uniform, he has appeared in the Far East Air Force Headquarters building in an open-necked shirt, pullover sweater and slacks."

The most serious charge in the report was that Nichols mistreated his men and that they had turned against him, complaining over his head to other air force officers, as well as to U.S. senators from their home states. The report said many officers and airmen who served in his unit "have shown little or no loyalty to Major Nichols, have utter contempt for Major Nichols' treatment of USAF personnel, and are perplexed that such a person should command a USAF squadron."

That Nichols would be perceived as a hard-nosed and arbitrary commander was hardly surprising. His spying instincts and aggressiveness, not his empathetic leadership skills, had propelled his rise to squadron commander. Not once during his career had he been back to the States to attend a military leadership school. He had always been too valuable as a field agent to train as a manager.

During the war, when panic ruled and his bosses were desperate for intelligence, most of the men who took orders from Nichols were Koreans—airmen and officers from the South Korean air force, along with North Korean defectors, deserters, refugees, and local criminals. In the air force and throughout the U.S. military, the treatment of Koreans was abrupt, often racist, and sometimes brutal. An unwritten rule for U.S. Army officers said "never ask a Korean to do anything: tell him." Nichols had authority to send Koreans on suicide missions—and often did so. Koreans were in no position to complain.

As for the Americans who worked for Nichols during the war, many were awed by the risks he took with his own life and they admired the relentlessness of his work ethic. They thought he was a decent man, although not especially warm. "Nick was a tough and demanding boss, but he was also a good guy," said Torres. "He was strict about parties and bringing girls on the base, but he was generally liked and respected," said Ronald F. Cuneo, a corporal who served as photographer on Nichols's base in the last year of the war. "He didn't mingle with us, but he took care of his people," said Raymond Dean, an air force supply sergeant who also spent the final year of the war on Nichols's base. "He knew every one of us by name. Sometimes in the evening, we would go walking in the mountains with his little dog Brownie."

But turnover among officers and airmen in Korea was high and the reputation Nichols won in wartime had faded by 1957. Most men serving under Nichols rotated in and out of his base in less than two years. Few were veterans of the Korean War and fewer still knew anything about Nichols's achievements. His junior officers typically had college degrees but no combat experience and most of his airmen were draftees counting the days until they could get out of Korea. Compared to the men Nichols commanded during the war, their tolerance for iron-fisted leadership was low.

Still, the specific descriptions of mistreatment in Colonel Dunn's report were skimpy and far from shocking. He accused Nichols of having "overwhelming confidence in his own standards of command and control," of writing sharply critical evaluations of his subordinates, and of failure to provide "adequate transportation" for his men for recreational activities or sick call.

But the report also said that Nichols was as good as ever as an intelligence officer.

"Major Nichols is a 'unique' individual and in some respects he can be labeled 'outstanding.' Through his personal contacts with the Chief of the Korean Air Force, President Rhee and other officials at all levels of the Korean government, he has performed a consistently splendid 'individual' job in keeping the USAF informed of activities and events in South Korea. He is as well informed on South Korean affairs and personalities as any American I know."

Nichols was aware of some of his management deficiencies, the report said. He had made "some effort to improve himself. . . . He has lost some weight, has disposed of some of his dogs, permits more reasonable utilization of Government transportation and sends me a statement to the effect that once a month he has appeared before USAF personnel in the uniform of a Major."

It was not nearly enough to appease his commander. Concluding his assessment of Nichols, Dunn wrote: "I consider the relief of Major Nichols from command, rotation to the Zone of Interior [the United States] and replacement by a new squadron commander as the most appropriate action available under the circumstances."

Colonel Dunn did not, however, spell out specifics that came close to justifying the sacking of the most-experienced, best-sourced American intelligence commander in Korea. The muddy imprecision of his report begs the question: What else was going on with Nichols in Korea that impelled the air force to fire him and send him home?

After Partridge left Tokyo, the Far East command launched two formal investigations of Nichols. The first, which generated a report called "Alleged Mistreatment of Military Personnel," was conducted by the 6002nd Air Intelligence Group, which supervised Nichols's unit from Tokyo. While it was under way, Nichols "challenged" the authority of an investigating officer who had been sent to his base near Seoul. A second inquiry was conducted by the Air Force Office of Special Investigations, the internal affairs unit Nichols had once worked for. The findings of these investigations were not contained in Nichols's military service record and have been destroyed. But a letter about the reports says they "revealed numerous instances of abuse of authority, mistreatment of subordinates, and poor leadership qualities on the part of Major Nichols." The letter did not specify what abuses of authority Nichols committed or how he might have mistreated subordinates.

There are, however, a number of tantalizing leads.

During most of his eleven years in Korea, Nichols had unsupervised access to very large amounts of cash. In his office at Oryu-dong, the base outside Seoul, he had cabinets stuffed with American dollars, South Korean won, and North Korean currency, some counterfeit, some genuine. This was the cash Nichols often tossed to agents bound for North Korea.

"There was so much money!" said Chung Bong-sun, the South Korean air force intelligence officer who worked with Nichols. "When he opened both doors of the cabinet, all I could see was cash. Nichols's houseboy told me there was also cash in other cabinets that he did not open in front of me."

As early at 1948, Nichols began bringing eye-popping quantities of American dollars to a photo lab run by Frank Winslow, then a twenty-one-year-old first lieutenant in the Army Signal Corps.

"My lab was just across from the American embassy and Nichols was a constant customer," Winslow recalled. "In fact, he was my best customer. Everyone knew he was a spook. He wore civvies and came into the lab with greenbacks in bags to be photographed. It was always a substantial amount of money."

At that time, U.S. currency in large quantities was an arresting sight in Seoul. The U.S. military in South Korea had created a kind of Monopoly money—military payment certificates (MPC)—in an attempt to keep dollars from flooding the local economy, distorting exchange rates, and fueling the black market. Most servicemen in Korea were not allowed to possess greenbacks, and when they arrived from the States, they had to convert all their cash to MPC, which they could then convert to South Korean won for purchases off base. Service members were also paid in MPC.

As an intelligence officer running spies into North Korea, Nichols had a legitimate need for dollars to pay off agents and buy information. But his access—combined with the near-complete absence of oversight that Nichols enjoyed—would also have given him an opportunity to become an expert in exchange-rate manipulation. That market could be exceptionally lucrative, especially to those who, like Nichols, had access to dollars over many years. He could sell dollars for won at the highly favorable black-market rate, then convert his mountains of won back into dollars at the official rate, reaping handsome, untraceable, and untaxed profits.

Frank Winslow never understood why Nichols wanted photographs of the cash. But given the frequency with which Nichols lugged bags of it into the photo lab, Winslow strongly suspected something illegal was going on. "I could see the value of the stuff he was dealing," he said. "It just seemed like he was cheating the system."

Winslow was not alone in his suspicion. Ed Evanhoe, an army intelligence officer in Seoul during and after the war, told military historian Michael Haas that he suspected Nichols was involved in black-market trading. Chung Bong-sun, the South Korean intelligence officer, said that before Nichols left Korea, there were widespread rumors that he was selling U.S. military equipment for large amounts of money. To recruit spies in North Korea, Nichols had developed contacts within criminal organizations in Seoul, which may have strengthened his network of black-market contacts.

There is nothing, however, in Nichols's military service record that accuses him of currency trading or black-market dealings, and he was never charged with any illegality while serving in Korea. Nichols does not refer to currency speculation in his autobiography, although it was common among officers and enlisted men in Korea and rarely punished. He did say that he used the government's postal savings account to make "regular, monthly deposits and was proud of a small but steadily increasing balance. . . . It may be of interest to mention that when I retired . . . my savings had increased to the thousands. I had enough to buy all the necessities of civilian life, a car, a home and so on."

Yet a large slice of the wealth he accumulated in Korea was in cash. When he returned to the States, he banked it in his brother Judson's freezer in Florida.

"Uncle Don had big bags of cash in our freezer, three or four bags, maybe a hundred thousand or a couple hundred thousand dollars," said Donald H. Nichols, Judson's son. "My father was very nervous about having it."

It was an understandable worry. In 1963, $200,000 had the buying power of $1.53 million in 2017. It was an exceptional sum for a just-retired air force major to have saved at all—let alone in cash.

Besides financial impropriety, it is also possible that the air force could have fired Nichols for homosexuality. As noted earlier, South Korean intelligence officers said Nichols often brought young Korean airmen to his office in the evening for sexual encounters. An air force letter in Nichols's military service record may support this explanation. Written in 1958, it says that if Nichols had not retired during the previous year, investigators "would have initiated action under the provision of air force regulation 36-2 to cause his elimination from the military service." That regulation was then the primary tool used to discharge officers for homosexuality—though it was also used to kick officers out of the service for abuse of personnel or insubordination. The letter concludes with this tough, albeit vague, recommendation: "every effort should be made to insure that [Nichols] never again be placed in a position to subject United States military personnel to such abuses."

If homosexuality was the reason for sacking Nichols, it is unlikely that the air force would have been so furtive about it. There was nothing subtle, vague, or indirect about official intolerance of homosexuals in the American armed forces during the 1950s.

Still another possible reason for Nichols's removal from Korea was that he had stayed too close for too long to Syngman Rhee, who had become a chronic irritant to U.S. intelligence agencies and the State Department.

"It was highly irregular for Nichols to have been there so long," said William V. Bierek, who in 1957 was a twenty-four-year-old first lieutenant working for Nichols at the spy base outside of Seoul. "People thought he was too powerful, getting politically involved in the Rhee administration, and endangering America. Colonel Dunn and others may have believed he would cause a potential political problem."

Rhee, who was eighty-two in 1957, had been annoying the U.S. military, State Department, and White House for more than a decade. He had also lost support among millions of South Koreans. They wanted a younger, more flexible, less belligerent leader with fresh ideas about how to improve the broken economy. Although Rhee won a third term as president in 1956, it was a far narrower victory than in 1952; his winning margin slid from 75 percent to 56 percent. More telling, the vice presidential candidate of Rhee's ruling party had lost.

In Washington, the director of the CIA, Allen Dulles, sensed weakness. He said the 1956 election "indicated a rather startling decline in President Rhee's influence" and worried that he would resort to violence to stay in power. The Eisenhower administration, after years of paying off Rhee with economic and military aid in return for not provoking another war, was sick of indulging him. A diplomatic dispatch from the American embassy in Seoul said that South Korea is still "dominated by the aging President Rhee, who, although staunchly anti-Communist and friendly to the free world, continues unimaginatively the somewhat sterile policies of past years." The embassy had been warning for years that Rhee was a risk to South Korea's future and America's reputation: "the personal prestige of [a man] approaching senility is an extremely precarious base for a nation's stability."

Like many long-serving, egotistical heads of state, Rhee could not understand why he was not universally beloved. What especially worried American diplomats after the 1956 election was that Rhee viewed his shrinking popularity not as a political problem to be addressed with smarter policies but as "a challenge to his 'rightful' authority." To meet the challenge, he reshuffled his cabinet, increasing the power of hard-line supporters and tightening his personal control over the national police. In a cable to Washington, the embassy warned that Rhee's determination to maintain control "creates increasing danger of trouble ahead."

While the American embassy was skittish and standoffish with Rhee, Nichols was not.

He maintained his special access to the president, according to his military service record, and it allowed him to walk into the president's office on "short notice." The South Korean leader, as he had during the war, continued to shower Nichols with honors and medals. In 1954, Nichols was made an honorary colonel in the South Korean air force, and was given pilot wings, along with an honorary law degree from Seoul National University. A year later Rhee gave Nichols a second Order of Military Merit for exceptional service to Korea.

In addition to Rhee, Nichols stayed in regular contact with senior South Korean intelligence officials who served the president by destroying his political opponents. Notably, Nichols stayed "very close" to Kim "Snake" Chang-ryong, Rhee's right-hand man for political intelligence and electoral intimidation. At his spy base, Nichols entertained Kim frequently. A major general in the South Korean army, Kim ran the country's counterintelligence corps as a personal intelligence shop for Rhee and often fed its reports to Nichols, who repackaged the information as "air intelligence" and sent it on to his bosses in Tokyo. One such report in late 1955 was based entirely on information from Kim's intelligence operation. It described a purported "attempted assassination of President Rhee." Staged assassination attempts around election time had become commonplace in Rhee's era. Historians have speculated that they were intended to bolster foreign and domestic sympathy for the president.

Much more real was Rhee's scheme to eliminate his most serious political rival. Cho Bang-am, a charismatic Left-leaning politician, had challenged Rhee in the 1956 presidential election and won 30 percent of the vote. Rhee saw this as an intolerable political threat, so his special military police went after Cho. They invented a North Korean espionage plot in 1957 and accused Cho of being a spy for Pyongyang. He was arrested and hurriedly convicted in 1958.

American diplomats followed the Cho affair with growing alarm and disgust. Shortly after he was arrested, a State Department memorandum said the evidence against him was "flimsy" and would "further disillusion popular hopes for improvements [in] the democratic process." After Cho was sentenced to death, the State Department warned Rhee that an execution would "effectively negate any success we may have had in developing political stability and maturity" in South Korea. The American ambassador in Seoul was instructed to "unofficially bring serious concern" to Rhee's government.

As events proved, the American embassy was right to worry about "trouble ahead." Cho was hanged. Fifty-two years later, the Supreme Court of Korea overturned the conviction, confirming the obvious: South Korea's founding leader had ordered Cho killed. The execution was called a judicial murder and an indelible stain on the country's history.

By 1957, when Nichols received his derogatory evaluation, Rhee's government was looking more and more like a tin-pot dictatorship. Things were "disintegrating," the British chargé d'affaires said in a conversation with his American counterpart. Rhee's enforcer and Nichols's friend, Kim "Snake" Chang-ryong, was assassinated by his own men.

At that point, Nichols's "very close friendship" with Rhee was probably perceived by the American embassy and the CIA as an unacceptable risk.

"You have got to realize what a ticking time bomb Nichols was after the war," said Michael Haas, a former air force colonel, special operations officer, and military historian who has examined Nichols's career and written two books about covert military operations in Korea. "The problem was that his postwar connections with the senior echelons of the South Korean government posed a threat to U.S. policy on the peninsula. No administration in Washington, no American ambassador in Seoul, could ever be sure what Nichols was telling the South Koreans or what operations he might be running into North Korea. Neither, for that matter, could the CIA."

No documentary evidence of State Department or CIA involvement in Nichols's dismissal has surfaced, and there is no hint of it in his military service record. But over the course of his long career in Korea, Nichols gave air force brass, U.S. diplomats, and senior intelligence officials plenty of reasons to sack him. Based on his assessment of the risk Nichols posed to American interests in Korea, Michael Haas suspects that high-level officials in the U.S. government made the call, quietly ordering Colonel Dunn to tell Nichols that it was time to go.

CHAPTER 10
Shocked

The day after he received his derogatory report, Donald Nichols was relieved of command. He was also ordered to rebut Colonel Dunn's evaluation and did so by composing twenty-five hundred words of carefully chosen, mostly apologetic prose.

None of his previous commanders, he wrote, had cared about the clothing he wore on duty. "As long as I can remember my superior officers never spoke of this matter or made mention of it to the effect it interfered with my work." Still, Nichols said he was happy to comply with Dunn's order to wear a full-dress uniform once a month to inspect his men. Nichols said he had long ago disposed of a dog that had bitten people and had relaxed his "austere" policies on recreational use of jeeps in the motor pool. As for being "rather 'Prussian' in my ways," Nichols acknowledged it was true, but said he had been trying for some time to be less so. As a result, "a certain degree of moral and emotional growth has been experienced both by myself and by the men in my command." Finally, Nichols complimented Colonel Dunn on his fairness and pledged to be a better, more solicitous, more humane leader in the future.

"I would like to state that my position as commander of the 6006th Air Intelligence Service Squadron has taught me much about many things and those corrective influences concerning myself will continue to be administered. Further, habits which tend to improve my outlook and mature my judgement [*sic*] in the various areas of human existence will be aggressively pursued."

His rebuttal reads like the argument of a confident career officer who expects contrition and flattery to soothe his boss's ruffled feathers—and perhaps win him another intelligence command. But it changed nothing.

After being replaced on July 27, 1957, he stayed in Seoul for a few months as a "commander's representative," apparently to help dismantle the covert unit that bore his name. Colonel Dunn was in a hurry. He ordered Nichols and his replacement, Captain James E. Kleinpeter, to attend a meeting on October 1 at the Bando Hotel in Seoul, where the American embassy had its offices. A plan was drawn up there to shut everything down. The fleet of boats Nichols had assembled for surreptitious travel north of the thirty-eighth parallel was given to the South Korean air force. North Korean uniforms, clandestine radios, and other special equipment were disposed of. North Korean currency and original copies of various stolen North Korean documents were sent to Japan. Agent training programs were canceled. The longtime senior Korean supervisor of Nichols's unit was fired.

At the Bando Hotel that day, the spy outfit known as NICK ceased to exist. In a sense, so did Donald Nichols. He returned to his base, where he ate alone in his quarters. Seven days later he vanished.

"At breakfast, we heard that Mr. Nichols was spirited off the base in a straitjacket," said William Bierek, the first lieutenant who worked for Nichols. "We were stunned because he had not shown one iota of mental illness. No explanation was given. Nothing more was said."

On October 8, 1957, Nichols was admitted for psychiatric evaluation at the 6407th Air Force Hospital in Tachikawa, Japan. Not far from Tokyo, it was a major treatment center for casualties from wars in Korea and Vietnam. When Nichols arrived, however, it was not immediately obvious to doctors that he was a casualty. There did not seem to be anything wrong with him.

"He had apparently been referred because of what was described as unusual behavior while on duty in Korea," according to his clinical record.

But it does not say what that unusual behavior might have been. During his eleven years in Korea, none of his superior officers, including Colonel Dunn, stated or even hinted in biannual evaluations of Nichols that he had mental health problems or that he struggled to manage the stress of spying on North Korea.

Psychiatrists at Tachikawa initially observed that Nichols was "oriented as to time, place, and person," although he seemed "quite anxious [and] stated that he did not know the reason for the request for evaluation but later volunteered that there was a personality clash with his commanding officer."

As his involuntary hospital stay dragged on into its tenth day, Nichols grew angry, violently so.

"This patient suddenly became disoriented, agitated, and broke a window with his fist," his clinical record says. "Despite inclement weather, he ran outdoors with only his pajamas on and had to be returned to the hospital by several attendants. He was then transferred [from an open hospital ward] to the psychiatric ward where he was noted to be agitated, disoriented, and very aggressive."

Locked in the psych ward, Nichols spent his time pounding his fist against the wall. At one point, he picked up a chair and tried to smash it through the window of the nurses' station. Doctors responded to his outburst by placing him on 400 milligrams of Thorazine a day. This, they said, "adequately sedated him."

Thorazine, a brand name for chlorpromazine, was the first effective antipsychotic drug. When Nichols was hospitalized in 1957, it had been on the market for only four years. But it had already revolutionized treatment of severely mentally ill patients who were considered hopeless and had been confined to nether regions of government institutions. Thorazine proved particularly effective in treating schizophrenia, a complex, long-term illness whose symptoms include hallucinations, delusions, and an inability to organize one's thoughts. Prior to his arrival at the hospital in Japan, there was nothing in Nichols's military service record or medical history to suggest he suffered from these symptoms. Nevertheless, air force psychiatrists diagnosed him as schizophrenic. For psychiatrists, nurses, and ward attendants, a major benefit of giving sizable doses of Thorazine to disruptive patients was that it made them sluggish and relatively easy to care for. That is how Smith, Kline & French, the American pharmaceutical company, initially marketed the drug to mental health professionals. "When the patient lashes out . . ." says a print advertisement from the early 1960s, "Thorazine quickly puts an end to his violent outburst."

This was true for Nichols in Japan, although his record says that even when heavily sedated, he was seething.

About a week after he was first dosed with Thorazine, the air force decided Nichols needed more psychiatric treatment than he could receive in Japan. He was flown to Eglin Air Force Base Hospital, located near the western tip of the Florida Panhandle, arriving on October 28, 1957.

A few days earlier, Nichols managed to send a letter to General Partridge, who was in Colorado commanding the North American Air Defense Command. He wrote that he was returning to the United States and asked his former boss for assistance in finding a new assignment. The letter did not mention that he was bound for more involuntary psychiatric treatment. Partridge wrote back immediately, sounded delighted to hear from Nichols, and offered help in job placement.

"Have your note announcing your return to the United States, and would like to know more about your future plans. There are several assignments in which you would do well, but I do not want to get into the act if you are already placed where you can be useful," Partridge wrote on October 28, clearly unaware that on that very day Nichols had checked in at Eglin hospital. "It is my understanding that you now have some 17 years' service and that you are anxious to fill the 20 necessary for retirement. Please let me know if this is correct and give me any other data which might be useful."

Nichols was placed in an open ward at Eglin, where air force psychiatrists made the same vague diagnoses as psychiatrists in Japan. "He gave the impression of suffering a chronic schizophrenic reaction without any really disturbing, acutely psychotic symptoms," his clinical report said. At Eglin, Nichols continued to complain about his former commanding officer, Colonel Dunn. Examining psychiatrists wrote that he was "quite evasive" and attributed it to his "clandestine intelligence activities. . . . Any information that was obtained is weaned only after repeated interviewing and apparently considerable thought on his part to avoid giving any information that might possibly be classified."

As for his violent behavior in the hospital in Japan, Nichols explained that it was due to nightmares. He complained, too, about the accumulated stress of his spy work. He regretted that "quite a few of his men were lost." He said he did not want to be locked up. He worried that North Korean assassins might be after him, but doctors noted that his "phobic type fears are apparently usually held in check." He was not having hallucinations or delusions, he was oriented as to time and place, his memory was intact, and "his intelligence is probably at least average."

Nichols wrote again and again to Partridge during his first two months at Eglin. With each letter, he became more candid about his "predicament" and more desperate for help. His first letter from Eglin acknowledged he was a patient at the base hospital, but did not say he was in the psychiatric ward.

"I am all mixed up at the moment on what I should do in the future," he told Partridge. "I feel like I should fill out the 20 years for normal retirement, however, am not sure. Please advise me on what I should do. Sir; I can never work for officers like Col Dunn or Col Hull again." Colonel Harris B. Hull had approved Dunn's recommendation that Nichols be removed from command. In his letter, Nichols told Partridge that the colonels "are both the type where either you play politics or else. In my case it has been the or else, this is the reason that I am now in a spot."

Partridge did not immediately reply to this letter, the first to make the general aware that Nichols believed his removal from Korea and forced hospitalization were driven by his commanders' political motivations.

The longer Nichols was in the psych ward, the more he brooded about his sanity. According to his clinical record, he became apprehensive about returning to duty, feared the responsibilities of command, and "frequently felt as though he might be going out of his mind."

On November 1, five days after Nichols arrived at Eglin, his case was presented to a conference of the psychiatric staff. "It was their opinion this man was a deteriorating schizophrenic," his record says. "He was obviously no longer of potential value to the service, and it was felt that he should probably be recommended for discharge or, rather, retirement."

Nichols was again put on Thorazine. This time, though, it was a far higher dose. A normal dosage at that time in a psychiatric hospital was 300 milligrams a day. In Japan, doctors gave him 400 milligrams a day. At Eglin, doctors who were struggling to keep him under control tripled the dosage to 1,200 milligrams a day. But it did not help. Nichols showed "only minimal improvement in his agitation and anxiety and some increase in [his] already considerable depression." His condition spiraled downward. He was having trouble thinking and concentrating. "He became more and more withdrawn and subsequently even more agitated and more depressed," his record states.

When nurses and attendants could no longer handle him on an open ward, he was moved to a closed psych ward. With Nichols clearly worse off than when he arrived at Eglin, psychiatrists dialed back his dosage of Thorazine. On November 21, they convened another meeting: "The problem was discussed with the staff and it was decided he should receive a course of electro-shock treatments."

Invented in Italy in the late 1930s, electroshock became commonplace in psychiatric hospitals across Europe and the United States in the 1940s and 1950s. The treatment sends an electric current through a patient's brain, causing epilepsy-like grand mal seizures that last from thirty seconds to two minutes. Some have compared the effect of electroshock to that of rebooting a computer and removing glitches. For reasons that were not (and are still not) understood, electroshock can alleviate symptoms for severely depressed, manic, and psychotic patients, as well as some schizophrenics. The beneficial effects are often immediate, but temporary. In many cases, years of maintenance treatments are prescribed.

Like Thorazine, electroshock makes patients easier to manage, reducing the workload of psychiatric caregivers. During and after World War II, U.S. military hospitals adopted electroshock as a standard treatment for soldiers suffering from shell shock, now known as posttraumatic stress disorder. Electroshock was used—and sometimes misused—on thousands of GIs. Some psychiatrists used it to "treat" homosexuality. In the late 1950s, one army hospital outside Denver administered twenty to twenty-five electroshock treatments to nearly every soldier admitted to the psych ward.

Electroshock, sometimes called electroconvulsive shock therapy (ECT), was often used for the convenience of doctors and nurses, medical historians say. "ECT stands practically alone among the medical/surgical interventions in that misuse was not the goal of curing but of controlling the patients for the benefits of the hospital staff," David J. Rothman, a medical historian at Columbia University, said at a National Institutes of Health conference in the 1980s.

Electroshock did not last long as a standard treatment in military or civilian hospitals. Largely because of Ken Kesey's 1962 novel, *One Flew Over the Cuckoo's Nest*, and the wildly successful 1975 film adaptation starring Jack Nicholson, it disappeared from common American psychiatric practice for nearly two decades. In the movie, Nicholson won an Oscar for playing Randle P. McMurphy, a petty criminal who feigns mental illness to escape hard labor in prison only to end up in an asylum under the care of the stone-hearted Nurse Ratched. In a terrifying scene, Nicholson's character is strapped to a bed by a scrum of white-coated attendants and given electroshock that flushes his face, convulses his body, and seems to sizzle his brain.

The movie, together with the introduction in the 1960s of antidepressant drugs that seemed less barbaric, pushed electroshock to the fringes of psychiatry until the mid-1980s, when clinical evidence showed its utility in relieving severe depression. Famous American personalities, like talk show host Dick Cavett, said it saved their lives. But questions remain about electroshock's effects on brain function, mortality, and long-term memory. Clinical evidence shows that it usually causes permanent memory loss for events that occurred immediately before, during, and after treatment.

Nichols started with fourteen consecutive rounds of electroshock. Based on his clinical record, they probably began on Monday, November 25, and continued daily until Sunday, December 8. After that, his treatments were "more widely spaced." He told his family he had a total of fifty electroshocks. Each began with a nurse smearing his right and left temples with a conducting gel and putting a rubber plug in his mouth so that he would not bite his tongue (although he told his brother he often bit his tongue). Each session ended with a savagely painful headache. Nichols showed "maximum improvement" after his eighth treatment, his record says. He then began to show "considerable organic confusion," even as treatments continued.

On December 4, with ten shock treatments done and four more to go, Nichols managed to write again to Partridge. This time he did not blame his hospitalization on politics or on his bosses. He acknowledged his status as a psychiatric patient, but chose not to report his electroshock treatment.

"Appreciate your concern for my predicament," Nichols wrote. "At present I am in a psychiatric ward. . . . Having been sent here due to a near nervous breakdown, it is now obvious that I may receive a medical discharge. However, I'm not sure this is the best way to leave the service. Please advise me as to whether I should finish my twenty years and receive a normal discharge and retirement, or accept a medical discharge now."

When Partridge read the letter at NORAD's command center in Colorado, it clearly gave him pause. His executive officer, Colonel Cecil Scott, wrote a note at the bottom of the letter, reminding his boss that he had already written to Nichols "on this subject." Beneath that note, Partridge scrawled, "What now?"

When Partridge failed to respond, Nichols sent him a Western Union telegram, dated December 19. It mentioned, yet again, that he was a patient at Eglin. Plaintively, it asked, "If you are ever down this way please stop in to see me."

The day after Christmas, Partridge replied: "I doubt that I will be able to journey in the direction of Eglin Field for some time to come but if I do get down that way, you may be sure that I will drop in to see you.

"Meanwhile, I should like to suggest that you relax and accept the medical procedures which the doctors suggest for you. If by chance you are retired with a medical disability, you will be far better off from a tax point of view than you would be if you completed your 20 years of service. Thus, it appears to me that you are going to be the winner either way. . . . Please accept my best wishes for a happy and prosperous New Year."

Nichols was given a convalescent leave over Christmas to visit his brother Judson and his family in Florida. While he was there, he told his relatives that he had been receiving shock therapy and that he would have to return to Eglin for more. "He said it was not health care," his nephew recalled, "but that the government wanted to erase his brain—because he knew too much."

———————————

The electroshock treatment Nichols received at Eglin was considerably more intensive—and disorienting—than he would likely have received today. Two or three treatments a week are now the norm for acutely ill patients, and the duration of the pulse of electricity sent through a patient's brain is briefer and more focused than in the 1950s. It is targeted to stimulate brain regions associated with mood while avoiding areas used in cognition.

Whatever the political reasons may have been for booting Nichols out of Korea and relieving him of command, his clinical record suggests that air force doctors believed they were helping him. Based on a review of that record, electroshock experts say Nichols almost certainly benefited from his stay at Eglin. "For the psychiatry of the day, his treatment was about right," said Edward Shorter, a professor of psychiatry and the history of medicine at the University of Toronto. By the time Nichols received electroshock in 1957, most U.S. military hospitals were using techniques that were less painful and more humane than what Jack Nicholson's character endured in *Cuckoo's Nest*, according to Dr. Max Fink, a psychiatrist who worked in military hospitals and began using "modified electroshock" in 1952. Modified treatment would have put Nichols to sleep with an anesthetic, covered his nose and mouth with a mask to deliver oxygen to his brain, and given him an intravenous dose of a drug called succinylcholine, which relaxes muscles during convulsions. Nichols would not have been at risk of a fractured jaw or of broken bones in his spinal column, a common side effect of unmodified shock therapy. "I think the doctors in this case did well and he was successfully treated for the time," said Fink, who has written a number of books on electroshock and has studied its efficacy for more than six decades.

While doctors Fink and Shorter agreed that electroshock treatment was appropriate for Nichols, they also believed that military psychiatrists misdiagnosed him. Based on the evidence in his clinical record, both said, Nichols was not schizophrenic. Fink and Shorter said the air force probably triggered his mental breakdown by demolishing his self-image as an effective intelligence commander.

"They clearly wanted to get rid of him and that must have been a colossal disappointment," said Shorter. "It is reasonable to believe that he had a severe psychiatric reaction to the sudden end of his career."

Nichols explained the overwhelming feeling of worthlessness he experienced when the air force sacked him and sent him home. In the most emotionally powerful passage in his autobiography, he wrote: "I [left the air force] in the category of an untouchable in 1957 . . . as an untouchable to anyone who had ever worked in the intelligence jobs of the Orient. I was a bastard orphan of the intelligence services without reference, protection, unit, assignment, indeed without a home."

His decade of high-wire stress as a spymaster, his fear of assassination, and his guilt about sending agents to their death in North Korea—all might have heightened his risk of mental illness. But his sudden fall from intelligence prince to psych-ward untouchable appears to have been the trigger for what today would be described as a reactive psychosis marked by severe depression.

Electroshock happens to be a highly effective treatment for such depression, producing positive responses in about 80 percent of patients, according to clinical research. This seems to have been true for Nichols. He was hardly ebullient when his daily electroshock treatments ended at Eglin, and it took two weeks for his "organic confusion" to clear up. But the overall result, his doctors said, was that he seemed "much more at ease, much more relaxed, and more sociable with only minimal evidence of depression. . . ." After visiting relatives on leave, he returned to Eglin in January 1958 in "good spirits, and it was felt that he had received maximum hospital benefit."

Although Partridge did not visit Nichols, the general was unable to stop worrying about him and sent at least one letter to psychiatrists at Eglin before Nichols was discharged on January 16, 1958. Their patient had endured eleven years of "tremendous physical and mental strain" in Korea, Partridge wrote, telling doctors to give Nichols "maximum permanent medical retirement."

"I have personally observed the apparent state of his physical and mental health deteriorate as a result of this service," Partridge wrote. He added, quite prophetically, "I have serious doubts as to his future service, usefulness, or even his ability to pursue a civilian vocation."

On April 2, 1958, the air force released Nichols from active duty, placing him on "temporary disability retirement." He was judged to be 70 percent disabled. His final diagnosis from Eglin was "schizophrenic reaction, paranoid type, chronic, severe, manifested by effectual disturbances, thinking disturbances, loosening of associations, marked agitated depression, etc." Psychiatrists said he was "mentally competent," but described his impairment as "marked" for military duty and "moderate" for life as a civilian. As far as air force doctors could determine, he never got much better.

In the spring of 1962, when he was thirty-nine, Nichols traveled to Montgomery, Alabama, for an extensive evaluation at Maxwell Air Force Base hospital. It was the final step before his permanent separation from the air force and it determined how much disability pay he would receive for the rest of his life. It was also the fourth time in four years that he had been ordered to report to an air force hospital. Based on the clinical notes for that visit, he was fed up with military psychiatrists.

"The patient was a very obese white male," his doctor wrote. "He would seem to disregard the examiner except when a specific question was asked and then he would answer appropriately in the shortest possible answer. Then he would seem to go back and withdraw in himself and be absorbed in his own thoughts. The slightest exertion seemed to drain all of his energy from him. If the patient tried to go into any detail he would tend to lose the train of thought and wander off. There were no apparent delusions and hallucinations even though the patient was preoccupied within himself. There seems to be a rather marked depression present. Patient complained of rather severe nightmares and at times would react to these and on one occasion recently was destructive [no details given]. The patient was obviously unable to pursue a sustained train of mental activity. His affect was markedly flat. The patient was oriented as to time, place, and person."

The air force concluded that Nichols had "severe mental illness" and reaffirmed that he was 70 percent disabled. His doctor wrote that he had "continued to deteriorate" since coming home from Korea and concluded his clinical report by writing, "The prognosis for any improvement is extremely poor."

In his autobiography, published nineteen years after he was discharged from the air force, Nichols did not write about his lockdown in psychiatric wards, running outside in the cold in his pajamas, pounding his fist against walls, throwing a chair in the nurses' station, seething through heavy doses of Thorazine, or enduring fifty rounds of electroshock. Like many Americans of his era, he surely viewed mental illness as an embarrassing sign of weakness. Fifteen years after Nichols's treatment, disclosure of electroshock destroyed the vice presidential hopes of U.S. Senator Thomas Eagleton of Missouri.

In all likelihood, Nichols viewed his psychiatric treatment as a trumped-up government excuse for ejecting him from the air force. It is also possible that he forgot many details about his treatment, owing to the memory-obliterating effects of electroshock. It is far less likely that he forgot about Colonel Dunn or the report that finished him as an air force intelligence commander, although neither the colonel nor his report appears in Nichols's autobiography.

Nichols did write effusively and at length about Syngman Rhee and how their friendship enabled him to become a successful spy. He offered no insights, however, into how that friendship might have cost him his career, sentenced him to the psych ward, and triggered his involuntary early retirement. Like a good spy, Nichols sanitized the narrative, writing: "For some reason which God alone knows, in late 1957, He saw fit to allow me to return from Korea."

CHAPTER 11
Adrift and Accused

After leaving Eglin Air Force Base Hospital, Donald Nichols moved in with his older brother Judson, who lived in central Florida with his wife, Nora Mae, and their four children. Near the small town of DeLand, they owned an old farmhouse that sat on concrete blocks, had asbestos siding, and needed work.

A devout Christian, Judson was a welcoming brother. He had always worried that Donald, more than any of his siblings, had been scarred as a boy by the sexual antics of their mother. Judson had recently landed a job as head of bus operations for Volusia County Schools. After years of struggling to feed and clothe his family, the job provided him with a regular salary, along with a realistic expectation that he and his wife could fix up their house. Still, they drove an old Plymouth. Like most people who came of age during the Depression, they worried about money. To supplement Judson's salary, the family raised ferns for sale in flower shops.

Donald's arrival was a seismic disturbance, and the tremors began even before he showed up in person. He sent the family an expensive set of fine china in a big aluminum trunk, each piece carefully wrapped in tissue paper. The children, ages two to fourteen, did not know what to make of the fancy, imported dinnerware, but quickly found a soothing use for the tissue: it replaced pages of the Sears, Roebuck catalog they had been using as toilet paper.

When he arrived in the flesh, Nichols was driving a new car, a white 1958 Chevrolet Bel Air with twin headlights and a V-8 engine. He was also carrying loads of money.

"You would have known Uncle Don only one day before he made you know that he was rich," said Donald H. Nichols, Judson's oldest son, then fourteen. "He had so much cash and he loved to show it off. He'd pull a wad out of his pocket, maybe a thousand dollars or two. The money was always a mystery to us the whole time we knew him. He never said where it came from. He didn't want anybody to know how much he had. It wasn't millions, but it was probably a few hundred thousand dollars."

After he moved into the farmhouse, Uncle Don, who had a loud and commanding voice, often issued orders to everyone in the household. He bought mountains of junk food—chips, crackers, candy bars, and Cokes— and shared it reluctantly with his nieces and nephews. He had a tiny 16-millimeter movie camera, a tool of the spy trade that intrigued the children. Stay away from it, he warned: it contains secrets from Korea.

In his Chevy, he took the family on rides that were often disturbing. At an all-you-can-eat chicken restaurant, he gorged on so much chicken that the owner called the police. At all-you-can-drink roadside juice stands, he guzzled orange juice until he threw up. At supermarkets, he would hijack grocery carts, taking them from parents distracted by their kids. Then he would rush to the checkout counter, buy everything in the cart, and race away in his Chevy, smiling broadly. Stopping at a roadside amusement park, he once ordered the entire family—including Judson and the reluctant Nora Mae—to get out of the car and go down a steep slide on a small rug. With his young nephew Donald riding shotgun, he drove his big car at more than 120 miles an hour on the back roads of central Florida, grinning and glancing sideways to gauge the terror in the eyes of his passenger.

"He was crazy Uncle Don, a kind of overgrown kid. You didn't want to grow up to be like him," Donald said. "He was looking desperately for fun. The things you would expect from a military guy like him—cigarettes, booze, and women—they were not in the picture. Instead, at the drop of a hat, he would do something stupid. It was all superficial, being crazy. He challenged me to a 'blender contest.' Mix up anything from the fridge and drink it. I put gumdrops, pickles, mustard in. He drank it all and threw up. It was good fun for kids, not so much for my parents."

Soon, three boys from Korea moved in—Uncle Don's adopted sons. In his autobiography, Nichols said he had "prepared for the exit of my sons" during his final weeks in Korea. It might also have been during this time that he arranged for the shipment of his cash back to Florida, a movement of funds that had to have been concealed from customs authorities.

The oldest adopted boy, Lee Tae Chon Nichols, turned sixteen in the summer of 1958. He had been one of Nichols's houseboys at the spy base outside Seoul. Naturalization records list his occupation as "cook" and show that he arrived in the United States on November 19, 1957, around the time Nichols checked into Eglin Air Force Base Hospital.

The second oldest, Bruce Nichols, whose Korean name was Kim Si Koo, was ten. He had also arrived in the United States the previous November. Records show that Bruce and Lee were born in Seoul.

The youngest, Donald "Donnie" Nichols II, was five. As explained previously, he arrived in the United States in 1955 because his adoptive father feared the boy was being stalked by North Korean assassins. Before Donnie showed up at Judson's house he had lived in Hollywood, Florida, with Nichols's eldest brother, Walter Sr., a local policeman, and his wife, Fern. Nichols would claim decades later that Donnie was the only child of his marriage to Kim In Hwa. But in the spring of 1958, he did not mention a wife who died in childbirth—he said Donnie was adopted.

In the DeLand farmhouse, seven children and three adults squeezed into three small bedrooms and shared one bath. It was crowded and tense. Nora Mae was unwilling to leave her children alone with her brother-in-law. Nichols treated his two older Korean boys less like sons and more like servants. They would, in time, become resentful and testy. It was clear to everyone that Donnie was Uncle Don's favorite. After several bumpy weeks with Judson's family, Nichols and his sons moved out.

He bought a nearly new house in South Florida. Located less than a block from the Fort Lauderdale Country Club, with four bedrooms and three baths, it was much larger and fancier than the homes of any of Nichols's brothers. The deed on the property in Plantation, a suburb of Fort Lauderdale, shows that on May 2, 1958, Nichols paid an unspecified amount of cash to take over a ten-thousand-dollar mortgage.

After enrolling his sons in local schools, Nichols began searching for something to do with the rest of his life. He was thirty-five and an exile from the military, the only American institution he understood. He did not—and probably could not—plug into the old-boy network that many retired intelligence officers use to arrange lucrative government contracts or jobs in corporate security. "I found the civilian touch isn't exactly 'Heaven' for retired military officers," he wrote. "[T]he majority of people I met didn't seem to give a damn about anyone but themselves."

Like many parents in a new town, he made friends through his children. He took neighbor boys fishing with his sons. He started a wholesale plant nursery and began buying real estate, purchasing at least three undeveloped parcels in Broward County. Most of the houses in his middle-class subdivision, called Country Club Estates, were two or three years old, and Nichols got to know his neighbors while discussing suitable trees and shrubbery to plant around the ranch-style houses. But he could not find a full-time job that suited him and was often bored.

"In addition to my inability to adjust to the change of pace from espionage to civilian life, I found it impossible to adjust to the new atmosphere which had taken place in Florida after my long absence," he said in his autobiography. "For lack of something better to do in those interminable days in Florida, I made a study of palms. . . . I continued as a lone wolf resting under and studying my stately friends, sometimes suppressing the desire to howl my melancholy song of affinity with these abnormal lords of the plant world."

Nichols did not appear to show symptoms of paranoid schizophrenia. In the 1960s, as his brother Judson and Judson's children saw him, he was cogent, articulate, certainly sane—though at times manic and often brooding. With family, he sometimes talked about his time in the psych ward, describing electroshock treatments as very painful. He repeatedly told them that the government wanted him to forget what he had done in Korea and that he, too, wanted to forget.

Yet he displayed his war medals in his house and told war stories: about massacres he had witnessed, tanks and MiGs he had captured, a secret trip into Manchuria, schemes that captured teams of North Korean agents, and his "very close friend" Syngman Rhee.

The more Uncle Don talked about Korea, the less his family trusted his stories.

"It was just his personality," recalled his nephew. "You never quite believed him or knew where you stood with him. I never saw a moment of introspection. I never saw the inside of the guy. He never questioned what he was doing with his life. Today, I would call him a phony. He was missing a tick. Empathy. He was missing empathy.

"You couldn't tell if he was bullshitting or not. He was a master manipulator. We thought he manipulated the air force to get a medical discharge. We thought this guy has figured a way to get a lifetime pension early. He claimed he knew Syngman Rhee, but we wondered if it was real. We never understood the importance of what he did. We flat-out missed it."

———

At six in the evening on December 18, 1965, Nichols telephoned a twelve-year-old neighbor boy and invited him to his home. The boy lived a few blocks away, on the far side of the Fort Lauderdale Country Club. He was a playmate of Donnie's, and Nichols had taken him along on a family fishing trip. But when Nichols invited the neighbor boy over, his three adopted sons were elsewhere.

"So I asked my mom and dad if I could go over to his house and they said yes," the boy said later in a sworn deposition. "I got on my bike and went over to his house and he said he had a Christmas present, which he didn't."

The boy said Nichols took him into the den and "started showing me these indecent pictures. . . . Naked ladies. And he undid my pants and started playing around with my personals; and after a while, he put his mouth to my personals, and I came to a climax and then he quit and gave me two dollars and I went home."

A few weeks later, the boy told his father what had happened and also described two similar sexual encounters with Nichols. The boy's alarmed father soon heard from other parents in Country Club Estates whose sons had told them similar stories. The parents wanted to know "what was going on." Five months later, on May 2, 1966, the father went to the Broward County Courthouse in Fort Lauderdale and swore out an affidavit accusing Nichols of assaulting his son.

Sheriff's deputies arrested Nichols four days later. A brief news story appeared the following day at the bottom of the local news page in the *Fort Lauderdale Sun-Sentinel*. Under a one-column headline, MAN CHARGED WITH ASSAULT, it identified Nichols by name, noted the charge of "indecent assault upon a child," and reported that he posted bail of twenty-five hundred dollars before his release from the county jail. The forty-three-word article did not disclose the age or sex of the child, nor did it include any biographical details, except Nichols's address. If the newspaper had learned that he was a retired air force major and a much-decorated veteran of the Korean War, it probably would have written more. But Nichols had been smart. In giving his occupation to deputies, he described himself only as "retired," according to the arrest record.

Nichols clearly felt stressed in the spring and summer of 1966. He appears to have tried to ease it with Coke, candy, and junk food. By the time he was arrested in May, his weight had ballooned to 320 pounds. His spy instincts also seem to have kicked in. Broward County property records show that he sold four parcels of land, including his house—all for cash, all on the same day, August 1, 1966. Three days after he signed paperwork for those land sales, Nichols was charged with a second sex crime. An arrest warrant accused him of the statutory rape of a fifteen-year-old girl.

In September, Nichols fled Florida, became a fugitive from justice, and attracted the attention of the Federal Bureau of Investigation. He took off in his car, along with Donnie and a pedigreed Chihuahua named Mama and her two puppies. In the most bald-faced lie in his autobiography, he explained his departure as a spur-of-the-moment lifestyle choice, a sudden response to the ennui of South Florida living.

"I decided one day this was not for me. When Donnie returned from school, I told him we were headed out. . . . [We] found ourselves on the open road, destination unknown. In the following weeks, we visited the states of Georgia, Alabama, Mississippi, Louisiana, Texas, New Mexico, Arizona, and California in search of a location pleasing to us where I thought I could raise my youngest. Eventually, we found ourselves in Guadalajara, Mexico. Choosing Mexico proved to be a wise move. I felt healing in myself."

While it was surely a relief to find sanctuary in Mexico, their journey was hardly that of a father seeking an amiable location to rear a son.

His flight was driven by panic. He faced a felony trial and five years in prison. After his arrest, Nichols knew that his sexual predilections, which he had indulged without legal consequences on his spy base in South Korea, were secrets he could no longer control. He could expect that testimony at the trial would disgust his brothers and their wives, as well as his neighbors in Country Club Estates.

Nichols's two older adopted boys did not leave Florida with him, and it is not clear whether he left them behind or they chose not to go. In his last will and testament, Nichols said that Lee and Bruce Nichols "deserted their brother Donald, II, and me in 1966." This suggests that he wanted them to come to Mexico and that they refused. In his autobiography, Nichols spun a slightly different story, writing that both of the older boys decided to go out on their own in 1966. Lee, who was twenty-five that year, had found work as a full-time cook in a local Chinese restaurant and his job came with a furnished apartment, Nichols claimed. He said that Bruce, then eighteen, left for California to become a surfer.

"He wasn't doing too good in school—was surf-board crazy." Their version of these events could not be learned. Bruce Nichols died in California in 1985 at thirty-seven; extensive efforts to locate Lee Nichols failed.

Whatever their reasons were for not going to Mexico, Nichols's relationship with both of them appears to have permanently soured when he fled Florida. Lee later told Judson Nichols that he never again wanted to see or talk to his adoptive father. Bruce had never gotten along with him. The two often fought and Nichols criticized Bruce in front of relatives for being "lazy." Both Lee and Bruce eventually cut off all contact with the man who had brought them to the United States. No evidence has emerged to suggest that Nichols sexually abused them, but family members later wondered about it. "In retrospect, I think it was very strange that Uncle Don had adopted three boys from Korea—and two of them would not want to have anything to do with him," said Diana Carlin, Nichols's niece.

Nichols would never forgive the boys for leaving him. In his will, under the heading "Adopted Sons," he declared: "I specifically make no provisions of any type [for Lee and Bruce]. I desire they get none of my earthly possessions at all. Memories are more than enough."

After four months of traveling across the United States, the Mexican getaway ran into a roadblock of Nichols's own inadvertent making. On the last day of 1966, a Saturday, he left a paper sack containing twenty-five thousand dollars on the counter of Colleen's Coffee Shop in Escondido, California—about forty miles north of the Mexican border. Before Nichols discovered his loss and could rush back to the coffee shop to claim the cash, a waitress had turned it over to police. To retrieve it, Nichols had to pay three visits to the Escondido police station, show identification, and repeatedly explain why he was Mexico-bound with a bag full of hundred-dollar bills. By his third visit, police had learned that he was a fugitive from Florida. He was arrested on Tuesday, January 3, on warrants for statutory rape and indecent assault on a child. Donnie, then twelve, was taken to a nearby emergency shelter for children. While Nichols was being booked into the San Diego County jail, deputies found a cashier's check for fifteen thousand dollars drawn on a nearby California bank, where Nichols had apparently just deposited another tranche of the cash he had in his car. His traveling money was equivalent, at the time, to about six times the average annual household income in America.

The *Los Angeles Times* and the *San Diego Union* wrote brief news articles about the arrest, and wire services picked up the story. Versions of it appeared in the *Miami Herald* and other newspapers in Florida. What made the arrest moderately newsworthy was not that it nabbed a former spymaster from the Korean War, as no one then realized who Nichols was or what he had done. The articles focused instead on the oddity of a former air force officer leaving behind such a sizable amount of cash. In any case, Nichols hired a lawyer and posted cash bail of $2,750. Then he secured his sack of money, collected his son and his Chihuahuas (it is not clear where the dogs were kept during Nichols's two nights in jail), and took off for Guadalajara, apparently forfeiting his bail money.

.   FBI agents were soon on the case. They went to the home of Judson Nichols, who by then had moved to Miami to serve as director of school bus transportation for Dade County. "We got a knock on the door, and it was couple of guys who wanted to talk to my dad about Uncle Don," said Judson's daughter, Diana, who was eleven at the time. "The FBI wanted to know if my dad had been in contact with him."

When Judson told the agents that he had talked to his brother on the phone, they insisted that he try to bring Donald back to Florida. "The FBI twisted my dad's arm," said Judson's oldest son, Donald, who years later became a defense lawyer. "My dad had an eighth-grade education. He wasn't much better educated than Uncle Don. The FBI used some legal mumbo jumbo, threatened my dad with charges that he was harboring a fugitive or aiding a fugitive."

The threat worked and Judson called his brother, urging him to come home to face charges. On the phone, Donald said he might consider returning if Judson came down to Mexico so they could talk in person. Judson flew to Guadalajara and spent a week with Donald and Donnie.

During that time, Donald allowed himself to be photographed by Judson—a rarity, as he often refused to allow his picture to be taken, especially when he was overweight. But in Mexico, he had something to show off, a new physique. He had lost more than a hundred pounds and was all but unrecognizable.

Judson secured his brother's promise to turn himself in. But in many conversations with Donald, he did not learn about the charge of indecent assault on the twelve-year-old boy. He had not seen the one short newspaper article about his brother's arrest and knew only about the statutory rape charge from the girl of fifteen. Judson's children say no one in their family ever learned about the charge involving the boy. "If my father and mother had known, they would have been very disgusted and would have completely cut off ties," Diana said.

When Judson returned to Miami, he hired a legendary South Florida defense attorney, Irwin J. Block, to help his brother. In the early 1960s, Block had helped represent Clarence Gideon in a landmark case, *Gideon v. Wainwright*, in which the Supreme Court established the right of a poor defendant to have a lawyer. In another celebrated Florida case, Block worked for nearly a decade without pay to get two black men off death row for a 1963 murder they had not committed. Block also defended clients who paid him extremely well. In all his cases, he was known and feared for his relentless pretrial preparation.

After Nichols surrendered at the U.S.-Mexican border on December 8, 1967, he was transported by Broward County sheriff's deputies from Nogales, Arizona, back to Fort Lauderdale. The stress of returning to the United States to face trial and possible imprisonment had apparently put Nichols off his healthful Mexican diet. When he was arrested in Nogales, Nichols had regained all the weight he lost in Guadalajara and weighed 325 pounds.

In Fort Lauderdale, Irwin Block had already gotten busy filing motions, one of which obtained Nichols's release on bail. He moved in again with Judson and family, bringing Donnie and several Chihuahuas into their house in Miami. As he had a decade earlier, Nichols also arrived with astonishing amounts of cash. Large-denomination bills were stuffed into his knee-high socks. "He had brought the money back from Mexico and wanted to put it into the freezer," said Diana Carlin, his niece. "I remember my mom was horrified. My dad said to Uncle Don that if he wanted to stay with us, he had to get the money out of the house."

Irwin Block, who was likely paid with some of this money, was quietly efficient and spectacularly effective in defending his new client. Nichols did not face a jury trial on the statutory rape charge. It was apparently dismissed after the girl who had accused him changed her story and blamed another man for assaulting her.

A trial on the charge of indecent assault on the twelve-year-old boy in Country Club Estates was held in late May 1968. It began after Block had taken a lengthy deposition from the boy, as well as from two other boys in the neighborhood who said Nichols had abused or tried to abuse them. Block also deposed the boys' fathers. Questions asked during the depositions elicited some confusion and discrepancies among the boys and their fathers about the dates of the assaults and when the boys reported them to their parents. No transcript of the trial was available in court records, but inconsistencies in the accusers' depositions might have weakened the state's case. After a four-day trial, a jury found Nichols not guilty.

Block also succeeded in keeping Nichols's name out of the newspapers. There appears to have been no press coverage of the trial in Fort Lauderdale or anywhere in South Florida. When military historians began writing about Nichols in the 1990s, they did not know about the accusations against him in Broward County in the 1960s. No one in Judson Nichols's family learned about the accusations from the boys in Fort Lauderdale until the author of this book found their depositions in 2016.

In his autobiography, Nichols did not write about the trial or thank Irwin Block for his legal work. Instead, he blandly said that he left Mexico due to "ill health" and because he "felt that Donnie needed an American environment." But in recounting his return to Florida, Nichols did include a singularly revealing passage that describes the kind of man he wished he could be. The portrait is painted in the words of two "female friends" who were supposedly talking about Nichols as he prepared to leave Guadalajara.

As his book reports their overheard conversation, they saw Nichols as an attractive, charismatic, and dangerously sexy man of mystery:

> Behind those baby green eyes there is a monster's bastard brain that won't quit. It runs all the time, it won't sleep and God help you if you get on the wrong end of his stick for love—or hate, for he was equally endowed with both emotions. You know he never just enters a room, he charges it, and everything including your windows and doors all seem to quiver under the strain of his presence. But this is just one of Nichols' many facets. He has a pack of dogs, collects antiques, stamps, coins, kids, old guns, etc.—as if they were running out of style. If he was ever short of them, he isn't now. Someday he has to settle down and build a twenty acre house just for his collection of kids and junk. If he does I bet you won't find standing room for the prevalence of his dog guests. He loves women, but damn if he'll let anyone know it, how do you get to a man like that?

CHAPTER 12

Nolo Contendere

After his acquittal, Donald Nichols moved out of his brother's house. With Donnie and the dogs, he drove four hours north on the Florida turnpike and settled in the central Florida town of Brooksville. He might have chosen the town, which then had a population of four thousand, because real estate was cheap. Legal fees had probably taken a bite out of his cash reserves.

Brooksville and surrounding Hernando County would one day be absorbed into the sprawl of suburban Tampa, but in the late sixties, the town and county were part of the rural segregationist South. The region had a notably sinister history of racist violence. Hernando County had the nation's highest lynching rate between 1900 and 1930. Brooksville was named after Preston Brooks, a champion of slavery who represented South Carolina in the U.S. House of Representatives in the nineteenth century. He became infamous in 1856 for using his cane to club and seriously injure a Republican U.S. senator from Massachusetts, the abolitionist Charles Sumner, in an assault on the Senate floor. Appreciative citizens of what had been Pierceville, Florida, celebrated the beating by changing their town's name to Brooksville. In all likelihood, Nichols did not know this story when he moved to town. But he surely would have noticed the Ku Klux Klan, which regularly paraded through town.

Before the move, Nichols had hatched a new plan. He would write a book about his life as a spy. He asked General Partridge to write a foreword. Retired by then, Partridge was happy to oblige. In the fall of 1968, he mailed Nichols five pages of praise. It began:

"If I were called upon to name the most amazing and unusual man among all those with whom I was associated during my military service, I would not hesitate for a second in picking out Donald Nichols as that individual. His name and deeds are unknown to the general public or even to the people of the military establishment, yet Nichols successfully directed and often assisted in carrying out a long series of extraordinary exploits that called for imagination, for a high order of organizational capability, for maximum operational skill under the most difficult circumstances and for personal courage far beyond the normal call of duty."

(Six years later, when Partridge participated in an air force oral history project, he was more measured, saying that while Nichols "was a genius; he finally went crazy, really, literally." Three years after that, in another interview with the air force, Partridge said that Nichols "finally fell apart mentally." It is not clear whether Nichols ever met in person with Partridge after returning to the United States. Partridge's judgment appears to have been strongly influenced by the clinical reports the general received from air force psychiatrists, with whom he exchanged letters in 1957.)

With Partridge on board, Nichols turned next to Serbando Torres, his closest wartime aide. Sounding like the squadron commander that he had once been, Nichols wrote to Torres and instructed him to put down on paper "right away" the details of the "dates, places, times" they had spent together before and during the war. "I expect a lot from you to fill in the wide hole covering [the] period you were with me," he wrote. He told Torres not to fret about security considerations. "Forget the classification," he said. "Trust me on this. I'll handle that angle. You put down, please, all you can remember." Torres was still serving in the air force when he received the letter in 1969, and he chose not to help Nichols.

Nichols pushed ahead with the book anyway, working on it sporadically throughout the 1970s. He found a local schoolteacher, Joynelle

Pearson, to assist him with organization and grammar. He asked his brothers and their wives to send him letters and share memories from childhood. He asked his former executive officer in Korea, Major George T. Gregory, to describe what he knew about their spy adventures during the war. Gregory came through with an account of his former boss that was even more positive, if less factually reliable, than what Partridge had sent him. Nichols included the entire fifteen pages from Gregory as a book chapter titled "The Unknown Lawrence of Korea." Nichols also asked the National Archives in St. Louis to send him a complete list of his twenty-one U.S. medals and decorations, as well as seven medals from the South Korean government.

Finally, Nichols found an air force veteran of the Korean War, Robert "Bobby" Meadows, who owned Brooksville Printing, to be his typesetter, book designer, editorial adviser, and publisher. On and off, the two veterans spent more than a year together in Bobby's print shop. They worked weekends and late into the night, arguing about text, photographs, and the cover design. Steve Wyatt, Bobby's son, who was thirteen when the book came together, said Nichols always wore black combat boots, blue jeans, and steel knee braces.

"We called him 'Iron Fist Don' and he didn't take no bull from anyone," Wyatt said. "If he said 'jump,' his son Donnie said 'how high.' I think he weighed about 260 pounds, but he wasn't that fat, just big. He kept telling my dad that he ought to make our customers stop smoking when they came into the shop. Sometimes he'd shout at them, 'Put out your damn cigarette.'"

Nichols, for all his irascibility, took to middle-class life in Brooksville. It was the closest he ever came to normality, and it lasted throughout the 1970s and into the mid-1980s. While he worked on his book, he bought real estate and rental properties in Hernando County and across central Florida, presumably paying with the cash he had carried from Korea to Mexico and back to Florida. He also bought a chicken farm and later sold it after failing to make a profit. His son Donnie attended Hernando High School and later bought a service station. Donnie was married in 1975, had two children in eight years, and became a business partner with his father, who in 1981 gave him power of attorney over all his affairs.

Air force doctors had diagnosed Nichols in the 1960s as a diabetic at risk of heart disease. He needed daily insulin shots. In the 1980s, as his knees, damaged from wartime parachute jumps, caused more pain and his mobility decreased, Donnie invited his father to move in with his family. There, Donald Sr. often watched television with his granddaughter on his lap. He joined the Mormon church, made friends at VFW posts around Hernando County, and researched his family's genealogical history. In Brooksville, Nichols let it be known that he was a retired colonel. Although he retired as a major in the air force, Syngman Rhee had bestowed on him the higher honorary rank.

As it had been throughout his life, Nichols's weight was a chronic issue and it continued to fluctuate wildly. He went on a watermelon-only diet in the 1980s, buying his melons from J. O. Batten, a Vietnam veteran and neighbor. "Colonel Nichols lost a hundred pounds eating my watermelons," said Batten.

Nichols even mended fences, for a time, with the air force. His former unit, the Office of Special Investigations, invited him to speak to cadets attending its academy at Bolling Air Force Base in Washington, D.C. Wearing leg braces, he spoke to students about spying in Korea. "I got the feeling he liked the attention," said Edward C. Mishler, a retired air force historian. "He liked to be praised for what he did." After a couple of visits, though, Nichols stopped coming to Bolling, apparently because he felt he was not getting the respect he deserved.

His autobiography, *How Many Times Can I Die?*, was published in 1981. The book's cover, the work of printer Bobby Meadows, was a drawing of a young, helmet-wearing airman against the backdrop of an American flag. In the drawing, blood drips from a corner of the airman's mouth and runs down his left cheek. It did not look a bit like Nichols, but he liked it and mailed many books to relatives and friends. For more than a decade, few people, including his relatives, read or paid much attention to the book. It was dedicated to his father, whom he described lovingly, and to his wayward mother. He wrote that he had forgiven her, but also said, "I wished every day that she would come back, and swore in my heart that I would not welcome her if she did."

He was required to submit his autobiography for review by air force intelligence and did so in 1980. After it came back from the censors, he wrote in the book's final pages that he was "well aware that there is much more that could have been included, but security dictated that some of this documentation was necessarily abbreviated." The one detail in the book that aroused international attention—after it was discovered by a few Korean War scholars and journalists in the late 1990s—was Nichols's description of the "unforgettable massacre" of civilians by South Korean forces that he witnessed near the town of Suwon. As noted earlier, Nichols knowingly lied in his book about the location of this mass killing, which he had actually witnessed near the town of Taejon. Still, his powerful eyewitness description found its way into a series of investigative Associated Press articles about civilian killings during the Rhee era and into a number of scholarly articles and books.

The autobiography did nothing to disturb the contented obscurity of Nichols's life in Brooksville. People there knew he had served in Korea, but not much more. He was silent about his dismissal from the air force, his electroshock treatment, and his diagnosis of mental illness. No one had heard about the charges of indecent assault in Fort Lauderdale. Drifting through middle age, Nichols enjoyed a long season of freedom from his past. As he wrote in the final pages of his autobiography, "The years in Brooksville have brought a new dimension to my life."

The tranquillity of those years was shattered on Sunday, June 23, 1985, when Nichols's son lost control of an ultralight drag-racing airboat traveling at seventy miles an hour on Lake Kissimmee, about two hours southeast of Brooksville. The boat went airborne and Donnie was thrown through a protective cage into the airboat's big propeller. He was pronounced dead on the lakeshore at age thirty-two.

For his father, Donnie's death was unbearable. "It was like popping a balloon; he went downhill fast," said Steve Wyatt, his friend at the print shop. Donnie's daughter, Lindsay, was seven at the time of her father's death. She remembers that afterward, her grandfather seemed lost. "The light went out of his life," she said. After Donnie died, conflict arose between Nichols and his son's widow, Linda. He moved out of their house and rented an apartment nearby. Nichols decided the time had come to write a will. The brief, rather bitter document denied inheritance rights to his estranged adoptive sons but aimed to protect his war medals, saying that none of them should "ever be sold, destroyed, traded or given away to anyone."

An unexpected invitation helped Nichols break out of his depression. His former intelligence comrades from the South Korean air force, many of whom had become rich businessmen or powerful members of the South Korean government, contacted him and offered to pay his expenses for a visit to Seoul in March 1987. They wanted to celebrate his service during the Korean War. It was an honor that Nichols had long felt was his due, and one that he had never received from the U.S. Air Force. He had not been back to South Korea since his involuntary departure thirty years earlier. He eagerly accepted.

En route from Tampa to Seoul, Nichols changed planes in Minneapolis. While waiting for his next flight, he invited his nephew Donald H. Nichols, the defense attorney who had lived there for many years, to come out to the airport. When his nephew spotted him, Uncle Don was sitting all alone in an empty part of the terminal. His hair had turned white. He was much more obese than he had ever been in the 1960s. Somehow he had squeezed into his old air force dress uniform. The front of his uniform jacket was covered with ribbons and medals from the Korean War.

"He told me about how he was going to meet all these bigwigs in South Korea, very important people," Nichols's nephew recalled. "It was all about what he was going to do. He was very proud. I don't remember that he asked me anything about my life."

When Nichols landed in Seoul, more than a hundred of his former South Korean colleagues met and cheered him at the airport. (Nichols later told a Florida newspaper that eight hundred well-wishers were there.) His visit was covered by Korea's national television news and as well as major newspapers and magazines in Seoul. Stories said that the South

Korean government had awarded Nichols medals for valor and described him as a close friend of Syngman Rhee. At that time, the Korean government had not yet investigated mass killings of civilians during the Rhee era; those inquiries began a decade later, in the late 1990s. Nichols's witnessing of those killings and his longtime friendships with murderers like Kim "Snake" Chang-ryong were not public knowledge. At one of many dinners held for him, a banner behind the head table read "WELCOME BACK!! MR. NICHOLS, HERO OF KOREAN WAR." During his four-week stay, Nichols slept at Kimpo (now called Gimpo) Airport, the former air base where he had worked as a spy. With no bed there big enough for him, his comrades chipped in to have one built.

After Nichols returned home, the *St. Petersburg Times,* then Florida's second-largest newspaper, learned about the hero's welcome he had received in Seoul and wrote a flattering article describing him as the father of "a key part of South Korea's espionage network." The story was accompanied by two photographs of Nichols, one with a plaque he brought home from Seoul, the other with his miniature 16-millimeter spy camera. It was the biggest splash of positive publicity he ever received in the United States.

Nichols's long stretch of relative normality ended in the summer of 1987, when his decades of predatory behavior finally caught up with him. He was sixty-four.

Two weeks after the "hero's welcome" story was published in the *St. Petersburg Times*, he was arrested at home. Three teenage boys, aged thirteen to fifteen, had complained to Brooksville police that Nichols masturbated in front of them in his apartment, while urging them to do likewise. They said he threatened to hurt them if they told their parents. The arrest did not come as a complete surprise to some people in Brooksville. "Colonel Nichols was always around younger boys," said J. O. Batten, the veteran who sold him watermelons. "There had been talk."

This time, press coverage was punishing. LEWD ACT CHARGED AGAINST DECORATED VET said a banner front-page headline in the Brooksville *Daily Sun-Journal.* Four days after his arrest, Nichols was still in custody. Police said his victims and their parents were "in fear of their lives." Nichols was reported to be under a suicide watch.

Coverage in the *St. Petersburg Times*, which needed to set the record straight about a local resident it had just lionized as a war hero, dug deeper. In addition to describing what the boys had gone through in Nichols's apartment, the newspaper looked closely at police records and found another molestation claim in Brooksville. It involved Nichols and a twenty-three-year-old man who had been a friend of Donnie's. The friend claimed Nichols abused him when he was eleven years old. Instead of going to the police, the young man had tried to extort money from Nichols. He showed up at a family memorial service for Donnie at Brooksville Cemetery demanding twenty thousand dollars in return for remaining silent and not going to the police.

Alicia Caldwell, a reporter for the *St. Petersburg Times,* reached Nichols by phone. He told her nothing much had happened with the three boys in his apartment. The whole business, he said, was not his fault: one of his accusers, a boy of fifteen, had asked him questions about sex and encouraged Nichols to fondle himself, which he did. "Because he encouraged me," Nichols told the newspaper. "I thought I was teaching him something. . . . I will admit to one instance."

This was not a persuasive argument at the Hernando County Courthouse. In late 1987, facing a humiliating and expensive trial, as well as near-certain conviction, Nichols pleaded nolo contendere to two felony counts of lewd and lascivious behavior in the presence of a child under sixteen. He was fined five hundred dollars, required to go into counseling as a sex offender, ordered to pay counseling costs for his victims, and sentenced to two years of "community control," a kind of house arrest. It banned him from any contact with children without the supervision of another adult.

When he was arrested in Fort Lauderdale in the 1960s, Nichols had received the support of his brothers and extended family. His kin believed in him then. But when sex charges surfaced again in 1987, relatives kept their distance. "I think the second criminal thing turned the whole family against him," said his nephew.

Community control did not go well. Nichols was arrested six months later for having unsupervised young boys in his home. The county prosecutor demanded he be sent to prison for three years. A judge agreed. But before Nichols could serve time, the same judge declared him mentally incompetent, and he was admitted to a private psychiatric hospital in nearby Tampa. Donnie's widow, Linda, whom he had named as the executor of his will, declined to become his guardian. In 1989, the psychiatric hospital in Tampa told the Hernando County court that Nichols would have to go elsewhere.

Nichols was then sent to the Veterans Administration Medical Center in Tuscaloosa, Alabama, where he was confined to the psychiatric ward. He hated the place. It made him depressed, according to court documents. With the help of John G. Jones, an ex–military friend from Hernando County who had agreed to become his guardian, Nichols devised what would be his last tactical plan: he would move back to central Florida and build a house near Jones, who would assist in his care and pay for it with Nichols's money. In a court hearing, financial records were presented showing that he had land and liquid assets worth $275,000, about $500,000 today. While Nichols remained in the psych ward, the "home plan" triggered motions and lawsuits that found their way, after three years, to a Florida appeals court. Among those who objected to his release was his daughter-in-law, Linda. Her lawyers argued that Nichols should stay in the hospital in Tuscaloosa because the home plan would diminish his medical and psychiatric care while draining his bank account.

Joining her in objecting to Nichols's release was the prosecutor back in Brooksville. He told the court that Nichols was "a pedophile who posed a danger to the children of Hernando County." If Nichols was found to be mentally competent and returned to Florida, the prosecutor said, the state of Florida would insist that he go to prison for three years.

If he was deemed mentally incompetent, the prosecutor said, he must be locked up in a state psychiatric hospital.

Nichols turned sixty-nine on February 18, 1992. His health had declined in the hospital in Tuscaloosa. He had lost weight, his memory deteriorated, and he could not be understood on the phone. He needed help getting in and out of bed. On May 20, an attendant found him on the floor of his hospital room. He was unconscious after an apparent stroke. He remained unconscious in intensive care until June 2, when he was pronounced dead.

EPILOGUE

A Spy's Grave

In *A Bright Shining Lie*, Neil Sheehan explains the American debacle in Vietnam through the life and death of John Paul Vann, a flawed hero of the war. Sheehan begins with Vann's grand funeral at Arlington National Cemetery. A horse-drawn caisson carried the coffin of the gallant and brilliant soldier who, in Sheehan's words, had tried to "redeem the unredeemable" war. There was a marching band, an honor guard, and a parade of important mourners, a Who's Who of the Vietnam era. It included senators and spies, antiwar crusaders and prowar columnists, senior generals blamed for losing Vietnam, and Vann's ex-wife along with her five fatherless children. "It was a funeral to which they all came," Sheehan wrote. "Those who had assembled to see John Vann to his grave reflected the divisions and the wounds that the war had inflicted on American society."

Few came to the funeral of Major Donald Nichols. He was buried in Brooksville three days after he died, with only his son's widow, two young grandchildren, and a handful of others in attendance. Most of his relatives did not know he was gone until months later. His death occasioned no coverage in the national press. Obituaries were brief in central Florida newspapers: a couple of sentences about his service in Korea. Nothing about sex crimes. Nothing about his "magnificent" and "impossible" achievements as a spymaster. The tragic arc of his life, from South Florida ragamuffin to King of Spies to serial pedophile, was unknown. As far as anybody understood at the time of his death, Nichols was just another worn-out and troubled veteran who had faded away.

Yet in its invisibility, his passing was as symbolically rich as the pomp and ceremony that marked the state funeral of John Paul Vann.

In life and in death, Vann had shone a spotlight on the conduct of his war. He wanted Americans to understand the folly of their military leaders. While his war was a singular tragedy for the United States, it was a tragedy performed in public. Vietnam sparked riots, but it also taught lessons that changed the conduct of the American military. The war's impact was even more profound in the hearts of millions of Americans who never again would trust so blindly in their government.

As for Nichols, his unnoticed death was of a piece with his undigested war. Most Americans never debated, let alone understood, the causes and conduct of the conflict in Korea, even though it killed GIs at a far faster clip than the Vietnam War did. Did it make sense for the United States to draw an arbitrary line across Korea, igniting war without end on the peninsula? Should the United States have passively acquiesced as Syngman Rhee's men murdered tens of thousands of South Koreans who might or might not have been Communists? Was it not just counterproductive but immoral for the U.S. Air Force to flatten every population center in North Korea with bombs and napalm?

Because questions about Korea went unasked, blunders in military strategy and errors in statecraft were not examined. Soon they were repeated. After the air force bombed and burned North Korea, it did the same thing in Vietnam and Cambodia, with the same unsatisfactory and morally reprehensible results. After the United States empowered and unleashed Rhee in South Korea, it repeated the strategy in many parts of the world, installing and supporting "anti-Communist" leaders in Africa, South America, and the Middle East.

Ignorance about the Korean War has also led to the cartoonish, ahistorical understanding many Americans still have of contemporary North

Korea. They know that a family of clownish-looking dictators named Kim has created a hermit state armed with nuclear weapons. They know that it is wildly belligerent toward the United States. But most do not know that the fears of North Korea's isolated citizens are firmly rooted in history: they are afraid that Americans might once again raze their country. Thanks to the bombs and napalm dropped by the U.S. Air Force during the Korean War, the Kim family is able to stoke anti-American hatred and perpetuate its rule, all while telling a terrifying, fact-based story that most Americans have never heard.

The quiet passing of Donald Nichols occasioned no examination of his behavior in Korea or the blinkered acceptance of it by his commanders. Nichols's battlefield achievements—assembling a team of code breakers that helped save the U.S. Eighth Army in the Pusan Perimeter, identifying weaknesses in Soviet-made tanks and fighter jets, and finding thousands of bombing targets behind enemy lines—altered the course of a major war of the twentieth century and saved an untold number of American and South Korean lives. For this, he deserved his medals. But his closeness to Syngman Rhee made him, at the very least, a passive accomplice to atrocities that occurred before and during the war. He attended mass executions of South Korean civilians, trained the murderous Korean National Police, and regularly sat in on torture sessions. While there is no documentary evidence or eyewitness testimony showing that Nichols personally took part in mass killings or torture, he acknowledged that his career benefited from the intelligence that torture extracted. If he had interfered "in the methods our Allies used during interrogation," Nichols said, "a good source of information would have dried up." In much the same way, Nichols was compromised by his closeness to Rhee. It gave him exclusive information, high-level contacts, and an inside-the-palace cachet that thrilled his commanders, who rewarded him with promotions, power, and autonomy. But the price of his proximity to the president was blindness. He did not see—or did not care to see—Rhee's criminal excesses or his incompetence. Nichols convinced himself that Rhee was "a great Democrat" and a "deeply trusted leader of the South Koreans."

In the confused early days of the Korean War, when the air force was utterly dependent on Nichols for expertise, he was allowed, even encouraged, to operate outside the normal military chain of command. When he got into a bloody shoot-out with agents who feared that Nichols would send them to die in North Korea, his behavior did not raise eyebrows: the gunfight in his own quarters with his own men never entered his military service record. When he pushed suspected double agents out of boats or aircraft, commanding officers in the air force did not know or did not care.

At moments in his autobiography, Nichols raised questions about the morality of his behavior, even if he was not honest or rigorous in examining it. He knew, for example, that he needed tighter supervision, complaining that he "received absolutely no training." He was unequipped, he said, to manage what he called his "legal license to murder."

"Who should have this kind of authority?" he wrote. "Perhaps, if I had the benefits of higher education, an education which included something of philosophy and an understanding of life and man and their interrelationships with morals, honor, and duty, it would be easier for me to assay our wartime conduct. . . . I was a small cog in a big machine, the one that had to do a lot of dirty work for higher headquarters."

Why was a poorly educated, minimally trained American agent allowed to befriend—and serve the interests of—a foreign head of state? Who allowed him to work for years with South Korean enforcers who sent severed heads to Seoul to demonstrate their loyalty? Who allowed Nichols to push people out of planes? To send hundreds of South Korean agents to their deaths in the North? There are no answers for these questions, in part because no one outside the Far East Air Forces knew enough about Nichols to ask them—until more than a quarter century after he was dead.

Nor is there an easy explanation for Nichols's decades-long pattern of secretly abusing young men and boys. The hospital-based psychiatric care Nichols received in the air force failed him—and the boys he later victimized in Florida. According to his clinical record, air force psychiatrists—between lockdowns, heavy doses of Thorazine, and multiple rounds of electroshock—never made much effort to explore his family history. They diagnosed and treated a "schizophrenic" who did not exist. They failed to notice or help the sexual predator who did.

———

Nichols put a lot of time, thought, and subterfuge into his final resting place.

He and his son Donnie are buried on opposite sides of a large, lichens-stained granite cross with NICHOLS engraved on it. The monument is easy to find in Brooksville Cemetery, a tidy, town-owned graveyard shaded by live oak trees draped in Spanish moss. On the spring morning I spent beside the grave, a tendril of moss, swaying in a warm breeze, caressed the top of the family headstone.

Nichols acquired the plot, which has enough space for six coffins, in 1976. He was then fifty-three years old, and eight years had passed since his acquittal in Fort Lauderdale for abusing boys; their anguished depositions were safely sealed away in Broward County court archives. He had established himself as a respectable parent in Brooksville, where he served as chairman of the Hernando County school board's comprehensive plan steering committee. By then, his marital status had also changed, at least on official records. Instead of being single, he was a widower. The change appears on Veterans Administration paperwork he filled out in the latter years of his life. He seems to have decided to become a widower while he was writing the autobiography that chronicled his wartime marriage to Kim In Hwa.

In Brooksville, as Nichols worked on his autobiography in the late 1970s, he arranged to have the marriage set in stone. Purchasing the monument for his future gravesite, he instructed that KIM HWA be engraved just to the right of DONALD. (Her death date was also added; his was left blank to be filled in later.) Between their names, the engraver added the word MAMA, an apparent reference to one of Nichols's favorite dogs. Soon after the monument was placed in Brooksville Cemetery, Nichols photographed it, and the photo appears on the final page of his autobiography, enshrining his seemingly normal heterosexual marriage and the sentimental ideal that he would one day rest beside his beloved wife. An undated photograph of a young Korean woman whom Nichols identified as Kim Hwa also appears in the book, as does a photo of his dog Mama.

Nichols provided Brooksville Cemetery with a metal box, eighteen inches wide, forty-eight inches long, that he said contained the cremated remains of his late wife. This vault was set in concrete next to the space reserved for him. But the cemetery has no information about when her remains might have been transferred from South Korea to Florida or, indeed, if her ashes are in the vault. "I have no clue what's in it," said Mike Hughes, manager of the cemetery. "It is kind of odd." It seems unlikely the transfer ever occurred. In 1953, when Kim Hwa supposedly died in childbirth, cremation was viewed in South Korea as an affront to Confucian values. It was extremely rare, especially for a supposedly married woman.

A second stone marker on the Nichols plot also signals the spymaster's sleight of hand. Engraved on it are the names of his mother, Myra, and father, Walter—even though the two never reconciled and neither is actually buried there. When Walter died in Broward County in 1940, his relatives paid to have his body transported to New Jersey for burial in a family plot. Myra remarried at least once, becoming Myra Wolf. She died with that name in 1978 in a nursing home in Hollywood, Florida, and was cremated in nearby Delray Beach. "I don't know what is under the headstone, to be honest with you," the cemetery manager said.

By uniting his parents on a stone near his grave and by engraving the name of his potentially nonexistent "wife" on his own headstone, Donald Nichols concocted a happy and conventional ending to a life that was tormented and strange. It satisfied his father's frustrated longing for a loving wife. It reconnected him to a mother he always hated but never stopped needing. It created an enduring tableau of Nichols as a devoted husband and family man.

In his autobiography, Nichols asked: "How does one de-train the mind of a trained agent?" In his case, it seems it could not be done.

He played one last spy trick in the graveyard. On the granite cross that stands over his grave, he hid the part of his life that was most important to him and to the country he served. The monument bears no reference to the U.S. Air Force. It does not mention his rank. It forgets the Korean War.

ACKNOWLEDGMENTS

First, a special acknowledgment to Kurt M. Marisa, a retired air force colonel who served as an intelligence officer in South Korea. He took an active interest in this project, opened doors in the air force bureaucracy, and helped connect me with air force veterans who knew and worked with Donald Nichols. Without Marisa's help, this book would have taken far longer to complete.

Michael E. Haas, also a retired air force colonel, was the first historian to examine Nichols's career in depth. I contacted him in the early, middle, and final stages of this book and each time he generously shared his scholarship, his insight as a former special operations commander, and his understanding of how the military bureaucracy functioned during and after the Korean War. He referred me to other experts and took time to read, correct, and improve an early draft of this book.

Members of the Nichols family were essential in making it possible to research this book, particularly Donald H. Nichols, who welcomed me into his home in Wisconsin, and Diana Carlin, who, in addition to granting many interviews, shared scores of family photographs. Both read and corrected early drafts. Their brother, Paul W. Nichols, also told me

ACKNOWLEDGMENTS

stories about his uncle. I'm grateful as well to Nichols's granddaughter, Lindsay Morgan, who met with me in Brooksville, Florida, and shared family photographs, letters, and her grandfather's medals.

Serbando J. Torres, the former air force sergeant who is often cited in this book, allowed me to see Nichols as Torres saw him during the Korean War, when Nichols was his immediate superior, close friend, and housemate. Torres spent many hours steering me through the factual minefield that was Nichols's military career. As we worked together on this book, he and I became friends. I am sad to write that he died on January 30, 2017. He was eighty-seven.

Other air force veterans of the Korean War who knew Nichols and shared memories include William Bierek, Ronald Cuneo, Raymond Dean, Jack Sariego, and Rowan Raftery. I also thank retired air force command historian Herb Mason and Edward J. Hagerty, a history professor at American Military University. Several retired officers from the Air Force Office of Special Investigations helped me understand that unit and Nichols's role in it. They include Dick Law, Ed Mishler, and Gene Mastrangelo.

For previously unseen Korean War–era photographs of Nichols, I am indebted to Frank Winslow, a former Army Signal Corps photographer who took pictures of Nichols in and around Seoul before the North Korean invasion.

A small legion of men and women at the National Archives and the Air Force Historical Research Agency spent many hours helping me find documents and photographs. In particular, at the archives in College Park I want to thank Eric van Slander, a reference archivist, and Timothy K. Nenninger, chief of the textual records reference branch. Both of them suggested new directions for research and provided contacts that helped me obtain Nichols's military service record from the National Archives in St. Louis. There, the chief of archival operations, William Siebert, personally located Nichols's service record and directed me to the air force officials who were authorized to release it. At the personnel headquarters of the air force in San Antonio, Sharon Hogue helped start the Freedom of Information process.

At the Air Force Historical Research Agency in Montgomery, Alabama, Maranda Gilmore located previously unreleased documents about Nichols, and Forrest Marion directed me to a rarely viewed official history of Nichols's spy unit. Senior archivist Archangelo DiFante expedited the declassification of several documents. At the MacArthur Memorial in Norfolk, Virginia, chief archivist James W. Zobel directed me to useful documents about General Charles A. Willoughby, MacArthur's chief of intelligence. To understand the use of electroshock treatment in the military in the 1950s, I was greatly assisted by two psychiatrists who are experts in the subject, Dr. Edward Shorter in Toronto and Dr. Max Fink in St. James, New York. Thanks, too, to the University of Washington's library system in Seattle, which greatly simplified my research by having nearly every important work on Korean War history on its shelves.

The South Korean part of my research was made possible by Yoon-jung Seo, a Seoul-based journalist and researcher. She located Korean War veterans, dug through archives, found obscure online links to Nichols, and translated everything from North Korean newspapers to sit-down interviews. I also want to thank South Korean war veterans who granted interviews. In Seoul, they include Yoon Il-gyun, Chung Bong-sun, Kim In-ho, Lee Kang-hwa, and Kim Ji-eok; and in Riverdale, New Jersey, Kim Ok-sung.

For reading drafts of this book and offering corrections and suggestions, I thank my friend and former *Washington Post* colleague Glenn Frankel and Allan R. Millett, a specialist on the history of the Korean War and Ambrose Professor of History at the University of New Orleans. As she has done in the past, Sheila Kowal also read this book and offered helpful suggestions. Any errors of fact or judgment, of course, are on me.

This is my third book related to Korea and I'm very fortunate that the principal editor for all them at Viking has been Kathryn Court. At Viking, Lindsey Schwoeri also edited this book and improved it considerably, and Gretchen Schmid helped pull its many pieces together. Literary agent Raphael Sagalyn nursed this project along from conception to completion—and came up with the book's title.

ACKNOWLEDGMENTS

Thanks to my daughter, Lucinda, and son, Arno, who have had no choice during their childhoods but to learn about the history of the Korean Peninsula. Above all, thanks to my wife, Jessica Kowal. She encouraged me to write this story and, as an adviser, editor, and shrewd encourager, greatly improved it.

NOTE ON SOURCES

Donald Nichols was a flagrantly unreliable narrator. His autobiography, *How Many Times Can I Die?*, is marred by self-flattering exaggeration, outright lies, and numerous omissions of critical events in his life. Yet his 1981 book is also an essential source that explains where he came from: a troubled Depression-era family and a poisoned relationship with his mother. His account of his early years is supported by family letters and my interviews with his relatives and military colleagues. The autobiography also includes extensive and credible accounts of torture and mass execution as practiced by Syngman Rhee's security forces. I was dubious about Nichols's description of working in a clandestine world that included severed human heads—until I found a U.S. Army photograph of him standing beside one. There are also passages in his book that tell painful truths about his own emotions, particularly the heartbreak he felt when he came home from Korea, left the air force, and joined the ranks of the "living dead."

My introduction to Nichols, though, was not his autobiography. It was a series of interviews with the former North Korean fighter pilot who became Kenneth Rowe. I was writing a book about Rowe and his 1953 escape from North Korea when he told me about his unforgettable meetings with a swaggering, Coke-swilling American spy who was astoundingly well informed about the inner workings of the North Korean air force. Besides being beefy and gruff, Rowe said, Nichols was a good listener and genuinely empathetic.

After hearing this, I located a previously unreleased intelligence report in the National Archives that Nichols had written about his debriefing of the North Korean pilot. The report was accurate, analytically sophisticated, and well written. It impressed me and made me wonder: Who was this mysterious overfed American intelligence operative? How did he manage to work as a spymaster for eleven years in South Korea? What happened to him?

In the three years since I began asking those questions, my research has focused on archival records, court documents, and interviews with surviving Korean War veterans in the United States and South Korea, as well as with members of Nichols's family and U.S. experts on military intelligence and covert operations.

In the United States, the primary source of written material for this book was Nichols's military service record, which I requested from the air force under the Freedom of Information Act. The previously unreleased 191-page document fundamentally changes historical understanding of Nichols's military career. The record contains biannual evaluations of Nichols's performance as an officer throughout his years in Korea, the clinical record of his psychiatric treatment in air force hospitals in Japan and the United States, and extensive narrative citations for the many medals that Nichols won. It also includes copies of two prewar letters from President Rhee to American ambassador Muccio in Seoul, asking that Nichols be allowed to stay in South Korea and act as a personal adviser to Rhee on air force matters. These letters are perhaps the strongest primary source evidence of the highly unusual relationship that developed between Rhee and Nichols.

At the Air Force Historical Research Agency (AFHRA) in Montgomery, Alabama, I used the Freedom of Information Act to obtain copies of embassy letters and air force documents that revealed a previously unknown attempt by army general Charles A. Willoughby, MacArthur's chief of intelligence, to toss Nichols out of Korea two months before the start of the Korean War. Other documents declassified upon my request at AFHRA detailed the improbable starring role that Nichols played in the first months of the war, as his commanding general in the Far East Air Forces hurriedly promoted him and boasted in cables to Washington of his special relationship with Rhee. These documents show that just because Nichols bragged shamelessly about being a very important intelligence agent, it didn't necessarily mean he was exaggerating.

The unusually close relationship between Nichols and General Earle E. Partridge is documented in Partridge's personal correspondence, his diary, and two rounds of oral history interviews that were conducted by the air force in the 1970s. Most of these sources are archived at AFHRA, although one key letter from Partridge was found only in Nichols's military service record.

While the air force was extremely helpful in opening up a large number of files about Nichols, it continues to block access to many others. At the National Archives in College Park, Maryland, there are index cards identifying hundreds of air intelligence reports written by Nichols in the run-up to the Korean War. According to the index cards, many of these reports detail North Korea's military buildup before its invasion of South Korea, together with the role played by the Soviet Union in supplying arms, aircraft, and training. When I asked to see these prewar reports, archivists could give me only near-empty boxes of file folders, each of which contained a single sheet of blue paper labeled "access restricted." That restriction, which normally does not apply to government documents that are more than fifty years old, was imposed by the air force in 2011. It did so to protect information that "would reveal the identity of a confidential human source or a human intelligence source," according to an official at the archives. No other explanation was available. So far, my efforts to obtain bulk or individual declassification of these historically important documents have failed.

In his autobiography, Nichols does not boast about—or even mention—his creation of the Korean code-break team that helped the U.S. Eighth

Army defend the Pusan Perimeter in 1950. The decoding operation was perhaps his most important wartime achievement and it is confirmed in now-declassified documents published by the National Security Agency, the air force, and the South Korean government, all of which are cited in the endnotes of this book. But I never would have known to search for those documents without the advice of Serbando Torres, who served with Nichols for three years in Korea. Twenty years old when the war started, Torres was part of the code-breaking operation and an eyewitness who kept photographs, documents, and letters. He was well placed to correct the many instances in which Nichols exaggerated and distorted his wartime experience, while confirming and explaining his real achievements. Nichols asked Torres to help with research for his autobiography in 1969, but Torres was then serving in the air force and declined. When I reached Torres in 2015, he was retired and eager to help me tell Nichols's story. We met at his home near Baltimore and spoke on the phone several times a month for the better part of a year. Torres died after this book was completed. By then, he had read the manuscript twice and told me in a letter that it was accurate, as far as he knew.

Nichols compartmentalized his life and kept secrets from nearly everyone. My numerous interviews with his nephew Donald H. Nichols and his niece Diana Carlin, who were teenagers when they lived with their uncle in Florida after the war, opened some of those secret chambers. They saw the bricks of cash Nichols brought home from Korea and stored in a freezer. They knew, too, about his flight to Mexico as a fugitive from sexual-assault charges in the 1960s. But Nichols hid the exact nature of those charges from his family and friends. In the fall of 2016, when I was nearly done writing this book, I found previously sealed criminal court records on sex charges in the Broward County Courthouse annex in Fort Lauderdale.

During the Korean War, more than 90 percent of the men Nichols commanded were Korean. In my efforts to find and interview these primary sources in Korea, I was assisted by Seoul-based journalist and researcher Yoonjung Seo. She helped me locate men—now in their eighties and nineties—who worked with Nichols before, during, and after the Korean War. When I traveled to Seoul, she translated for interviews; she also conducted her own interviews. The South Korean consulate in Seattle also assisted in locating some of these men.

Two retired South Korean air force officers were particularly important in providing insights and new information about what Nichols did and did not do in Korea:

Retired general Yoon Il-gyun, a South Korean air force intelligence officer who later directed the Korean Central Intelligence Agency (now the National Intelligence Service), worked with Nichols during the war and traveled with him on many missions. In interviews for this book and in his own books and other writings, Yoon explained that Nichols planned and supervised key intelligence missions that succeeded in salvaging crucial parts of a Soviet MiG-15 fighter and a Soviet T-34 tank. But Yoon also said Nichols was not actually on the ground and in harm's way during these operations, which won Nichols, respectively, the Distinguished Service Cross and the Silver Star. Yoon's eyewitness version contradicts official U.S Air Force accounts of these missions and raises questions about whether Nichols should have been awarded America's second- and third-highest military honors for valor.

Retired colonel Chung Bong-sun, who worked for Nichols for nearly a decade, provided eyewitness details about the large sums of money that Nichols controlled and literally threw at his agents. Chung also explained how Nichols's close relationship with Syngman Rhee gave the American spymaster extraordinary power and influence inside the South Korean government. Chung said, too, that he carried out Nichols's orders to transport young Korean airmen to Nichols's private quarters for sexual encounters.

In researching the Korean years of Donald Nichols, U.S. military records and State Department documents were by far the most credible and important primary sources of written information. But the Syngman Rhee Presidential Papers at Yonsei University Library in Seoul also contain important and previously unnoticed documents (presidential appointment entries and a letter from Rhee's wife, which are cited in this book) that confirm the relationship between Nichols and Rhee. It seems likely that Nichols's close involvement with the Korean National Police, the South Korean army, and Rhee generated even more revealing primary source documents that are kept in the archives of the South Korean security forces. These records, though, have not yet been made available to researchers.

NOTES

EPIGRAPHS

v **"Ask yourself: Is there a man":** Donald Nichols, *How Many Times Can I Die?* (Brooksville, FL: Brooksville Printing, 1981), 132.

v **"How long can we defend":** John le Carré, "To Russia, with Greetings: An Open Letter to the Moscow *Literary Gazette*," *Encounter*, May 1966, 3–6.

INTRODUCTION: The Spy Who Came in from the Motor Pool

1 **promoted in India to master sergeant:** Nichols's military service record says he was a master sergeant—a rank typically held by an enlisted man with seventeen years of service—when he left India at the age of twenty-two with less than five years of service (part 2, 4); the USAF released his service record from the National Archives in St. Louis to the author on March 14, 2016, under the Freedom of Information Act (FOIA). Also, an article in the *Post Review*, a base newspaper at the Army Air Corps base in Kearns, Utah, says Nichols became a master sergeant at age nineteen, which made him one of the youngest master sergeants in the army at the time; article quoted in Nichols, 108; also see Nichols, 86–95.

2 **his team of Korean cryptographers:** This is detailed in chapter 5, "Code Break Bully."

2 **called him "magnificent":** These superlatives come from air force general Earle E. Partridge, commander of the Fifth Air Force in the first year of the Korean War: in a signed photograph given to Nichols, date unknown, family collection; Partridge war diaries, vol. 2, April 18, 1951, IRIS 126019, 168.7014, Air Force Historical Research Agency (AFHRA), Montgomery, AL; Partridge

in Air Force Oral History Program, April 25, 1974, IRIS 01019869, 567, AFHRA; Partridge in Nichols, 6; Partridge in "Air Interdiction in World War II, Korea and Vietnam," Office of Air Force History, Washington, DC, 1986, 50.

3 **His officer efficiency reports:** Nichols's military service record, part 3, 1–27.

3 **"only one of his kind":** Ibid, part 3, 21.

3 **Quick tempered and pushy:** Author interviews with retired USAF master sergeant Serbando J. Torres, Baltimore, MD, 2015–16. Torres worked and lived with Nichols for three years before and during the Korean War. Interviews in person in Baltimore and by phone.

3 **up to 260 pounds:** Nichols's weight is mentioned in his 1957 officer efficiency evaluation. Nichols's military service record, part 3, 3.

3 **"No Korean could match":** Author interviews with South Korean air force colonel (ret.) Chung Bong-sun, Seoul, South Korea, November 4–5, 2015.

3 **Unlike the agency's very best:** See Evan Thomas, *The Very Best Men* (New York: Touchstone, 1995), 15–125.

3 **he was astoundingly unschooled:** U.S. Census 1940, Hollywood, Broward County, Florida; roll: T627_577; 1B; enumeration district: 6-36.

3 **"big pay day":** Nichols, 56.

3 **shaving cream up to his:** Author phone interview with Raymond Dean of Craig, OK, October 3, 2014. Dean served as an air force supply sergeant in Korea under Nichols in Detachment 2, 6004th Air Intelligence Service Squadron (AISS), from 1952 to 1953.

4 **wads of it:** Author interviews with Nichols's niece Diana Carlin by phone in Greensboro, NC, and his nephew Donald H. Nichols in Webster, WI. Interviews took place on multiple dates in 2015 and 2016.

4 **cash on a coffee shop:** "25,000 in Sack Leads to Jail," *Los Angeles Times*, January 5, 1967, 3. Details of the fugitive life of Nichols are in chapter 11, "Adrift and Accused."

4 **"an invaluable man":** Colonel Frank E. Merritt, Air Force Oral History Program, December 8, 1977, IRIS 01028635, 17, AFHRA; Partridge, AF oral history interview, 1974, 567; Partridge quoted in "Air Interdiction in World War II, Korea and Vietnam," Office of Air Force History, Washington, DC, 1986, 50.

4 **"performed the impossible":** George E. Stratemeyer, "The Three Wars of Lt. Gen. George E. Stratemeyer," ed. William T. Y'Blood, Air Force and Museum Program, 1999, 197, https://archive.org/stream/TheThreeWars/TheThree Wars_djvu.txt.

4 **"justifiable exception" to military policy:** Stratemeyer cable to USAF HQ, October 1, 1950, in Balchen report note cards, part 1, IRIS 1031199, AFHRA.

5 **called him "Mr. Nichols":** Author phone interview with Ronald F. Cuneo, October 24, 2015. A retired air force corporal, Cuneo lives in Hypoluxo, FL, and served under Nichols in 1953.

5 **more than seven hundred agents:** "History of Detachment No. 2, 6004th AISS," Far East Air Forces (FEAF) History, vol. II, tab 36, November 1953, 53, AFHRA.

5 **agents who parachuted over:** Interview with Brigadier General (ret.) Kim Chong-sup, last commander of South Korean AF Office of Special Investigations, conducted by Christine E. Williamson, USAF Office of Special Investigations historian, Seoul, South Korea, February 28–March 3, 2000, 2. On file at USAF, Office of Special Investigations HQ, Andrews AFB, MD.

5 **"They knew it meant lives":** Nichols, 132.

5 **air force, which Nichols helped:** Details on the role Nichols played in helping to create a separate South Korean air force are in chapter 2, "Rhee and Son."

5 **Nichols gave rice to:** Author interviews with several U.S. and South Korean officers and enlisted men who worked for Nichols during the war.

5 **he threatened those families:** Nichols, 135.

5 **"a pretty body":** Ibid., 133.

6 **fabricated a self-serving story:** Yoon Il-gyun, *Korea-U.S. Joint Espionage Secrets—6006th Unit* (Paju City, South Korea: KSI Publishing Group, 2005), 23–27; also, researcher Yoonjung Seo interviewed Yoon in Seoul, August–November 2015. Medal episode is described in depth in chapter 6, "Any Means Necessary."

6 **he embellished his achievements:** Author interview with Torres, who said Nichols "dreamed up a lot of baloney." These exaggerations are detailed throughout this book, especially in chapter 4, "Dark Star."

6 **"the King of U.S. spies":** Jung Byung-joon, *Clashes on the 38th Parallel and Formation of War,* 6th ed. (Kyoha-eup, Paju City, South Korea: Han Cheol-Hee Publishing, 2014), 658.

6 **Stalinist-style show trial:** This is detailed in chapter 8, "Famous in Pyongyang."

6 **bounty on his head:** Dean E. Hess, *Battle Hymn* (New York: McGraw-Hill, 1956), 139.

6 **suspect was summarily shot:** Author interview with Chung.

6 **dogs joined him for meals:** Nichols's military service record, part 3, 2.

6 **Nichols never disputed:** The 1950 killing of 5,000 to 7,000 South Korean civilians near Taejon is blamed exclusively on North Korean forces in the official American history of the early stages of the Korean War; see Roy Appleman, *United States Army in the Korean War: South to the Naktong, North to the Yalu, June–November 1950* (Washington, DC: Center of Military History, U.S. Army, 1992), 587–88. Historical understanding of the mass killings near Taejon

in 1950 has been complicated because there were two rounds of them. Nichols witnessed the first and by far the largest mass killing in July, when South Korean forces shot several thousand South Korean civilians who had been held as suspected Communists in local jails. The second round of killing occurred in and around Taejon after September, when retreating North Korean forces killed at least 40 American soldiers and several hundred South Korean troops. See chapter 4, "Dark Star," for details on this massacre and Nichols's role.

6 **South Korea refused to investigate:** Charles J. Hanley and Jae-Soon Chang, "Summer of Terror: At Least 100,000 Said Executed by Korean Ally of U.S. in 1950," *Asia-Pacific Journal* 6, issue 7, no. 0 (July 2, 2008), first published by the AP, May 18, 2008; see also AP Web site for documents, photos, and videos, http://hosted.ap.org/specials/interactives/_international/korea_mass killings/index.html?SITE=AP.

7 **"one of history's great men":** Nichols, 113.

7 **"He demonstrated considerable":** Nichols's military service record, part 6, 16–20.

7 **"trying to destroy my memory":** Author interviews with Diana Carlin and Donald H. Nichols.

7 **would have been thrown out:** Nichols's military service record, part 6, 12.

7 **"With Uncle Don":** Author interview with Diana Carlin.

7 **"How did I, an uneducated":** Nichols, 136.

8 **"I was a fifth wheel":** Ibid., 163.

8 **ranks of the "living dead":** Ibid., 132.

8 **"the graveyard of an image":** Ronald Steel, "The Man Who Was the War," *New York Times Book Review*, September 25, 1988.

9 **air force credited Nichols:** Robert Frank Futrell, *The United States Air Force in Korea, 1950–1953* (Washington, DC: U.S. Air Force, 1983), 502.

9 **population of the country:** Nicholas Eberstadt and Judith Banister, *The Population of North Korea* (Berkeley, CA: Institute of East Asian Studies, University of California, 1992), 32. Authors had access to statistics from the North Korean Central Statistics Bureau.

9 **General Curtis E. LeMay:** General Curtis E. LeMay, head of Strategic Air Command during the Korea War, in "Strategic Air Warfare," ed. Richard H. Kohn and Joseph P. Harahan, Office of Air Force History, Washington, DC, 1988, 88, https://www.scribd.com/document/50163700/Strategic-Air-Warfare; http://www.afhso.af.mil/shared/media/afhistory/strategic_air_warfare.pdf.

9 **widely regarded as a war crime:** For details on U.S. Air Force bombing of North Korea, see Blaine Harden, *The Great Dictator and the Fighter Pilot* (New York: Viking, 2015), 6–7, 66–70. Also see Sahr Conway-Lanz, *Collateral Damage: Americans, Noncombatant Immunity, and Atrocity after World War II* (New York: Routledge, 2006), 83–121.

9 **"add sparkle to tedious histories":** Kenneth P. Werrell, *Sabres over MiG Alley* (Annapolis, MD: Naval Institute Press, 2013), 94.

9 **he praised him without qualification:** John Dille, *Substitute for Victory* (New York: Doubleday, 1954), 45.

10 **"better left un-detailed":** Nichols, 111.

10 **"founding fathers" of its covert:** Diane Putney, "Air Force HUMINT 40th Anniversary," U.S. Air Force Special Activities Center booklet, Fort Belvoir, VA, undated.

10 **"In peacetime, you lock":** Author phone interview with Herb Mason at Hurlburt Field, FL, October 21, 2015.

CHAPTER I: Nichols of Korea

15 **ascendancy in Arabia:** Scott Anderson, *Lawrence in Arabia* (New York: Anchor Books, 2013), 3.

15 **"sideshow of a sideshow":** Ibid., 4.

16 **"substitute for World War III":** William Stueck, *The Korean War: An International History* (Princeton, NJ: Princeton University Press, 1995), 3.

17 **"pronounced lack of interest":** Nichols's military personnel record, part 3, 27.

17 **He often ate dinner alone:** Letter to author from William Bierek, February 2, 2016. As a first lieutenant in the air force, Bierek served under Nichols in Korea in 1957.

17 **it is a "natural tendency":** Nichols letter to Partridge, May 27, 1955. From Personal Collection of Earle E. Partridge, January 1, 1954, to January 1, 1959, IRIS 126058, AFHRA.

17 **Nichols rarely read a book:** Author interview with Donald H. Nichols.

17 **"Everyone has a skeleton":** Nichols, 117.

18 **"Have Fun in Japan":** Clay Blair, *The Forgotten War: America in Korea, 1950–1953* (New York: Doubleday, 1987), 28, 989n49.

18 **"gonorrhea, diarrhea, and Korea":** Lieutenant General John R. Hodge, speaking in Korea to newly arrived troops, November 1947, quoted in Paul W. Edwards, *Korean War Almanac* (New York: Facts on File, 2006), 26.

18 **"article of faith":** Ed Evanhoe, *Dark Moon* (Annapolis: Naval Institute Press, 1995), 3.

18 **bathed naked in the kitchen:** Author interviews with Donald H. Nichols and Diana Carlin.

18 **Nichols often spoke disparagingly:** Author interviews with Torres. He recalled several occasions when Nichols said he "hated" women. He said it was because his mother abandoned him and his brothers.

19 **he threatened to kill himself:** Author interviews with Donald H. Nichols and Diana Carlin.

19 **give the place more swank:** *The WPA Guide to Florida: The Federal Writers' Project Guide to 1930s Florida* (New York: Pantheon Books, 1984 repr.), 320.

19 **shoveled chicken manure:** Nichols, 36–38.

19 **his "psychopathic" bingeing:** Ibid., 34.

19 **Donald had nice green eyes:** Author interview with Diana Carlin. Nora Mae Swengel was Carlin's mother. Nora Mae later married Judson Nichols, Donald's older brother.

20 **"I am sorry I had":** Letter from Walter Nichols Sr. to Private Donald Nichols, October 28, 1940, family records.

20 **"tickled to death":** Ibid., October 3, 1940.

20 **"To hell with her now":** Ibid., October 24, 1940.

20 **"My biggest regret in life":** Nichols, 68.

21 **"Our higher brass evidently forgot":** Ibid., 93.

21 **"crates of other items":** Ibid., 95–96.

22 **"Nichols brothers were an explosion":** Author interview with Donald H. Nichols.

22 **repressed confusion about his sexuality:** Author interviews with Nichols's niece, nephews, and U.S. and South Korean air force colleagues give a consistent picture of a man who rarely, if ever, interacted with women outside of his family. In his autobiography, he mentions that he hated and loved his mother all his life.

24 **"an impossible situation":** Douglas MacArthur to George Marshall, September 18, 1945, War Department classified message, Harry S. Truman Presidential Library, http://www.trumanlibrary.org/whistlestop/study_collections /koreanwar/documents/index.php?documentdate=1945-09-18&documentid =kr-6-15&pagenumber=1.

24 **"use your best judgment":** Blair, 39.

25 **"same breed of cats":** The "same breed of cats" statement that damaged Hodge's reputation was taken out of context, according to William R. Langdon, a political adviser in Korea to the State Department. Langdon said that at a press conference in Seoul in 1945 Hodge was narrowly discussing the attitude of the Korean people toward Korean police who served under Japanese colonial rule when he said, "Koreans consider them the same breed of cats as Jap policemen." A visiting group of American correspondents misunderstood the statement as a broad comparison of Koreans to Japanese when they wrote their stories, Langdon said in a cable to Washington. In any case, Hodge's reputation for evenhandedness was permanently damaged in Korea by the stories. Langdon, though, does acknowledge that U.S. commanders were biased—mostly out of ignorance and language issues—toward wealthy landowners when they initially arrived in Korea: "As for favoring plutocracy in, and excluding popular left wingers from Military Government, it is quite

probable that at the beginning we may have picked out a disproportionate number of rich and conservative persons. But how were we to know who was who among this unfamiliar people? For practical purposes we had to hire persons who spoke English, and it so happened that these persons and their friends came largely from moneyed classes because English had been a luxury among Koreans." Langdon, "The Acting Political Adviser in Korea to the Secretary of State," *Foreign Relations of the United States [FRUS]: Diplomatic Papers, 1945, The British Commonwealth, The Far East*, vol. VI, November 26, 1945, d834. https://history.state.gov/historicaldocuments/frus1945v06/d834.

25 **he was a racist:** For the single most authoritative account in English of this often overlooked period of Korean history, see Allan R. Millett, *The War for Korea, 1945–1950: A House Burning* (Lawrence, KS: University of Kansas Press, 2005).

25 **"The American people rejoice":** State Department memorandum for the president, Truman Library, September 14, 1945, 2, https://www.trumanlibrary.org/publicpapers/index.php?pid=144&st=&st1=.

25 **Hodge hustled the Japanese out:** Millett, 59.

25 **"The Koreans themselves have":** MacArthur to Marshall, op. cit.

25 **"older and more educated Koreans":** Ibid., 3.

26 **"declaration of war" on "communistic":** Hodge to MacArthur, *FRUS*, November 25, 1945, d826, https://history.state.gov/historicaldocuments/frus1945v06/d826.

26 **Hodge's orders were:** Millett, 60.

26 **"edge of a political-economic":** Hodge to MacArthur in MacArthur to Joint Chiefs of Staff, *FRUS*, vol. 6, d835, December 16, 1945, https://history.state.gov/historicaldocuments/frus1945v06/d835.

27 **Soviets got off to:** "Political Information: Public Opinion and Discontent in North Korea," *U.S. Central Intelligence Group Report*, September 1947 (declassified January 6, 2001). For more on the emergence of North Korea, see my book *The Great Leader and the Fighter Pilot*, 15–62.

27 **believed he could walk:** Hongkoo Han, "Wounded Nationalism: The Mingsaengdan Incident and Kim Il Sung in Eastern Manchuria" (PhD diss., University of Washington, 1999), 365.

27 **"sun of mankind":** Kim Il Sung, *With the Century* (Pyongyang: Foreign Language Publishing House), 7:lv.

27 **North Koreans have been starved:** See David Hawk, *The Hidden Gulag*, 2nd ed. (Washington, DC: Committee for Human Rights in North Korea, 2012); Harden, *Escape from Camp 14*, updated ed. (New York: Penguin, 2015); Kang Chol-hwan and Pierre Rigoulot, *The Aquariums of Pyongyang* (New York: Basic Books, 2001); and Kim Yong, *Long Road Home* (New York: Columbia University Press, 2009).

28 **Hodge warned his officers:** See Millett for a detailed discussion of this period, 82–90.

28 **police made a bloody hash:** Ibid.

29 **American plot "to colonize Korea":** "Memorandum for the Officer in Charge: Anti-American and Anti-Military Government Activities," Counter Intelligence Corps, Seoul, June 20, 1947, 701–2, RG-331, entry A1 134-A, box 78, CIC Activities, N/S Korea, ZF015133, 701–2, National Archives, College Park, MD (NACP).

29 **"making use of Hirohito's residue":** Ibid., 698.

29 **civilians were reported killed:** *CIC Monthly Information Report,* Korea events, September–October 1946, January 17, 1947, 4, RG-331, entry A1 134-A, box 78, CIC Activities, N/S Korea, NACP.

29 **"fall easy prey to agitators":** Ibid., 3.

29 **Americans fought protesters:** Ibid.

30 **thirty thousand Koreans were imprisoned:** Bruce Cumings, *The Origins of the Korean War* (Princeton, NJ: Princeton University Press, 1981), 1:259–62.

30 **"Russian propaganda program":** Hodge to MacArthur, *FRUS,* vol. 8, d556, October 28, 1946, https://history.state.gov/historicaldocuments/frus1946 v08/d556.

30 **"idea was born":** "History of Detachment No. 2."

30 **"We invented it for":** Nichols, 117.

30 **Nichols did not personally invent:** Korea Headquarters CIC, *Annual Progress Report for 1947,* 1, RG-407, entry 427, WWII Operation Reports, box 14855, NACP.

CHAPTER 2: Rhee and Son

31 **university credentials "evoked awe":** Chong-Sik Lee, *Syngman Rhee: The Prison Years of a Young Radical* (Seoul: Yonsei University Press, 2001), 131.

32 **"His intellect is a shallow one":** Central Intelligence Agency, "Personality of Rhee Syngman," October 28, 1948, 9. The profile is listed as appendix A to CIA, "Prospects for Survival of the Republic of Korea," ORE 44–48, Truman Library, http://www.trumanlibrary.org/whistlestop/study_collections /korea/large/documents/pdfs/kr-8-7.pdf#zoom=100.

32 **"my son Nichols":** Researcher Yoonjung Seo interview with Yoon Il-gyun, former head of South Korea's Central Intelligence Agency and retired ROK Air Force general, in Seoul, November 5, 2015.

32 **"sincere friend of Syngman Rhee":** Nichols, 113.

32 **"President Rhee has recommended Nichols":** Stratemeyer to air force headquarters, op. cit.

32 **"Mr. Nichols' case was unique":** FEAF Intel History, vol. I, July 1948 to June 1950, 720.600, 8, AFHRA. Part of excerpt declassified at author request, October 1, 2015.

33 **"Mr. Nichols had our full trust":** Author interview with Chung.

33 **masterminded the executions:** Kim Dong-choon, "Forgotten War, Forgotten Massacres—the Korean War (1950–53) as Licensed Mass Killings," *Journal of Genocide Research* 6, no. 4 (December 2004): 538, 543n58.

33 **"Kim Chang-ryong was":** Author interview with Kim Dong-choon, professor of social sciences at Sungkonghoe University, Seoul, November 4, 2015. He was a standing commissioner on South Korea's Truth and Reconciliation Commission from 2005 to 2010. Also, Rhee's refusal to delegate power to talented people was criticized by State Department officials. Gregory Henderson, a State Department political officer who served in Seoul at that time, wrote that "Rhee's greatest single fault is his inability to work closely with anyone of ability.... [He has a] life-long and almost pathological suspicion of anyone who he considers as a possible rival to himself." Henderson, "A Memorandum Concerning U.S. Objectives in Korea," November 30, 1950, Cambridge, MA, Department of State, RG 59, 795, 1950–54, NACP.

34 **"Nichols was held in awe":** Author phone interview with Gene Mastrangelo, air force lieutenant colonel (ret.), February 20, 2016.

34 **Rhee personally requested:** Rhee to Muccio, August 26, 1949, Nichols's military service record, part 5, 19.

34 **"draws his information":** John J. Muccio letter to Major General Charles A. Willoughby, head of intelligence in the Far East Command, May 16, 1950, FEAF Intel History, vol. 1, part IV, January–June 1952, K720.600, IRIS 2-6031, AFHRA. Declassified at author request, October 15, 2015.

34 **Rhee was "personally interested":** Colonel W. H. S. Wright letter to assistant chief of staff, Far East Command, May 17, 1950, FEAF Intel History, vol. 1, part IV, January–June 1952, K720.600, IRIS 2-6031, AFHRA. Declassified at author request, October 15, 2015.

34 **he met with Nichols at least five times:** Presidential appointment book of Syngman Rhee for 1951, March 5–6, April 29, May 12, and August 13. File 8, documents 00100022, 00100042, 00100047, 00100090, Syngman Rhee Presidential Papers, Yonsei University Library, Seoul.

35 **"Incredibly, no one in the U.S. government":** Author e-mail exchange with Haas, October 28, 2016.

35 **"It was not a breach":** Nichols, 114.

36 **She did not allow him:** Lee, 4.

36 **"impetuous . . . arrogant, heedless":** Ibid., 42.

37 **"It seems he was never":** Bruce Cumings, *Origins of the Korean War,* 1:190.

37 **"He was a master":** Ibid., 431.

38 **Joint Chiefs of Staff concluded:** Matthew B. Ridgway, *The Korean War* (New York: Doubleday, 1967), 12.

38 **"would in no way constitute":** Dean Acheson, *National Security Council Progress Report on the Implementation of National Security Council Report 8/2*, Truman Library, July 19, 1949, 2, http://www.trumanlibrary.org/whistle stop/study_collections/koreanwar/documents/index.php?documentdate =1949-07-19&documentid=kr-7-6&pagenumber=1.

38 **"Leftist regime in South Korea":** CIA, "The Current Situation in Korea," March 18, 1948, ORE 15-48, 1–7.

39 **As historian Allan R. Millett:** Millett, 143.

39 **Rhee's forces fought back:** Hun Joon Kim, *The Massacres at Mt. Halle: Sixty Years of Truth Seeking in South Korea* (Ithaca, NY: Cornell University Press, 2015), 14–15.

39 **Forces loyal to Rhee:** Ibid.; the number of people killed on Cheju Island is an estimate that some historians, including Millett, dispute. *The War for Korea, 1945–50*, 303n74.

39 **Soldiers shot villagers trying to escape:** Ibid.

39 **"soldiers came to burn down":** Ibid.

40 **Nichols became "especially close":** Muccio to Willoughby, op. cit.

40 **Nichols delivered a truckload:** Yoonjung Seo interview with Kim Bok-dong, Seoul, July 14, 2015.

40 **"As an active, circulating agent":** Nichols, 120.

40 **CIA used waterboarding:** Human Rights Watch, "USA and Torture: A History of Hypocrisy," December 9, 2014, https://www.hrw.org/news/2014 /12/09/usa-and-torture-history-hypocrisy.

40 **"slow drowning and much pain":** Nichols, 120.

41 **"burned repeatedly on their testicles":** Ibid.

41 **head apparently was that of:** See Millett, 204; Sheila Miyoshi Jager, *Brothers at War: The Unending Conflict in Korea* (New York: W. W. Norton, 2013), 53.

41 **"I have seen these things":** Nichols, 121.

41 **"In most cases I did not approve":** Ibid., 120.

42 **"It became a snow-balling":** Ibid., 118.

42 **"Nick went over to see Syngman":** Author interview with Torres.

43 **"may cause Mr. Nichols":** These previously unreleased letters between Rhee and Muccio are in Nichols's military service record, part 5, 19.

43 **greeted each other with hugs:** Author interviews with Torres and Chung Bong-sun.

43 **"unique operation which I":** Nichols, 122.

43 **South Korea "was utterly incapable":** Robert K. Sawyer, *Military Advisors in Korea: KMAG in Peace and War* (Washington, DC: Center of Military History, U.S. Army, 1988), 93–94.

44 **Cho Boo-yi, became a noncommissioned:** Author interview with Torres.

45 **attached to KMAG:** A Far East Air Forces Intelligence history says: "With the withdrawal of the United States Air Force from Korea, Far East Air Forces was threatened with the loss of its most valuable intelligence agent in the Far East, Mr. Donald Nichols. Mr. Nichols' case was unique in that he had served in Korea since May 1946 and, in that time, had developed such friendly personal relations with high-ranking Korean personalities that President Syngman Rhee himself requested that [Nichols] be permitted to remain in Korea. . . . To prevent the loss of this highly qualified agent, FEAF sought to have him attached to the Korean Military Advisory Group. In this, FEAF received the assistance of the American Ambassador to Korea, Mr. John J. Muccio, who exerted his influence to have Mr. Nichols retained in Korea. As a result of Ambassador Muccio's interest [in a letter dated September 12, 1949], General Headquarters Far East Command approved a FEAF request to place seven agents, including Mr. Nichols, on indefinite temporary duty in South Korea and attach them to KMAG for logistic support." FEAF Intel History, vol. I, July 1948–June 1950, 8, AFHRA.

45 **"Kiss My Ass Good-bye":** Millett, 213.

45 **president's advisers also worried:** See Max Hastings, *The Korean War* (New York: Touchstone, 1987), 42–43.

45 **"we will gradually starve":** Rhee letter to Robert T. Oliver, September 30, 1949. Full text in Robert T. Oliver, *Syngman Rhee and the American Involvement in Korea, 1942–1960* (Seoul: Panmun Book Co., 1978), 251–52.

45 **In Moscow, he assured Stalin:** For an account of Kim Il Sung's persistence in courting Stalin and winning his backing for the invasion of South Korea, see my book *The Great Leader and the Fighter Pilot*, 48–60.

46 **churn out reports:** Futrell, "U.S. Air Force Operations in the Korean Conflict: 25 June–1 November 1950," FEAF, July 1, 1952, 101–71, AFHRA. This history says "it was the Nichols' reports which largely formed the basis for estimates made by KMAG, the embassy, and FEAF."

46 **In one special report:** Donald Nichols, "Review of North Korean Air Power and Its Potentialities," *Air Intelligence Report*, February 28, 1950, FEAF Intel History, vol. V, July 1948–June 1950, 120.600, AFHRA.

46 **"civil war in Korea is":** Cable from commanding general, FEAF, Tokyo, to chief of staff, USAF, Washington, DC, February 25, 1950. Reprinted in *Korean Liaison Office—Tactical Liaison Office* (Chuncheon, South Korea: Institute of Asian Culture Studies, Hallym University, 1996), 420–23.

47 **Who the hell is Donald:** These questions are paraphrased versions of issues mentioned in a State Department "Memorandum of Conversation" dated

April 3, 1950. The memo questions the reliability of Nichols's reports from Korea. Found in *Korean Liaison Office—Tactical Liaison Office*, 420.

47 **"action should and will be":** Ibid.

CHAPTER 3: Muzzling Mr. Nichols

48 **"win over by sheer friendship":** Nichols, 117.

48 **"legal-illegal looky-looky":** Ibid.

48 **met with Soviet and North Korean:** Ibid.

49 **surveillance flights over North Korea:** Ibid., 123; medal citations in Nichols's military service record describe similar flights that he made throughout the first year of the war, part 4, 45.

49 **took pictures with a Leica:** Detail about the Leica from Torres; the photos Nichols took of the April 1950 execution are in RG 319, entry (NM-3) 85A, Records of the Army Staff, Office of the Assistant Chief of Staff (G-2), Intelligence, Collections and Dissemination Division, Document Library Branch, Army Intelligence Document File, 1950–55, container 4273A, ID #66337, NACP.

49 **"No newspaper correspondents":** Bob E. Edwards, "Photographs of Communist Execution at Seoul, Korea," April 26, 1950 (fifteen photographs), RG 319 entry (NM-3) 85A, Records of the Army Staff. Office of the Assistant Chief of Staff (G-2), Intelligence, Collections and Dissemination Division, Documents Library Branch. Army Intelligence Documents File, 1950–55, container 4273A, ID #66337, NACP.

50 **"I don't believe they bothered":** Author interview with Torres.

50 **"Mr. Nichols is the most":** Nichols's military service record, part 3, 42–44.

51 **"there will be no":** These cables from Willoughby are quoted in James F. Schnabel, *U.S. Army in the Korean War, Policy and Direction: The First Year* (Washington, DC: U.S. Army Center of Military History, 1992), 62.

51 **"No more baffling":** William Manchester, *American Caesar: Douglas MacArthur, 1880–1964* (Boston: Little, Brown, 1978), 3.

52 **"dream world of self worship":** Stueck, *Rethinking the Korean War* (Princeton, NJ: Princeton University Press, 2004), 113.

52 **chief interpreter of intelligence:** Millett, 98–99. For an extended and withering dissection of Willoughby, see David Halberstam, *The Coldest War* (New York: Hyperion, 2007), 372–77.

52 **called Willoughby "my pet fascist":** Andrew Gordon, *A Modern History of Japan* (New York: Oxford University Press, 2009), 237.

52 **both looked down their noses:** Millett, 99.

52 **colleagues would accuse Willoughby:** Blair, 377; Millett, 98–99.

53 **"lowest possible reliability evaluation":** Matthew M. Aid, "US Humint and Comint in the Korean War: From the Approach of War to the Chinese

Intervention," 38. This paper is chapter 2 of Richard J. Aldrich et al., *The Clandestine Cold War in Asia, 1945–65* (London: Frank Cass, 1999).

53 **"in direct competition":** Ibid., 35.

53 **he barely had enough soldiers:** Blair, 41, 78.

53 **"followed by an invasion":** CIA, *Baptism by Fire: Analysis of the Korean War* (Washington, DC: CIA Center for the Study of Intelligence, 2013), 8.

54 **"discount reports and rumors":** "On the 20th Anniversary of the Korean War: An Informal Memoire by the ORE Korean Desk Officer" (draft manuscript, undated), copy reprinted in *Korean Liaison Office—Tactical Liaison Office*, 384.

54 **policy makers had to focus:** Schnabel, 63.

54 **never rose to that level:** Ibid., 64.

54 **Willoughby also scolded Nichols's:** "History of Detachment 2," 6–7. Quoted in Edward J. Hagerty, *The Air Force Office of Special Investigations 1948–2000* (Washington, DC: Department of the Air Force, 2009), 104, 132n33.

55 **"Mr. Nichols refused to agree":** FEAF Intel History, part IV, July 1948 to June 1950, 82–94; excerpts in Balchen report note cards, part 1, IRIS 1031199, AFHRA.

55 **attached to the Korean:** See endnote on page 219 for explanation of how Nichols came to be attached to KMAG.

55 **burned in 1951:** Letter to Willoughby from Gordon W. Prague, December 11, 1952, 5. MacArthur Archives, RG-23, box 9, folder 4.

55 **ambassador's written response:** Letter to Willoughby from Muccio, May 16, 1950, op. cit. A similar letter from Colonel W. H. S. Wright, chief of staff of KMAG, was written to Willoughby on May 17, 1950. It is at AFHRA in the same file and it also says that Nichols was much too useful to be transferred out of Korea. This letter was declassified at the author's request on October 15, 2015.

57 **He had not been privy:** Partridge, AF oral history interview, April 25, 1974, IRIS 01019869, 572–75, AFHRA.

57 **he met Ambassador Muccio:** Ibid.

57 **"incautious with his own life":** David J. Gurney, "General Earle E. Partridge, USAF: Airpower Leadership in a Limited War" (thesis at School of Advanced Airpower Studies, Air University, Maxwell AFB, AL, June 1998, 72). The biographical details in this section come from Gurney's thesis, which is based on four oral history interviews with Partridge conducted by the air force between 1966 and 1977.

58 **Like Nichols, Partridge had no:** Ibid.

58 **"If the powers say bomb":** Ibid., 62.

58 **"illegal as a three dollar bill":** Partridge, AF oral history interview, 1977, IRIS 1028633, K239.0512-111, 63–64, AFHRA.

59 **"you know zero":** Ibid., 51.

59 **an intercepted message:** Schnabel, 63n9; author interview with Torres, who said he typed this report in the spring of 1950.

59 **"preparing to invade South Korea":** Eighteen of these reports are part of a group of documents in the FEAF Intel History, vol. 5, July 1948 to June 1950, 720.600, AFHRA, that were declassified at the author's request on October 15, 2015.

59 **"Some ass at General MacArthur's":** Nichols, 123.

60 **Nichols exaggerated his accomplishments:** A history that Nichols apparently wrote of his own air force unit "has throughout a distinctly self-aggrandizing tone." Hagerty, 104, 132n33.

60 **he was no better than army:** Peter G. Knight, "MacArthur's Eyes" (PhD diss., Ohio State, 2006), 66.

60 **"it was suppressed by somebody":** Partridge, AF oral history interview, 1974, 567.

60 **indeed a major intelligence failure:** CIA, *Baptism by Fire*, 10.

60 **Truman was embarrassed:** Ibid.

CHAPTER 4: Dark Star

65 **his agitation turned to anger:** Hagerty, 104.

66 **an afternoon round of golf:** Partridge, Korean diary, vol. 1, June–October 1950, 22, IRIS 126018, AFHRA.

66 **"Had I known":** Partridge, AF oral history interview, 1974, 572.

66 **"If Washington only will not":** John Allison, *Ambassador from the Prairie* (Boston: Houghton Mifflin, 1973), 129.

68 **"a grinning nincompoop":** Steven Casey, *Selling the Korean War* (Oxford: Oxford University Press, 2008), 36.

68 **"must be corrected":** Partridge diary, vol. 1, 34–35.

68 **left its personnel files:** Edwards, *Korean War Almanac*, 42.

69 **"legend to the South Korean":** Stratemeyer to USAF headquarters, op. cit.

69 **"start the victorious march":** The president of the Republic of Korea (Rhee) to President Truman, July 19, 1950, *FRUS*, vol. VII, 1950, 429–30, https://history.state.gov/historicaldocuments/frus1950v07/d326.

69 **white sheet tied:** Hagerty, 104.

70 **"units immediately sought safety":** Nichols, 127.

70 **"I was a loner":** Ibid., 126.

70 **Nichols was not a loner:** The Bronze Star citation from the air force says Torres "distinguished himself by meritorious service in the conduct of his duties between the period of 25 June to 1 August 1950 as assistant" to Nichols. It also says that Torres "elected" to stay in an area that was "constantly endangered."

71 **"we better skedaddle":** Author interview with Torres.

71 **"I was the only American":** Nichols, 127.

71 **He was not the only:** Author interview with Torres and with Frank Winslow, a lieutenant in the U.S. Army Signal Corps who was with a KMAG group in Seoul on June 27–28 trying to find a way across the river. Winslow interviewed in Bellingham, WA, April 17, 2016.

72 **Nichols did not get wet:** Torres's version of the river crossing is supported by a letter he wrote on February 26, 1951, to air force headquarters in Tokyo. The letter certifies that Torres was aware that Nichols had lost his CIC identification badge while crossing the Han, apparently during the jostling that occurred while boarding the boat. A copy of the letter was sent to the author by Torres.

72 **B-29s bombed Seoul's railway station:** Futrell, *U.S. Air Force in Korea*, 29.

72 **"most ground information":** Lieutenant Colonel O'Wighton D. Simpson, "Fifth AF Intelligence at Beginning of Korean War," interview, December 1950, K-768.1504A-27, supp. doc. 17, AFHRA.

73 **Nichols had "performed the impossible":** Stratemeyer diary, 197.

73 **Nichols snuck back into Suwon:** Stratemeyer cable, 2; Futrell, *U.S. Air Force in Korea*, 34.

73 **Nichols volunteered to fly:** Nichols's military service record, part 4, 45.

73 **"a highly successful strike":** Ibid., 38.

73 **Soldier's Medal for heroism:** Ibid., 46.

73 **won a Purple Heart:** The Purple Heart was awarded to Nichols on July 31, 1950, by Partridge "for wounds received in action against an enemy on 23 July." The order for the medal is in Nichols's military service record, part 4, 46; the battlefield action is described in a September, 27, 1950, cable that Stratemeyer sent to USAF headquarters in Washington to justify the rapid promotions of Nichols. See Stratemeyer cable, 2, op. cit.

73 **"largely instrumental for the many":** Nichols's military service record, "Award of the Silver Star," citation, part 4, 52.

73 **forces struggled to stop them:** Blair, 172.

74 **"aware of the extreme danger":** Nichols's military service record, "Award of the Silver Star" citation, part 4, 52.

74 **"morale of our troops went up":** Nichols, 129.

74 **attacks with rockets and napalm:** Millett, *The War for Korea, 1950–1951: They Came from the North* (Lawrence, KS: University Press of Kansas, 2010), 230.

75 **"reading documents inside the tank":** Yoon Il-gyun, *Korea-U.S. Joint Espionage Secrets—6006th Unit* (Paju City, South Korea: KSI Publishing, 2005), 15–18.

75 **"performance recognized by decoration":** Nichols's military service record, part 3, 18.

75 **he requested the complete text:** Ibid., part 4, 1.

75 **"cannot ever be sold":** Nichols's will, Hernando County Courthouse, Brooksville, FL, June 30, 1992, 5.

76 **"I saw young Americans turn":** Higgins quoted in Max Hastings, *The Korean War* (New York: Touchstone, 1987), 81.

76 **losing 58,000 men:** Roy E. Appleman, *United States Army in the Korean War: South to the Naktong, North to the Yalu, June–November 1950* (Washington, DC: U.S. Army Center of Military History, 1992), 262–64.

76 **invasion as an excuse:** See reporting by AP journalists Charles J. Hanley and Jae-Soon Chang, "Summer of Terror," July 4, 2008, http://apjjf.org/-Charles-J.-Hanley/2827/article.html. Much of this is detailed at length in reports of the South Korean Truth and Reconciliation Commission.

77 **MacArthur was informed:** "The Political Adviser in Japan (Sebald) to the Secretary of State," Tokyo, December 19, 1950, *FRUS*, 795.00/12, telegram, https://history.state.gov/historicaldocuments/frus1950v07/d1072.

77 **no attempt to alert:** Author interview with Torres, who was working for Nichols as his clerk at the time of the massacre and would have been asked to type up any report about it.

77 **"I witnessed SK forces executing":** Nichols to Torres, January 2, 1969. In this letter, Nichols asked Torres for help in research for his life story and asked him for details about their time together, including Nichols's attendance at the massacre in Taejon.

78 **calling them a "fabrication":** In 1950, the U.S. Embassy in London denounced stories by Alan Winnington, a reporter for the British Communist *Daily Worker* who entered Taejon with North Korean forces. He wrote that the killings occurred over several days, with between 3,000 and 4,000 victims buried in shallow graves. He wrote, too, that witnesses said that U.S. officers in jeeps "supervised the butchery." See Hanley and Chang report for AP reports; also, AP has an online multimedia project about the Taejon massacre at http://hosted.ap.org/specials/interactives/_international/korea_mass killings/index.html?SITE=AP.

78 **"North Koreans had perpetrated":** Appleman, 587.

78 **military officers witnessed the killing:** Lieutenant Colonel Bob E. Edwards, "Execution of Political Prisoners in Korea," Report No. R-189-50, Records of the Army Staff, Office of the Assistant Chief of Staff (G-2) Intelligence, Collections and Dissemination Division, Document Library Branch, Army Intelligence Document Files, 1950–55, RG-319, box 4622, NACP. Also, author interview with Winslow, the army photographer who said that he was invited to watch the Taejon massacre but declined because he said he had seen and photographed a killing in April that Nichols attended and did not want to see another one.

78 **reports from the CIA:** In a memo to Truman, the director of the CIA said South Korean police in Taejon were executing suspected Communists "in an effort to both eliminate a potential 5th column and to take revenge. . . ." Memorandum from CIA director R. H. Hillenkoetter to Truman, July 3, 1950, Truman Library, Papers of Harry S. Truman, president's secretary's files, NLT 78-60, http://www.foia.cia.gov/document/specialcollectionkorean warintelligencememos1948-19501950-07-12pdf. An army intelligence cable titled "Execution of Political Prisoners in Korea" says that the killing of "1800 political prisoners at Taejon, requiring three days" was part of "some rather bloody executions by South Korean Police since the war started." The author of this cable, which included eighteen graphic photographs of bodies in ditches and South Korean shooters, was Lieutenant Colonel Bob E. Edwards, the same U.S. Embassy military attaché who three months earlier had been with Nichols at the killing of thirty-nine prisoners near Seoul. Edwards blamed the Taejon killing and other atrocities that summer on Rhee's government, writing that "orders for the executions undoubtedly came from top level. . . ." Edwards memo on Taejon, op. cit.

78 **they were afraid to talk:** Hanley and Chang, op. cit.

78 **"still alive and squirming":** *2007 Report on Executions*, 237, quoted in Jager, *Brothers at War*, 95, 507n98.

79 **"mercy shot was not administered":** Sergeant Frank Pierce, "Shooting of Prisoners of War by South Korean Military Police," August 11, 1950, NACP, http://www.545thmpassn.com/Korea.htm.

79 **Muccio met with Syngman Rhee:** Muccio to General Walker, August 25, 1950, RG-84, Korea-Seoul Embassy, 1950–56, box 1, NACP.

79 **"I wouldn't have these terrible":** Nichols, 128.

80 **"it didn't seem to bother him":** Author interview with Torres.

CHAPTER 5: Code Break Bully

81 **no longer an acceptable strategy:** See Blair, 34–35, 186–87; Edwin P. Hoyt, *The Pusan Perimeter* (New York: Stein and Day, 1984), 107.

82 **"we will die fighting together":** Appleman, *South to the Naktong*, 208.

82 **"die where you are":** Ibid.

82 **unable to control their fear:** Millett, *They Came from the North*, 224.

82 **"exhausted, dispirited, and bitter":** T. R. Fehrenbach, *This Kind of War* (New York: Macmillan, 1963), 157.

82 **frequent outbreaks of fighting:** Stanley Sandler, ed., *The Korean War: An Encyclopedia* (New York: Garland Publishing, 1995), 325.

83 **cryptographer for Kim Il Sung:** Hop Harriger, "A Historical Study of the Air Force Security Service and Korea: June 1950 to October 1952," U.S. Air Force Security Service, October 2, 1952, 23, 34; author interview with Torres.

83 **had ignored North Korea:** Jill Frahm, "SIGINT and the Pusan Perimeter," National Security Agency, 2000, https://www.nsa.gov/about/cryptologic -heritage/historical-figures-publications/publications/korean-war/sigint-and -pusan-perimeter.shtml.

83 **one self-taught Korean linguist:** Patrick D. Weadon, "SIGNET and COM- SET Help Save the Day at Pusan," National Security Agency, 2000, https:// www.nsa.gov/about/cryptologic-heritage/historical-figures-publications /publications/korean-war/sigint-comsec-save-day.shtml; Thomas R. Johnson, "American Cryptology During the Korean War: Opening the Door a Crack," *Studies in Intelligence* 45, no. 3 (2001).

83 **Americans were helpless:** Johnson.

84 **he made it safely:** Statement from Cho in Harriger, 8–11.

84 **"This I could not refuse":** Ibid., 12.

85 **took Walker out on battlefield:** Partridge diary, July 28 and 31, 1950.

85 **same table with Cho's men:** Harriger, 12.

85 **Murray "didn't have the Korean":** Simpson, op cit.

85 **"Murray's mission became entangled":** Thomas R. Johnson, *American Cryptology During the Cold War, 1945–1989, Book I: The Struggle for Central- ization, 1945–1960* (National Security Agency, 1995), 42. Declassified in 2007.

85 **"a severe jurisdictional battle ensued":** Ibid.

86 **"Lt. Murray is proceeding to Korea":** Harriger, 20.

86 **again ordered Murray out:** Johnson.

86 **"struggle for empire" that Nichols:** Harriger, 23.

87 **"came out with each shovelful":** Appleman, 208.

87 **"time is running out":** "Crisis in Korea," *New York Times*, July 31, 1950.

88 **"straight and hard for Pusan":** Appleman, 247.

88 **In his hurry to invade:** Critique of Kim's war tactics is based on author interviews with Joseph S. Bermudez, chief analytics officer at AllSource Anal- ysis Inc. Using classified and open source information, Bermudez studied North Korea for more than thirty years.

88 **more than fifteen thousand sorties:** Millett, *They Came from the North*, 230.

89 **"no prize for being almost":** Fehrenbach, 187.

89 **"amazing, utterly amazing":** Woolnough's oral history, quoted in Mat- thew Aid, *The Secret Sentry* (New York: Bloomsbury Press, 2009), 8, 325n8.

89 **"secretly dreams about":** Ibid., 27.

89 **severe shortage of Korean:** John Milmore, *#1 Code Break Boy* (West Con- shohocken, PA: Infinity Publishing, 2002), 42; Aid, *The Secret Sentry*, 27.

89 **decoded information that Nichols:** Simpson, op. cit.

90 **"appears to have been":** Johnson, "Opening the Door a Crack: American Cryptology During the Korean War," CIA, 2001, http://www.foia.cia.gov /sites/default/files/document_conversations/44/2001-01-01 pdf.

90 **"his untiring efforts":** Stratemeyer memo to air force headquarters, op. cit.

90 **Nichols received the country's:** The South Korean Order of Military Merit, second class, was awarded to Nichols on August 21, 1951, by Syngman Rhee. In listing reasons for the award, the first was: "He obtained and decoded enemy's communication messages by establishing a communication center and provided information to the UN Forces."

91 **Nichols found forty-eight agents:** Yoonjung Seo interview with Kim Bok-dong, translator for Nichols, Seoul, July 14, 2015.

91 **"One Korean agent had":** Hagerty, 105.

91 **"discard all their clothing":** Ibid.

91 **"Koreans were sent to die":** Author interview with Lee Kang-hwa, Seoul, November 5, 2015.

91 **"probably morally reprehensible":** Robert Burns, "CIA Calls Spying in Korean War 'Reprehensible,'" AP, April 4, 2000.

92 **"I strenuously oppose this move":** See Stratemeyer, 126; Partridge diaries, 68, 78, 81, 111, 114.

CHAPTER 6: Any Means Necessary

93 **Kim Il Sung was confused:** Shen Zhihau, "Sino-North Korean Conflict and Its Resolution During the Korean War," *CWIHP Bulletin*, no. 14/15 (Fall 2003–Spring 2004), 11.

93 **"extremely unfavorable conditions":** Evgeniy P. Bajanov and Natalia Bajanova, "Korean Conflict, 1950–1953: The Most Mysterious War of the 20th Century—Based on Secret Soviet Archives" (unpublished manuscript, CWIHP, Wilson Center, Washington, DC), 77.

94 **"a scarcity of strategic targets":** A. Timothy Warnock, ed., *The USAF in Korea: A Chronology 1950–1953* (Washington, DC: Air Force Historical Research Agency, 2000), 18.

94 **"We came out prepared":** Major General Emmett O'Donnell, "Evaluation of the Effectiveness of the USAF in the Korean Campaign," November 29, 1950, IRIS 00472436, K168.041-1, vol. 6, part 2, AFHRA.

94 **found seventy thousand:** The South Korean Order of Military Merit, second class, was awarded to Nichols on August 21, 1951, by Syngman Rhee. In listing reasons for the award, the second was: "He seized about 70,000 enemy air force related documents including information on air base and supply storage locations so they could be bombed."

94 **tried to intercept Chinese radio:** Larry Tart, *Freedom Through Vigilance: History of U.S. Air Force Security Service* (Conshohocken, PA: Infinity Publishing, 2010), 3:1236.

94 **"such action is not probable":** CIA, *Baptism by Fire*, 13.

95 **The agency told Truman:** Ibid.

95 **"They had created a fantasy":** Hastings, *The Korean War*, 129–30.

96 **"because of MacArthur's personality":** Quoted in Aid, *The Secret Sentry*, 32, 328n31, citing Office of the Secretary of Defense Historical Office, oral history interview with General M. B. Ridgway, April 18, 1984, 20–21, DoD FOIA Reading Room, Pentagon, Washington, DC.

96 **"number-one pain":** Author interview with Sidney Rittenberg, an American who translated for Mao, in Gig Harbor, WA, September 10, 2013.

96 **"extremely childish" military mind:** Shen, 12.

97 **Nichols stole portraits:** Author interview with Torres.

97 **"red, revolving, overstuffed chair":** Dille, 46; theft of Kim Il Sung's chair by Nichols also mentioned in Tart, *Freedom Through Vigilance*, 1236.

97 **Muccio blamed it on Willoughby:** Partridge diary, December 16, 1950.

97 **"all get on the same":** Futrell, "USAF Intelligence in the Korean War," op. cit.

97 **"destroy every means":** Futrell, *U.S. Air Force in Korea*, 221.

97 **"we tried to burn":** Homer Bigart, "Why We Got Licked," *Look*, January 30, 1951.

98 **400 MiG-15s took control:** Robert F. Dorr, Jon Lake, and Warren Thompson, *Korean War Aces* (London: Osprey, 1995), 16.

98 **Pentagon lied about:** For a more detailed account, see my book *The Great Leader and the Fighter Pilot*, 102–3.

99 **avoiding air combat:** Futrell, *U.S. Air Force in Korea*, 289.

99 **nothing like it had existed before:** Nichols's unit was "the first covert collection agency of a tactical nature in the history of the U.S. Air Force," writes Lieutenant Colonel Lawrence V. Schuetta, *Guerrilla Warfare and Airpower in Korea, 1950–53* (Maxwell AFB, AL: Air University, 1964), 77.

100 **explicitly limited his "administrative burden":** *Historical Report for 6004th AISS*, Tokyo, May, June 1951, K-SQ-Intel-6004-#1, 1950–57, 3, AFHRA.

100 **"all hell broke loose":** Evanhoe, 15–16.

100 **"stop all efforts":** Ibid.

101 **"he was a dumb":** "Historical Notes: Giving Them More Hell," *Time*, December 3, 1973, http://content.time.com/time/magazine/article/0,9171,908217,00.html.

101 **"information of inestimable value":** Citation for Nichols for the Distinguished Service Cross, General Order No. 159, FEAF, June 22, 1951.

101 **"coolly and efficiently photographed":** Ibid.

101 **dismantled the MiG:** These details appear in "Operation MiG" in the Fifth Air Force history, January 1, 1951, to June 30, 1951, IRIS 00521685, K730.01 vol. 2, 72, AFHRA; also in "They Snatched a MiG," *American Legion* 67, no. 5 (November 1959): 45. The magazine story gives Nichols a pseudonym, Mike Roberts, and says he is "an old hand at intrigue" and "a shadowy figure."

101 **"I never saw so much":** Nichols, 131.

102 **As Yoon tells the story:** Yoon has given his detailed and consistent account of the April 17, 1950, MiG rescue in three separate forms: an interview with researcher Yoonjung Seo in Seoul on October 29, 2015; in his 2005 memoir, op. cit.; and in *The Korean War Testimonies* (Seoul: Republic of Korea Air Force Headquarters, 2001), 595.

102 **Yoon presented Nichols:** Plaque of appreciation given to Nichols by Yoon in Seoul on April 4, 1987.

102 **changed American assumptions:** "Operation MiG," op. cit.

103 **"a wonderful piece of work":** Partridge diary, April 18, 1951.

103 **"by any means necessary":** Schuetta, 77.

103 **"legal license to murder":** Nichols, 132.

103 **"the Korean political situation":** Partridge diary, April 28, 1951.

103 **"very helpful" adviser and informant:** Francesca Donner (wife of Syngman Rhee) to Robert T. Oliver, May 4, 1951. File 88, document 0090010-12, Syngman Rhee Presidential Papers, Yonsei University Library, Seoul.

104 **"Mr. Nichols hugged and kissed him":** Author interview with Chung.

104 **"took turns giving him":** Author interview with Kim In-ho, Seoul, November 5, 2015.

105 **no "rehabilitation" of homosexuals:** Rhonda Evans, "U.S. Military Policies Concerning Homosexuals," Center for the Study of Sexual Minorities in the Military, University of California, Santa Barbara, 2001.

105 **standards of conduct to be:** Nichols's military service record, part 3, 40.

105 **wear metal braces:** Author interview with Steve Wyatt, owner of the Florida print shop that published Nichols's book, Brooksville, FL, March 23, 2016.

106 **"everyone else had better jump":** Nichols, 130.

106 **"some fool has to do":** Ibid., 135.

106 **shot three agents to death:** Kim Gye-son quoted in Korean-language blog *Guwolsan guerrilla unit comrades*, October 31, 2007, http://blog.daum.net/hidkki55/13160967.

107 **"he shot me out of":** Lee Kun Soon, interviewed on February 12, 1965, in *Korean War Testimonies*, 615.

107 **"audacious yet level-headed":** Nichols's military service record, part 3, 38, 40.

107 **Only the general was responsible:** Fifth Air Force, "Special Activities," periodic history, January 1, 1951, to June 30, 1951, IRIS 00521685, K730.01, vol. 2, 51, AFHRA.

107 **"He didn't care for human rights":** Lee Kun Soon, op. cit.

108 **a flight over the Han:** Sariego served as an airman second class in 1952, according to "History of Detachment No. 2." The information about the flight that dropped a North Korean colonel over the Han River comes from an e-mail Sariego sent to the author on November 25, 2014.

108 **"let the enemy do it":** Nichols, 135.

108 **"if there were any regulations":** Partridge to Nichols, April 26, 1955, Partridge personal correspondence, January 1, 1954, to January 1, 1959, IRIS 12608, 168.7014-4, vol. 6, AFHRA.

CHAPTER 7: Empire of Islands

109 **"no enemy can take":** Partridge diary, May 19, 1951.

110 **just him and three air force:** Author interview with Torres.

110 **"an organization of tremendous":** "History of Detachment No. 2," 53.

111 **he laughed and sometimes:** Author interview with Chung.

112 **an ambitious mission:** Details about the June 1, 1951, mission are in a letter from Nichols to the Fifth Air Force deputy for intelligence, June 2, 1951. Letter is exhibit 11 in "History of Detachment No. 2."

112 **"they were to steal":** Ibid., 5–22.

112 **ship high off the mudflat:** Ibid., 5.

113 **"I can contribute much more":** Nichols's letters to FEAF headquarters requesting "additional overseas extension," dated only as 1950, in Nichols's military service record, part 5, 23.

114 **promoting him to major:** The promotion was by Special Order #308, Far East Air Forces, December, 3, 1951, in Nichols's military service record, part 5, 1.

114 **"the tremendous opportunities":** "History of Detachment No. 2," 24.

114 **"infiltration and exfiltration":** Ibid.

114 **One North Korean whom Nichols:** Author interview with Kim Ji-eok, Seoul, November 3, 2015. Kim was eighty-two at the time.

114 **destroyed 75 percent of Pyongyang:** Air Force 548th Reconnaissance Technical Squadron, "Bomb Damage Assessment of Major North Korean Cities," appendix B, tab 1, K720.323A, AFHRA.

118 **"effectiveness as a stopping weapon":** Quoted in Robert M. Neer, *Napalm: An American Biography* (Cambridge, MA: Belknap Press of Harvard University Press, 2013), 103.

118 **"lasting burning effect":** Nichols, "Enemy Locomotive Repair Shop Located near Ssangga, North Korea," November 30, 1952, AF510886, RG 341, entry (NM15) 268, Records of Headquarters U.S. Air Force (Air Staff), Office of the Deputy Director for Intelligence and Collection and Dissemination, Dissemination Control Division, Documents Branch, Air Intelligence Report Files, box 1381, NACP.

118 **"heartily endorsed napalm":** Air Force Research Studies Institute, "Communist Military Casualties Inflicted by Airpower in Korea," June 26, 1950, to July 27, 1953, IRIS 00468000, K110.7034-3, AFHRA.

118 **"first choice weapon":** Ibid.

118 **napalm was its "primary weapon":** Balchen files, part 1, unsorted note cards, IRIS 1031199, AFHRA.

118 **"goal of burning the city":** Cumings, *Origins of the Korean War*, 2:753.

118 **twice as much napalm:** Neer, 99.

119 **nearly every man-made structure:** See an extended discussion of the bombing and its morality in Conway-Lanz, *Collateral Damage*, 83–121.

119 **"we have been attacking":** Partridge diary, December 16, 1950.

119 **"you know you've accomplished":** Conrad C. Crane, *American Airpower Strategy in Korea, 1950–1953* (Lawrence, KS: University Press of Kansas), 65.

120 **"Fifth Air Force's preference":** "Communist Military Casualties Inflicted by Airpower in Korea," op. cit., 3.

120 **"effects of air power":** Colonel Jean H. Daugherty to Nichols, mission letter, November 12, 1952, "History of Detachment No. 2," exhibit 14.

120 **told to travel to their:** Author interview with Kim Ji-eok.

120 **acceptable loss rate:** Daugherty to Nichols, op. cit., 5.

121 **"one of the crewmen":** This account is included in Nichols's biography as a separate chapter written by George T. Gregory in 1969. Nichols, 146–61.

121 **"increasing flow of reports":** "History of Detachment No. 2," 43.

121 **"most important single collector":** Futrell, *United States Air Force in Korea*, 502.

121 **hand-grenade factories:** The target list comes from dozens of air intelligence reports signed by Nichols. Air Intelligence Reports, April 17, 1951, to December 23, 1952, AF305754 to AF510886, RG 341, entry (NM-15) 268, Records of Headquarters U.S. Air Force (Air Staff), Office of the Deputy Director for Intelligence and Collection and Dissemination, Dissemination Control Division, Documents Branch, Air Intelligence Report Files, boxes 664–1381, NACP.

121 **aircraft repair shop disguised:** Air Intelligence Information Report, "Pyongyang Downtown Airfield and Nearby Installations," Detachment No. 2, 6004th AISS, September 28, 1951, AF371112, AFHRA.

121 **"proper maps and annotated photos":** "History of Detachment No. 2," 59–60.

122 **agents were apparently still:** Futrell, *United States Air Force in Korea*, 670.

122 **destroyed more of North Korea:** Ibid., 688

122 **"to get airpower off":** Ibid.

122 **bombing failed to stop:** Crane, 178.

123 **"our planes couldn't strafe":** Nichols, 139.

123 **ordered him to remove:** "History of Detachment No. 2," 65.

CHAPTER 8: Famous in Pyongyang

124 **"He was always paranoid":** Author interview with Donald H. Nichols.

124 **his name was on:** Author interview with Torres.

124 **from $7.50 to $200,000:** The first estimate is from Dean E. Hess, *Battle Hymn* (New York: McGraw-Hill, 1956), 139. The second is from Nichols in Mike Copeland, "Retired Air Force Colonel Gets a Hero's Welcome on Korean Trip," *St. Petersburg* (FL) *Times*, July 10, 1987, Hernando section, 1.

124 **three attempts were made:** Nichols, 122; Yoon, 48; author interview with Chung Bong-sun.

124 **official party newspaper:** *Rodong Sinmun*, August 7, 1953, 2.

125 **infiltrated agents into high positions:** Robert Scalapino and Chong-Sik Lee, *Communism in Korea* (Berkeley, CA: University of California Press, 1972), 1:442–43.

125 **"How great is Comrade Kim":** Baik Bong, *Kim Il Sung Biography* (Tokyo: Maraisha, 1969), 2:393.

126 **"I am a running dog":** Quoted in Kim Nam-sik, *Namnodang jongu* (Seoul: Tol Pegae, 1984), 504.

126 **"I will accept with gratitude":** Quoted in Andre Lankov, *From Stalin to Kim Il Sung* (New Brunswick, NJ: Rutgers University Press, 2002), 97.

126 **the testimony was wildly implausible:** Lankov, 92–100; Dae-Sook Suh, *Kim Il Sung: The North Korean Leader* (New York: Columbia University Press, 1988), 130–35.

126 **"is hardly convincing":** Dae-Sook Suh, 132.

127 **three thousand American dollars:** *Rodong Sinmun*, August 7, 1953, 2.

127 **"broke up numerous commy cells":** Nichols, 119.

128 **"impossible to separate truth":** Scalapino, 446.

128 **"Such devotion to duty":** Nichols's military service record, officer performance evaluation for May 1, 1953, to December 8, 1953, part 3, 24.

128 **"keep those secrets to myself":** Nichols, 197.

128 **No government records:** In Seoul, researcher Yoonjung Seo made repeated attempts to locate any South Korean records of Nichols's marriage, the birth of Donald Nichols II, and the death of Kim In-hwa. If the records ever existed, they are now unavailable because of privacy laws. They may have been destroyed during war or discarded later as part of bureaucratic housekeeping.

129 **told the same thing:** Nichols's military service record, part 6, 18.

129 **hinted that he was the boy's father:** Author interview with Diana Carlin.

129 **"3 adopted Korean children":** Nichols to Torres, January 2, 1969.

130 **his bride was nineteen:** Nichols, 196.

130 **war was then:** These details about the day come from Edwards, *Korean War Almanac*, 159–60.

130 **he had "never been married":** Nichols's military service record, op. cit.

130 **he did not mention:** In a letter Nichols sent to Torres in 1969, he wrote, "I'm still single." Nichols to Torres, January 2, 1969.

131 **moved his spy base:** "History of Detachment No. 2," 56.

131 **It had a parade ground:** Description of base layout from February 2, 2016, letter to author from William V. Bierek, who served there in 1953 as a first lieutenant.

132 **The pilot from North Korea:** This section is based on scores of author interviews with No Kum Sok—now known as Kenneth Rowe—between 2012 and 2016. No's story is told in my book *The Great Leader and the Fighter Pilot*.

136 **the first report about No's:** Nichols, Air Intelligence Information Report, Ro [*sic*] Kum Sok, North Korean People's Army Air Force, September 24, 1953, 6. USAF Intelligence Reports, 1942–64, AF 59786-597495, box 1793, 631/52/54/5; AF 592236, box 1758, 631/52/53/6, NACP.

136 **won commendations for Nichols:** "Semiannual History of 6002th Air Intelligence Service Group," July–December 1953, 130, K-GP-Intel-6002-HI, AFHRA.

137 **"You can't cooperate with smallpox":** Stephen Jin-Woo Kim, *Master of Manipulation: Syngman Rhee and the Seoul-Washington Alliance, 1953–1960* (Seoul: Yonsei University Press, 2001), 65.

137 **would view him as weak:** Ibid., 127.

137 **"Why are you murdering":** Ibid., 92.

138 **"biggest trouble came from Rhee":** Chang-jin Park, "The Influence of Small States upon the Superpowers," *World Politics* 28, no 1 (October 1975): 97.

138 **high price in "blood and suffering":** Jin-Woo Kim, 101.

138 **"too horrible to contemplate":** Minutes of discussion at White House with Korean delegation, Hagerty diary, July 27, 1954, *FRUS*, 1952–54, vol. 15, part 2, 1845, https://history.state.gov/historicaldocuments/frus1952-54v15p2/d923.

138 **"the stubborn old fellow":** Ibid., 1839.

139 **singled out Nichols:** "A Report on the Present Status of Foreign Intelligence Units and Guerrilla Forces in Korea," January 27, 1954. File 247, document 00759109-00750121, Syngman Rhee Presidential Papers, Yonsei University, Seoul.

CHAPTER 9: Sacked

143 **Nichols wrote him and asked:** Nichols to Partridge, February 23, 1954, personal correspondence of Partridge, IRIS 126058, 168.7014-4, vol. 6, AFHRA.

143 **"Although Nichols has been":** Partridge to O'Donnell, February 26, 1954.

144 **often did, according to:** Nichols's military service record, part 3, 2–3.

NOTES

144 **"the utmost confidence"**: Partridge to Nichols, April 26, 1955.

144 **created a ragged peace:** On July 25, 1954, Chinese fighters attacked two U.S. Navy fighters; on February 4, 1955, eight U.S. Sabre jets engaged twelve MiG-15s over the Yellow Sea, with one MiG shot down. *Korean War Almanac*, 428.

144 **killing three American pilots:** Ibid.

144 **"continuing effort shall be exerted":** "History of Detachment No. 2," 70.

145 **Squadron was in better shape:** "History of 6002 AISS," 173.

145 **"for the purpose of expediting":** Ibid., 170.

145 **"Major Nichols should be promoted":** Nichols's military service record, part 3, 15.

146 **"He is an invaluable man":** Ibid.

146 **"involving command of USAF personnel":** Ibid., part 3, 4.

146 **"minimum action considered appropriate":** Ibid., part 3, 2.

147 **"allowed himself to gain weight":** Ibid., part 3, 2–3.

147 **"no loyalty to Major Nichols":** Ibid., part 3, 4.

148 **"never ask a Korean":** Haas, 64.

148 **"He was strict about parties":** Author phone interview with Cuneo.

148 **"He knew every one of us":** Author phone interview with Dean.

149 **"a consistently splendid 'individual' job":** Nichols's military service record, part 3, 2.

149 **"relief of Major Nichols":** Ibid.

149 **Nichols "challenged" the authority:** Ibid., part 3, 3.

150 **have been destroyed:** The reports would have been destroyed as part of routine procedures after Nichols was discharged from the air force, according to Dick Law, a retired colonel who served for thirty years in the air force Office of Special Investigations.

150 **"revealed numerous instances":** Letter from Captain Hays Bricka to Commander, Continental Air Command, Mitchel AFB, NY, December 8, 1958. Nichols's military service record, part 6, 12.

150 **"all I could see was cash":** Author interview with Chung.

150 **"he was my best customer":** Author interview with Winslow.

151 **he suspected Nichols was involved:** Author interview with Haas.

152 **"Uncle Don had big bags":** Author interview with Donald H. Nichols.

152 **"air force regulation 36-2":** Bricka letter, op. cit.

153 **"People thought he was":** Author phone interviews with and letter to author from Bierek, a retired lawyer who lives in Hillsboro, OR, January–March, 2016.

153 **"startling decline in President Rhee's":** National Security Council meeting, June 7, 1956, box 7 NSC Series, Papers as President, Dwight D. Eisenhower Presidential Library, Ann Whitman file, 2.

153 **"somewhat sterile policies":** "Situation and Short-Term Prospects of the Republic of Korea," dispatch from American embassy in Seoul to State Department, November 21, 1957.

153 **"an extremely precarious base":** Donald Stone MacDonald, *U.S.-Korean Relations from Liberation to Self-Reliance* (Boulder, CO: Westview Press, 1992), 192.

154 **"creates increasing danger":** Ibid., 168.

154 **He maintained his special access:** Nichols's military service record, part 3, 15.

154 **made an honorary colonel:** Nichols's family copy of Rhee's March 24, 1954, letter making Major Nichols an honorary colonel in the South Korean air force.

154 **a second Order of Military:** "History of 6002nd Air Intelligence Service Group," January–June 1955, 171, K-GP-Intel-6002-HI, AFHRA.

154 **Nichols stayed "very close":** Author interview with Chung Bong-sun. Chung said Nichols met nearly every week with Kim Chang-ryong until Kim was assassinated by his own men.

154 **Nichols entertained Kim frequently:** Ibid.

154 **Kim ran the country's:** Fred Charles Thomas Jr., U.S. diplomat stationed at the American embassy in Seoul in the 1950s, Foreign Affairs Oral History Project, March 8, 1995, 67. Library of Congress, http://www.loc.gov/item/mfdipbib001171.

154 **"attempted assassination of President Rhee":** Donald Nichols, "Concerning the Attempted Assassination of Rhee," *Air Intelligence Report*, October 19, 1955, AF703568, RG 342, box 1102, NACP.

155 **"further disillusion popular hopes":** "The Arrest of Cho Bong-am," memorandum from Parsons to Jones, Washington, DC, February 3, 1958, *FRUS*, Korea, 1958–60, vol. XVII, 444, https://history.state.gov/historicaldocuments/frus1958-60v18/pg_433.

155 **"unofficially bring serious concern":** Editorial note 226, *FRUS*, Korea, 1958–60, vol. XVIII, https://history.state.gov/historicaldocuments/frus1958-60v18/pg_461.

155 **execution was called:** "Cho Bong-am Unjustly Executed: Supreme Court," *JoongAng Daily*, January 21, 2011; "Cho Bang-am's Name Cleared 52 Years After His Execution," *Kyunghyang Shinmun*, January 21, 2011.

155 **Things were "disintegrating":** "Memorandum of Conversation," Dugald Malcolm, British chargé d'affaires, and T. Eliot Neil, deputy chief of mission, U.S. Embassy, Seoul, January 5, 1957, RG 59, 795B.00/7-257, NACP.

155 **"ticking time bomb Nichols was":** Author phone and e-mail interviews with Haas, August 2, 2016. Haas's books and document research were commissioned by the air force.

CHAPTER 10: Shocked

157 **"corrective influences concerning myself"**: Nichols's military service record, part 3, 9.

158 **spy outfit known as NICK:** "History of 6002nd Air Intelligence Service Group," July 1–December 31, 1957, K-GP-Intell-6002-HI, 12-180, AFHRA.

158 **ate alone in his quarters:** Letter to author from Bierek, February 2, 2016.

158 **"spirited off the base":** Author phone interview with Bierek, January 4, 2016.

158 **"unusual behavior while on duty":** Nichols's military record, part 6, 17.

159 **pounding his fist:** Clinical and descriptive details comes from Nichols's military record, part 6, 16–20.

160 **he was seething:** Ibid.

160 **asked his former boss:** The letter was not found but its content can be inferred from the response it elicited from Partridge.

160 **"Please let me know":** Partridge to Nichols, October 28, 1957, Partridge personal correspondence, op. cit.

161 **he was "quite evasive":** Nichols's military service record, part 6, 19.

161 **"intelligence is probably":** Ibid.

161 **"I am now in a spot":** Nichols to Partridge. This letter is undated but appears to have been sent soon after Nichols arrived at Eglin AFB hospital in late October or early November 1957. It acknowledges receipt of Partridge's letter of October 28. Partridge personal correspondence, op. cit.

162 **A normal dosage:** Author phone interview with Dr. Max Fink, a psychiatrist and expert on electroshock therapy and psychoactive drugs who treated military patients in the 1950s, August 1, 2016, St. James, NY.

162 **rebooting a computer:** Katherine Q. Seelye, "Kitty Dukakis, a Beneficiary of Electroshock Therapy, Emerges as Evangelist," *New York Times*, December 31, 2016, http://www.nytimes.com/2016/12/31/us/kitty-dukakis-electroshock -therapy-evangelist.html.

163 **electroshock treatments to nearly:** Alan A. Stone, "Electroconvulsive Rx: A Memoir and Essay (Part 1)," *Psychiatric Times*, September 14, 2010.

163 **"ECT stands practically alone":** Sandra G. Boodman, "Shock Therapy: It's Back," *Washington Post*, September 24, 1996.

165 **brain regions associated with mood:** Owes Tirmizi, "Electroconvulsive Therapy: How Modern Techniques Improve Patient Outcomes," *Current Psychiatry* 11, no. 10 (October 1, 2012).

165 **"his treatment was about right":** Author phone interview with Edward Shorter, Toronto, August 1, 2016.

166 **"bastard orphan of the intelligence":** Nichols, 144–45.

167 **positive responses in about:** American Psychiatric Association, "What Is ECT," https://www.psychiatry.org/patients-families/ect.

167 **"much more at ease":** Nichols's military service record, part 6, 20.

167 **"serious doubts as to":** Partridge letter quoted in hospital records at Eglin, Nichols's military service record, part 6, 20.

169 **"God alone knows":** Nichols, 163.

CHAPTER II: Adrift and Accused

170 **He had always worried:** Author interview with Diana Carlin.

171 **"he loved to show it off":** Author interview with Donald H. Nichols.

171 **rides that were often disturbing:** These accounts come from author interviews with Donald H. Nichols and Diana Carlin; phone interview with nephew Paul W. Nichols, Tellico Plains, TN, November 17, 2015.

172 **"fun for kids":** Author interview with Donald H. Nichols.

172 **"prepared for the exit of my sons":** Nichols, 185.

173 **After several bumpy weeks:** Author interviews with Donald H. Nichols, Diana Carlin, and Paul W. Nichols.

173 **"a damn about anyone":** Nichols, 165.

173 **"howl my melancholy song":** Ibid., 166, 168.

175 **"started showing me these":** Deposition given by a boy on May 10, 1968, in Fort Lauderdale, related to a felony charge against Nichols for indecent assault on a child. Case no. 66-7298, Broward County Courthouse, Fort Lauderdale, FL. Name is not included for privacy reasons.

175 **"what was going on":** Deposition given by the father of the boy on May 7, 1968. Name is not included for privacy reasons.

175 **"indecent assault upon a child":** "Man Charged with Assault," *Fort Lauderdale Sun-Sentinel*, May 7, 1966, B1.

175 **described himself only as "retired":** Broward County Sheriff's Department arrest record, 66-12245, May 6, 1966.

175 **weight had ballooned:** Ibid.

175 **he sold four parcels:** Warranty deeds, 66-88618, 19, 20, Broward County property records, Fort Lauderdale, FL, August 1, 1966.

176 **rape of a fifteen-year-old:** Warrant, *State of Florida v. Donald Nichols*, August 4, 1966, IC no. 67-8-4665, docket no. 3, 4519.

176 **"I felt healing in myself":** Nichols, 169.

176 **"deserted their brother":** Nichols's will, op. cit., 5.

177 **"wasn't doing too good":** Nichols, 169.

177 **permanently soured when he fled:** Nichols's will, op. cit.

177 **he never again wanted:** Author interview with Diana Carlin.

177 **"Memories are more than enough":** Nichols's will, op. cit.

177 **on the counter of Colleen's:** "$25,000 in Sack Leads to Jail," *Los Angeles Times*, January 5, 1967.

177 **warrants for statutory rape:** AP, "Lot of Loose Cash Brings Arrest of Floridian," *Panama City* (FL) *News Herald*, January 5, 1967, 5.

178 **cashier's check for fifteen thousand:** "Man Who Left $25,000 in Cafe Faces Charge," *San Diego Union*, January 6, 1967, D4.

178 **wire services picked up:** UPI, "Broward Fugitive Held in California," *Miami Herald*, January 6, 1967, A22.

178 **posted cash bail:** *San Diego Union*, op. cit.

178 **apparently forfeiting his bail:** San Diego County Sheriff's Department said records of the arrest have been destroyed.

178 **Judson told the agents:** In response to a Freedom of Information inquiry about the FBI's effort to find Nichols, the bureau said that "records that may have been responsive to your request were destroyed on Nov. 1, 1992, and August 1976."

178 **if Judson came down:** Judson Nichols died in 1981. This account comes from his children Diana and Donald H.

179 **legendary South Florida defense attorney:** Jacqueline Charles and Carli Teproff, "South Florida Defense Attorney Irwin Block, Who Helped Get Innocent Pitts and Lee off Death Row, Dies at 87," *Miami Herald*, February 15, 2015.

179 **his relentless pretrial preparation:** Tributes to Block, who died in 2015 at age eighty-seven, said he won cases "because of the damage he had done in depositions and pretrial motions." See Florida court of appeals judge Kevin Emas in a tribute to Block in *Justice Building Blog*, http://justicebuilding .blogspot.com/2015/02/irwin-block-has-died.html.

179 **Nichols surrendered at:** Broward County Sheriff's Department arrest record, 67-8-4665, December 8, 1967.

179 **weighed 325 pounds:** The weight is on his arrest record.

180 **blamed another man for assaulting:** Author interview with Diana Carlin. There are no court records on this charge other than the initial arrest warrant from August 4, 1966.

180 **a jury found Nichols:** *State of Florida v. Donald Nichols*, felony order of acquittal, Broward County, May 16, 1968, case no. 66-7298. There is no transcript of the trial in county records.

180 **No one in Judson Nichols's family:** Author interviews with Diana Carlin and Donald H. Nichols. I told them in 2016 about sealed depositions I had been allowed to open in Broward County court archives.

180 **left Mexico due to:** Nichols, 180.

181 **"Behind those baby green eyes":** Ibid., 181.

CHAPTER 12: Nolo Contendere

182 **the nation's highest lynching rate:** Dan DeWitt, "Hernando's 100-Year-Old Courthouse Part of Long, Slow Journey to Justice," *Tampa Bay Times*, October 3, 2013, http://www.tampabay.com/news/courts/hernandos-100-year-old-courthouse-part-of-long-slow-journey-to-justice/2145517.

183 **"the most amazing and unusual":** Partridge to Nichols, sent from Colorado Springs, CO, October 30, 1968. Letter was reprinted verbatim as the foreword to Nichols's book. Copy of letter from Torres.

183 **"he finally went crazy":** Partridge, AF oral history interview, April 25, 1974.

183 **"fell apart mentally":** Partridge, AF oral history interview, 1977, 63–64.

183 **"I expect a lot":** Nichols to Torres, January 2, 1969.

184 **"The Unknown Lawrence of Korea":** Nichols, 146–61.

184 **"'Put out your damn cigarette'":** Author interview with Steve Wyatt, Brooksville, FL, 2015–16.

184 **bought a chicken farm:** *Sun Bank and Trust Co. v. Jones*, Fifth District Court of Appeal of Florida, no. 93-1861, December 14, 1994, http://bit.ly/2ctnOeO.

185 **gave him power of attorney:** "Durable Power of Attorney," Hernando County, FL, clerk's office, no. 82-13682, November 20, 1981.

185 **"eating my watermelons":** Author phone interview with J. O. Batten, commander of VFW Post 8713, Brooksville, FL, September 26, 2016.

185 **not getting the respect:** Author phone interview and e-mails with Edward C. Mishler, Sanford, NC, January 19, 2016.

186 **"I would not welcome her":** Nichols, 12.

186 **"documentation was necessarily abbreviated":** Ibid., 191.

186 **aroused international attention:** See articles, cited above, by AP journalists Charles J. Hanley and Jae-Soon Chang, and AP Web site project.

186 **"The years in Brooksville":** Nichols, 180.

186 **Donnie was thrown:** Karen Datko, "Father of 2 Killed by Propeller of Airboat," *St. Petersburg Times*, June 25, 1985, Hernando section, B1.

187 **"The light went out":** Author interview with Nichols's granddaughter, Lindsay Morgan, in Brooksville, FL, January 31, 2016.

187 **"or given away to anyone":** Nichols's will, 4.

188 **"MR. NICHOLS, HERO OF KOREAN WAR":** Coverage of Nichols's visit to Seoul appeared over two weeks in March 1987 in a number of South Korean media outlets. The detail about the bed comes from Yoon Il-gyun, who worked with Nichols in the 1950s and welcomed him back to Seoul. He was interviewed on October 29, 2015, by researcher Yoonjung Seo.

188 **a flattering article:** Mike Copeland, "Retired Air Force Officer Gets a Hero's Welcome on Korean Trip," *St. Petersburg Times*, July 10, 1987, Hernando section, 1.

188 **the biggest splash:** The newspaper is now called the *Tampa Times* and is the largest daily in Florida.

188 **threatened to hurt them:** David Cox, "Lewd Act Charged Against Decorated Vet," *Daily Sun-Journal*, Brooksville, FL, July 28, 1978, 1; Alicia Caldwell, "Retired Officer Faces Lewd Behavior Charges," *St. Petersburg Times*, July 28, 1987, Hernando section, 1.

188 **"There had been talk":** Author interview with Batten.

189 **"in fear of their lives":** *Daily Sun-Journal*, op. cit.

189 **"I was teaching him something":** Caldwell, "Retired Officer Tells About Sex Incident," *St. Petersburg Times*, July 30, 1987, Hernando section, 1.

189 **It banned him from any contact:** Caldwell, "Sentence Imposed in Case of Fondling," *St. Petersburg Times*, December 24, 1987, Hernando section, 1.

190 **Nichols was arrested:** Caldwell, "Sex Offender Arrested Again," *St. Petersburg Times*, May 31, 1988, Hernando section, 1.

191 **he must be locked up:** These details are in the judgment of *Sun Bank and Trust Co. v. Jones*, op. cit. John G. Jones was Nichols's guardian.

191 **he was pronounced dead:** Ibid.

EPILOGUE: A Spy's Grave

192 **"a funeral to which":** Neil Sheehan, *A Bright Shining Lie* (New York: Random House, 1988), 3, 4.

194 **"source of information":** Nichols, 119–20.

194 **"a great Democrat":** Ibid., 113.

195 **"received absolutely no training":** Ibid., 136.

195 **"I was a small cog":** Ibid., 132.

196 **enough space for six coffins:** Brooksville Cemetery records, shared by Mike Hughes, cemetery administrator, in phone interview, e-mails, and copied documents during 2015–16.

196 **where he served as chairman:** Caldwell, *St. Petersburg Times*, July 28, 1987, op. cit.

196 **Veterans Administration paperwork:** Nichols's military service record, part 6, 1.

197 **photo appears on the final:** Nichols, 199.

197 **an affront to Confucian values:** Douglas J. Davies and Lewis H. Mates, *Encyclopedia of Cremation* (Aldershot, England: Ashgate, 2005).

197 **his body transported:** Walter I. Nichols's death certificate, Bureau of Vital Statistics, Florida, issued to author on October 11, 2016. Walter died on

November 27, 1940, at the age of fifty-three. A family photograph shows Walter's name, along with the dates of his birth and death, on a large Nichols headstone in Maple Grove Cemetery in Hackensack, NJ.

197 **cremated in nearby Delray Beach:** Myra Wolf's death certificate, Bureau of Vital Statistics, Florida, issued to author on October 11, 2016. Myra died on May 29, 1978, at the age of eighty-seven.

197 **"How does one de-train":** Nichols, 132.

BIBLIOGRAPHY

Aid, Matthew M. *The Secret Sentry: The Untold History of the National Security Agency.* New York: Bloomsbury Press, 2009.

Aldrich, Richard J. *The Hidden Hand: Britain, America and Cold War Secret Intelligence.* London: John Murray, 2001.

Anderson, Scott. *Lawrence in Arabia: War, Deceit, Imperial Folly and the Making of the Modern Middle East.* New York: Anchor Books, 2013.

Appleman, Roy E. *South to the Naktong, North to the Yalu: U.S. Army in the Korean War, June–November 1950.* Washington, DC: Office of the Chief of Military History, Department of the Army, 1961.

Baik Bong. *Kim Il Sung: Biography. Vols. I–II.* Tokyo: Miraisha, 1969.

Bajanov, Evgeniy P., and Natalia Bajanova. "The Korean Conflict, 1950–1953: The Most Mysterious War of the 20th Century—Based on Secret Soviet Archives." Unpublished, undated manuscript, Cold War International History Project, Wilson Center, Washington, DC.

Blair, Clay. *The Forgotten War.* New York: Doubleday, 1987.

Breuer, William B. *Shadow Warriors: The Covert War in Korea.* New York: John Wiley & Sons, 1996.

Casey, Steven. *Selling the Korean War: Propaganda, Politics, and Public Opinion in the U.S., 1950–1953.* Oxford: Oxford University Press, 2008.

Central Intelligence Agency. *Baptism by Fire, CIA Analysis of the Korean War: A Collection of Previously Released and Recently Declassified Intelligence Documents.* Washington, DC: CIA Center for the Study of Intelligence, 2014.

Clark, Donald N. *Living Dangerously in Korea: The Western Experience, 1900–1950*. Norwalk, CT: EastBridge, 2003.

Clark, Mark W. *From the Danube to the Yalu*. New York: Harper & Brothers, 1954.

Coleman, Craig S. *American Images of Korea*. Elizabeth, NJ: Hollym International, 1990.

Collins, Robert. "Marked for Life: Sungbun, North Korea's Social Classification System." Washington, DC: Committee for Human Rights in North Korea, 2012. http://www.hrnk.org/uploads/pdfs/HRNK_Songbun_Web.pdf.

Conway-Lanz, Sahr. *Collateral Damage: Americans, Noncombatant Immunity, and Atrocity After World War II*. New York: Routledge, 2006.

Crane, Conrad C. *American Airpower Strategy in Korea, 1950–1953*. Lawrence, KS: University Press of Kansas, 2000.

Cumings, Bruce. *The Korean War*. New York: Modern Library, 2011.

———. *Korea's Place in the Sun*. New York: W. W. Norton, 1997.

———. *Origins of the Korean War*. 2 vols. Princeton, NJ: Princeton University Press, 1981.

Davis, Larry. *Air War Over Korea*. Carrollton, TX: Squadron/Signal Publications, 1982.

Dean, William F. *General Dean's Story*. New York: Viking, 1954.

Dildy, Douglas C., and Warren E. Thompson. *F-86 Sabre vs MiG-15: Korea 1950–53*. Oxford: Osprey Publishing, 2013.

Eberstadt, Nicholas, and Judith Banister. *The Population of North Korea*. Berkeley, CA: Institute of East Asian Studies, University of California, 1992.

Edelstein, David M. *Occupational Hazards: Success and Failure in Military Occupation*. Ithaca, NY: Cornell University Press, 2008.

Edwards, Paul M. *Korean War Almanac*. New York: Facts on File, 2006.

Evanhoe, Ed. *Dark Moon: Eighth Army Special Operations in the Korean War*. Annapolis, MD: Naval Institute Press, 1995.

Fehrenbach, T. R. *This Kind of War*. New York: Macmillan, 1963.

Futrell, Robert Frank. *The United States Air Force in Korea, 1950–1953*. Washington, DC: United States Air Force, 1983.

Goncharov, Sergei N., John W. Lewis, and Xue Litai. *Uncertain Partners: Stalin, Mao, and the Korean War*. Stanford, CA: Stanford University Press, 1993.

Gurney, David J. "General Earle E. Partridge USAF: Airpower Leadership in a Limited War." Thesis, School of Advanced Airpower Studies, Air University, Maxwell Air Force Base, AL, June 1998.

Haas, Michael E. *Apollo's Warriors: U.S. Air Force Special Operations During the Cold War*. Maxwell Air Force Base, AL: Air University Press, 1997.

———. *In the Devil's Shadow: U.N. Special Operations During the Korean War*. Annapolis, MD: Naval Institute Press, 2000.

Hagerty, Edward J. *The Air Force Office of Special Investigations, 1948–2000*. Andrews Air Force Base, MD: Air Force Office of Special Investigations, 2008.

Halberstam, David. *The Coldest Winter*. New York: Hyperion, 2007.

———. *The Fifties*. New York: Fawcett Columbine, 1993.

Han, Hongkoo. "Wounded Nationalism: The Minsaengdan Incident and Kim Il Sung in Eastern Manchuria." PhD diss. University of Washington, 1999.

Harden, Blaine. *Escape from Camp 14: One Man's Extraordinary Odyssey from North Korea to Freedom in the West*. New York: Viking, 2012.

———. *The Great Leader and the Fighter Pilot*. New York: Viking, 2015.

Haruki, Wada. *The Korean War: An International History*. Translated by Frank Baldwin. Lanham, MD: Rowman & Littlefield, 2014.

Hastings, Max. *The Korean War*. New York: Touchstone, 1987.

Hawk, David. *The Hidden Gulag*. 2nd ed. Washington, DC: Committee for Human Rights in North Korea, 2012.

Hoyt, Edwin P. *The Pusan Perimeter: Korea, 1950*. New York: Stein and Day, 1984.

Hwang, Ha-yong (aka Kil-yong). *My Father's War*. Edited by Hwang-sung. Indianapolis, IN: Dog Ear Publishing, 2008.

Hwang, Su-kyoung. *Korea's Grievous War*. Philadelphia: University of Pennsylvania Press, 2016.

Jager, Sheila Miyoshi. *Brothers at War: The Unending Conflict in Korea*. New York: W. W. Norton, 2013.

Kang Chol-hwan and Pierre Rigoulot. *The Aquariums of Pyongyang*. New York: Basic Books, 2001.

Kim, Stephen Jin-Woo. *Master of Manipulation: Syngman Rhee and the Seoul-Washington Alliance, 1953–1960*. Seoul: Yonsei University Press, 2001.

Kim Il Sung. *With the Century*, Vols. 1–7. Pyongyang: Foreign Languages Publishing House, 1996.

———. *Works*. Vols. 1–46. Pyongyang: Foreign Languages Publishing House, 1984.

Korean Liaison Office–Tactical Liaison Office. (Collection of declassified U.S. military intelligence reports on North Korea's invasion in 1950, with commentaries.) Chuncheon, South Korea: Institute of Asian Culture Studies, Hallym University, 1996.

Lankov, Andrei. *From Stalin to Kim Il Sung: The Formation of North Korea, 1945–1960*. New Brunswick, NJ: Rutgers University Press, 2002.

Lee, Chong-Sik. *Syngman Rhee: The Prison Years of a Young Radical*. Seoul: Yonsei University Press, 2001.

MacDonald, Callum A. *Korea: The War Before Vietnam*. New York: The Free Press, 1986.

MacDonald, Donald Stone. *U.S.-Korean Relations from Liberation to Self-Reliance*. Boulder, CO: Westview Press, 1992.

Manchester, William. *American Caesar: Douglas MacArthur, 1880–1964*. Boston: Little, Brown and Company, 1978.

Mansourov, Alexandre Y. "Stalin, Mao, Kim, and China's Decision to Enter the Korean War." *Cold War International History Project (CWIHP) Bulletin*, no. 6/7 (1995/1996): 94. http://www.wilsoncenter.org/sites/default/files/CWIHP _Bulletin_6-7.pdf.

Marshall, S.L.A. *The River and the Gauntlet: The True Story of the Most Brutal Battle of the Korean War*. New York: Warner Books, 1952.

Martin, Bradley K. *Under the Loving Care of the Fatherly Leader*. New York: Thomas Dunn Books, 2004.

Millett, Allan R. *The War for Korea, 1945–1950: A House Burning*. Lawrence, KS: University Press of Kansas, 2005.

———. *The War for Korea, 1950–1951: They Came from the North*. Lawrence, KS: University Press of Kansas, 2010.

Milmore, John. *#1 Code Break Boy: Communications Intelligence in the Korean War*. West Conshohocken, PA: Infinity Publishing, 2012.

Neer, Robert M. *Napalm: An American Biography*. Cambridge, MA: Belknap Press of Harvard University Press, 2013.

Nichols, Donald. *How Many Times Can I Die?* Brooksville, FL: Brooksville Printing, 1981.

Noble, Harold Joyce. *Embassy at War*. Seattle: University of Washington Press, 1975.

Oberdorfer, Don. *The Two Koreas*. New York: Basic Books, 2001.

Oliver, Robert T. *Syngman Rhee: The Man Behind the Myth*. New York: Dodd Mead and Co., 1954.

———. *Syngman Rhee and American Involvement in Korea, 1942–1960*. Seoul: Panmun Book Co., 1978.

Pantsov, Alexander V., with Steven I. Levine. *Mao: The Real Story*. New York: Simon & Schuster, 2012.

Person, James F. "New Evidence on North Korea in 1956." *CWIHP Bulletin*, no. 16 (Spring 2008): 471. http://www.wilsoncenter.org/sites/default/files/CWIHP Bulletin16_p51.pdf.

Ridgway, Matthew B. *The Korean War: How We Met the Challenge*. New York: Doubleday, 1967.

Rittenberg, Sidney, and Amanda Bennett. *The Man Who Stayed Behind*. New York: Simon & Schuster, 1993.

Salter, James. *The Hunters*. New York: Vintage Books, 1999.

Scalapino, Robert, and Chong-Sik Lee. *Communism in Korea*. Vols. *1–2*. Berkeley, CA: University of California Press, 1972.

Schnabel, James F. *U.S. Army in the Korean War, Policy and Direction: The First Year*. Washington, DC: U.S. Army Center of Military History, 1992.

Seidov, Igor. *Red Devils over the Yalu: A Chronicle of Soviet Aerial Operations in the Korean War, 1950–53.* West Midlands, UK: Helion & Company, 2014.

Seiler, Sydney A. *Kim Il-Song, 1941–48: The Creation of a Legend, the Building of a Regime.* Lanham, MD: University of America Press, 1994.

Service, Robert. *Stalin: A Biography.* Cambridge, MA: Belknap Press of Harvard University Press, 2005.

Sheehan, Neil. *A Bright Shining Lie: John Paul Vann and America in Vietnam.* New York: Random House, 1988.

Shen Zhihua, *Mao, Stalin and the Korean War: Trilateral Communist Relations in the 1950s.* Translated by Neil Silver. London: Routledge, 2012.

———. "Sino–North Korean Conflict and Its Resolution During the Korean War." *CWIHP Bulletin*, no. 14/15 (Fall 2003–Spring 2004): 10. http://www.wilson center.org/sites/default/files/CWIHPBulletin14-15_tableofcontents_0.pdf.

Shen Zhihua and Yafeng Xia. "China and the Postwar Reconstruction of North Korea, 1953–61." Working paper 4, North Korea International Documentation Project, Woodrow Wilson International Center for Scholars, May 2012: 7. http:// www.wilsoncenter.org/sites/default/files/NKIDP_Working_Paper_4_China_and _the_Postwar_Reconstruction_of_North_Korea.pdf.

Short, Philip. *Mao: A Life.* New York: Henry Holt, 2000.

Sok, No Kum, with J. Roger Osterholm. *A MiG-15 to Freedom.* Jefferson, NC: McFarland & Company, 1996.

Stone, I. F. *The Hidden History of the Korean War.* New York: Monthly Review Press, 1952.

Stratemeyer, George E. *The Three Wars of Lt. Gen. George E. Stratemeyer,* Edited by William T. Y'Blood. Air Force and Museum Program, 1999. https://archive .org/stream/TheThreeWars/TheThreeWars_djvu.txt.

Stueck, William. *The Korean War: An International History.* Princeton, NJ: Princeton University Press, 1995.

———. *Rethinking the Korean War.* Princeton, NJ: Princeton University Press, 2004.

Suh, Dae-Sook. *Documents of Korean Communism: 1918–1948.* Princeton, NJ: Princeton University Press, 1970.

———. *Kim Il Sung: The North Korean Leader.* New York: Columbia University Press, 1988.

Szalontai, Balazs. *Kim Il Sung in the Khrushchev Era: Soviet-DPRK Relations and the Roots of North Korean Despotism: 1953–1964.* Washington, DC: Woodrow Wilson Center Press, 2005.

Thomas, Evan. *The Very Best Men: Four Who Dared: The Early Years of the CIA.* New York: Simon & Schuster, 1995.

Time-Life editors with Richard B. Stolley. *The American Dream: The 50s.* Alexandria, VA: Time-Life Books, 1998.

United Nations. *Report of the Commission of Inquiry on Human Rights in the Democratic People's Republic of Korea.* February 7, 2014. http://www.ohchr .org/EN/HRBodies/HRC/CoIDPRK/Pages/ReportoftheCommissionofInquiry DPRK.aspx.

U.S. Air Force. Declassified Air Intelligence Information Report on Ro Kum Sok and Other Interrogation Documents, 1953–54. RG 341 USAF Intl. Repts., 1942–64, AF 59786-597495, box 1793, 631/52/54/5; AF 592236, box 1758, 631 /52/53/6. National Archives, College Park, MD.

U.S. Air Force. "History of Detachment 2, 6004th Air Intelligence Service Squadron." Far East Air Forces History, November 1953, vol. II, tab 36, Air Force Historical Research Agency, Montgomery, AL.

U.S. Air Force Directorate of Intelligence. "Maintenance of Falcon." *Air Intelligence Digest*, February 1955, 6–15.

———. "The Story of No Kum Sok," *Air Intelligence Digest*, September 1954, 28–34; October 1954, 36–41; January 1955, 32–36; February 1955, 20–22.

———. "These USAF Pilots Flew the MiG." *Air Intelligence Digest*, December 1953, 6–11.

———. "12 Minutes to Freedom: The Story Told by the North Korean Pilot Who Flew from Sunan to Seoul." *Air Intelligence Digest*, November 1953, 32–37.

Weathersby, Kathryn. "Dependence and Mistrust: North Korea's Relations with Moscow and the Evolution of Juche." Working paper 08-08, U.S.-Korean Institute at Johns Hopkins School of Advanced International Studies (SAIS), December 2008, 4. http://uskoreainstitute.org/wp-content/uploads/2010/09/USKI -WP08-8.pdf.

———. "Ending the Korean War: Considerations on the Role of History." Working paper 08-07, U.S.-Korean Institute at SAIS, December 2008. http://uskorea institute.org/wp-content/uploads/2010/02/USKI-WP08-07.pdf.

———. "The Impact of the Wartime Alliance on Postwar North Korean Foreign Relations." Unpublished paper courtesy of author.

———. "New Findings on the Korean War," Washington: *CWIHP Bulletin*, no. 3 (Fall 1993): 1. http://www.wilsoncenter.org/sites/default/files/ACF1BD.pdf.

———. "North Korea and the Armistice Negotiations." http://www.koreanwar .com/conference/conference_contents/contents/text/04_kathryn_weathers by.pdf.

———. "Should We Fear This? Stalin and the Danger of War with America." Working paper 39, CWIHP, Woodrow Wilson International Center for Scholars, Washington, DC, July 2002. http://www.wilsoncenter.org/sites/default /files/ACFAEF.pdf.

Werrell, Kenneth P. *Sabres over MiG Alley.* Annapolis, MD: Naval Institute Press, 2013.

Zhang, Xiaoming. *Red Wings over the Yalu: China, the Soviet Union, and the Air War in Korea.* College Station, TX: A&M University Press, 2002.

Photo Collections and Videos

AP interactive site on mass killings in South Korea, http://hosted.ap.org/specials/interactives/_international/korea_masskillings/index.html?SITE=AP.

Donald Nichols execution photos in Lieutenant Colonel Bob E. Edwards, "Photographs of Communist Execution at Seoul, Korea," April 26, 1950. RG 319, entry (NM-3) 85A, Records of the Army Staff, Office of the Assistant Chief of Staff (G-2), Intelligence, Collections and Dissemination Division, Document Library Branch, Army Intelligence Document File, 1950–55, container 4273A, ID #66337, National Archives, College Park, MD.

Taejon massacre photos in Lieutenant Colonel Bob E. Edwards, "Execution of Political Prisoners in Korea." Report No. R-189-50, Records of the Army Staff, Office of the Assistant Chief of Staff (G-2), Intelligence, Collections and Dissemination Division. Document Library Branch, Army Intelligence Document File, 1950–55, RG-319, box 4622, National Archives, College Park, MD.

INDEX

INDEX

Bodo League massacre, 6–7, 77–80, 186, 211–12*n*, 224–25*n*
Boeing B-17 Flying Fortresses, 58
Boeing B-29 Superfortresses, 72–73, 94, 98, 110, 118
Bradley, Omar N., 53
Bright Shining Lie, A (Sheehan), 192–93
British Royal Navy, 112
Bronze Star, 222*n*
Brooks, Preston, 182
Brooksville, Florida, 182–87
Brooksville Cemetery, 192, 196–98
Brooksville Daily Sun-Journal, 189
Brooksville Printing, 184
Broward County Courthouse, 175, 196
Brownie (dog), 72, 148
"bug out fever," 87
Burma, 1, 21
Butterfingers, 3

Caldwell, Alicia, 189
Carlin, Diana, 7, 131, 177, 178, 180
Cavett, Dick, 164
Center of Military History, 78
Central Intelligence Agency (CIA), 2
 Center for the Study of Intelligence, 90
 during Korean War, 5, 78, 91–92, 94, 95, 97, 100
 North Korea's military buildup and intelligence failures, 60–61
 Rhee and, 32, 38, 153–54, 155
 waterboarding, 40
Cheju Island, 57, 99
Cheju uprising, 39, 57, 218*n*
Chevrolet Bel Air, 171–72
China
 during Korean War, 94–99, 119, 125, 130
 armistice, 123, 137–39
 Opium Wars, 29
Cho Bang-am, 154–55
Cho Boo-yi, 44
cholera, 28
Chongchon River, 102
Chong-Sik Lee, 128
Chosun Dynasty, 36
Cho Yong Il, 83–86
Chung Bong-sun, 3, 33, 104, 151
CIA. *See* Central Intelligence Agency
Civilian Conservation Corps (CCC), 20

Clark, Mark, 138
Class C spies, 116–17
Coca-Cola, 3, 133, 171
codebreaking, 2, 82–86, 89–90, 94
Colleen's Coffee Shop, 177
Collins, Tom, 135
Communism in Korea (Scalapino and Lee), 128
Communist Party of Korea, 28–29, 30, 39
Congressional Medal of Honor, 51
Conrad, Joseph, 8
Cook, Eugene G., 128
counterfeit currency, 111, 150–51
Counter Intelligence Corps (CIC), 1, 22, 28–29, 30, 38, 71
Country Club Estates, 173, 175, 176, 180
Crabb, Jarred, 66
Cumings, Bruce, 37
Cuneo, Ronald F., 148

Dae-Sook Suh, 126
Dai-Ichi Seimei Building, 51, 95
Dandong airfield, 135
Dean, Raymond, 148
Democratic Youth Alliance, 28–29
Detachment 2 of 6004th Air Intelligence Service Squadron, 99–100, 104–8, 110–13, 144–45
Dille, John, 9
Distinguished Flying Cross, 73
Distinguished Service Cross, 5–6, 103
Donner, Francesca, 42, 103
Dulles, Allen, 153
Dulles, John Foster, 138
Dunn, Frank L., 146–49, 153
Duvall, Robert, 117–18
dysentery, 1, 21, 82

Eagleton, Thomas, 169
Edwards, Bob E., 49, 225*n*
Eglin Air Force Base Hospital, 7, 160–67, 172
Eighth United States Army
 Korean War, 81–85, 89, 90, 95, 96, 130
 Battle of Pusan Perimeter, 81–82, 86–89
 post–Korean War, 103, 109–10
Eisenhower, Dwight, 137–39, 153
electroconvulsive shock therapy (ECT), 163